SOCIAL WORK
IN AFRICA

AFRICA: MISSING VOICES SERIES

Donald I. Ray, General Editor

ISSN 1703-1826

University of Calgary Press has a long history of publishing academic works on Africa. *Africa: Missing Voices* illuminates issues and topics concerning Africa that have been ignored or are missing from current global debates. This series fills a gap in African scholarship by addressing concerns that have long been overlooked in political, social, and historical discussions about this continent.

SOCIAL WORK IN AFRICA

Exploring Culturally Relevant Education and Practice in Ghana

LINDA KREITZER

UNIVERSITY OF
CALGARY
PRESS

AFRICA: MISSING VOICES SERIES
ISSN 1703-1826 (PRINT) ISSN 1925-5675 (ONLINE)

University of Calgary Press
2500 University Drive NW
Calgary, Alberta
Canada T2N 1N4
www.uofcpress.com

LIBRARY AND ARCHIVES CANADA CATALOGUING IN PUBLICATION

Kreitzer, Linda, 1955–
   Social work in Africa : exploring culturally relevant education and practice in Ghana / Linda Kreitzer.

(Africa, missing voices series, ISSN 1703-1826 ; 10)
Includes bibliographical references and index.
Issued also in electronic formats.
ISBN 978-1-55238-510-4

   1. Social work education—Africa—Western influences. 2. Social work education—Africa—History. 3. Universities and colleges—Africa—History. 4. Social service—Africa—Western influences. 5. Social service—Africa— History. 6. Social service—Ghana—History. 7. Africa—Civilization. 8. Curriculum change—Social aspects—Africa. 9. Curriculum change— Social aspects—Ghana. I. Title. II. Series: Africa, missing voices series ; 10

HV11.8.A35K74 2012   361.3071'16   C2012-901032-4

The University of Calgary Press acknowledges the support of the Government of Alberta through the Alberta Multimedia Development Fund for our publications. We acknowledge the financial support of the Government of Canada through the Canada Book Fund for our publishing activities. We acknowledge the financial support of the Canada Council for the Arts for our publishing program.

Government of Alberta   Canadä   Canada Council for the Arts   Conseil des Arts du Canada

Cover Photo: Balme Library named after a British citizen Mr. David Balme, the Principal of the University College of the Gold Coast, later known as the University of Ghana, Legon. Photo courtesy of the author.

Cover design, page design, and typesetting by Melina Cusano

Table of Contents

Adinkra Symbols

Preface

The journey towards initiating and ultimately writing this book (my PhD research) did not begin with my first visit to Ghana in 1994. It began as a young child watching slides of my father's visits to Africa. My own courage and confidence to travel came from my parents, who throughout their lives travelled the world, making it a normal part of life's experience. My own travels outside my country of the United States began in 1972 with a backpacking trip with my sister at the young age of 17. In 1981, I moved to London, England, where I experienced my first cross-cultural living experience. I learned what it was like to be a privileged immigrant and to live and work in a different culture. During the thirteen years I lived in England, I took advantage of the opportunities to travel to many parts of the world in order to experience and learn about other cultures. This interest in other cultures paralleled my training and practice in social work and led naturally to an interest in combining my two passions. In particular I was drawn to learning how social work had developed and was currently manifested in other countries, particularly non-western countries.[1] Specifically, I discovered and learned how other cultures provided social supports for people at the individual, group, and community level. I was interested in knowing if social workers (or their equivalents) were present in other countries, what social and professional role they filled, and what education they received in their country. In the past twenty-two years, this journey has included lengthy times spent in Britain, Ghana, Armenia, Canada, and a Liberian refugee camp.

From 1994 to 1996, I taught social work at the University of Ghana, Legon, in the Social Work Unit through the British non-government organization Voluntary Services Overseas (VSO). At the same time I was reading James Midgley's (1981) book *Professional imperialism: Social work in the Third World*. As I taught western social work theory and methods to African students in Ghana I became uncomfortably aware that I too was part of this professional imperialism. Over the past ten years I have questioned why I was needed in Ghana to teach social work and why 'western knowledge' was so revered. I wanted to know if western-style social work theory and practice was appropriate in all countries of the world, and, if not, what alternatives have been created in order for the curriculum to be more culturally relevant.

To further educate myself in regards to the above questions, in 2000, I became involved with the International Federation of Social Workers and the International Association of Schools of Social Work and have attended their conferences at the international and African regional level. I continue to be interested in social work in other parts of the world. I see that it continues to flourish in some places and continues to struggle in others, including Africa. At its best, social work reflects the society in which it is operating. It should be a dynamic profession, changing and evolving with the needs of the people of the country and continent. However, this evolution can be both positive and challenging, particularly when countries are politically, socially, and economically unstable. It is my impression that western social work curriculua (theories, values, and practice) are still transferred to other countries in a top-down fashion instead of evolving naturally from a grassroots base. Why is this so? Why is it that 90 per cent of books in the social work library in Africa are western? This forces students to adapt western textbooks to their own situation when they should be having textbooks of their own. How far can one push adaptation to a point where it stifles learning? These and other questions will be part of the contents of this book.

On a more personal level, in combining my interest of international work and social work I have had to come to terms with my own place in this world, one in which I am a privileged white western woman who was socialized to believe in a certain way about the world. My journey has included challenging these worldview assumptions and challenging the profession of social work as a white, western professional entity. I have also been challenged by my own racism, particularly concerning Africans. Over the years I have been privileged to work with many Africans that have helped me reduce this irrational prejudice. I have endeared myself to Africa and its people and wish to continue this connection at both a personal and a professional level.

Many people, places, animals, spirits, and objects were part of this journey. First and foremost, I am grateful to my PhD research group in Ghana for giving their time, knowledge, and experience to be part of the

2002/2003 research project that provided the impetus for this book. The research group included: Ziblim Abukari, Adu-Gyamfi Jones, Kwaku Afram, Joanna Mensah, Salima Imoro, Patience Antonio, George Dah, Nana Boatema Afrakoma II, and Comfort Sackey. My thanks also go to Dr. Maureen Wilson, Dr. Timothy Pyrch, and Dr. Donald Ray for their encouragement over the years. My thanks also extend to the great people of Ghana at the Department of Social Work and their helpfulness while I was there on my various visits. I am grateful particularly to Prof. Nana Araba Apt, whose friendship and encouragement has been exceptional. I want to thank Prof. Lengwe Mwansa at the University of Botswana for his insight into the Association for Social Work Education in Africa. Finally, I thank both the International Federation of Social Workers (IFSW) and the International Association of Schools of Social Work (IASSW) for giving me the opportunities to present at their conferences as part of my process of thinking and learning about social work in Africa. This has allowed me to develop my thoughts from a thesis to a book. Finally, I thank Steve Brechtel for his loving support and editorial help during this process of writing. To all of you, thank you from the deepest part of my heart.

Introduction: Situating the Context

The African continent has a rich and ancient history of which much has been forgotten and remains unacknowledged by the world today. With the expansion of European civilization into Africa in the 1800s (Congress of Berlin, 2000) came the assumption that Africa was a continent to be explored and exploited, having no relevant history or culture (Hegel, 1956; Kuykendall, 1993; Pakenham, 1991) and thus was a land free to be conquered and civilized. However, it is clear that Africa had a long involved, complex and cultured history with an immense diversity of ethnic groups living on a continent, complete with appropriate social, economic, and political infrastructures. In terms of governance, "Africa was probably more democratic than most other parts of the world, including Europe" (Tandon, 1996, p. 296). Kuykendall (1993) emphasizes that "customs, laws, and traditions were the constitution and these structured the society ... and from these structures stability and perpetuity were maintained" (p. 579). An example of these laws and customs can be seen in the region of Africa that is now known as West Africa, which was divided into kingdoms in pre-colonial times (Ray, 1986). Life was mainly rural, with clans settling in different regions. The centre of the social system in pre-colonial West Africa was the kinship institution. Defined as "patterns of behaviour associated with relatives in a society, together with the principles of governing these behaviours" (Nukunya, 1992, p. 11), this system uplifted and supported the running of societies. It served as a way to administer rules and principles of seniority, succession, and residence patterns concerning customary law (Rattray, 1929). Within the kinship system were descent groups called clans and lineages (Busia, 1951; Nukunya, 1992). Intertwined in these systems was a religious belief system that depended heavily on the guidance and punishment by ancestors throughout life.

The Asante Kingdom had a chieftaincy system in place whereby the king (divisional level) was to administer the Division, look after the spiritual, physical, and emotional welfare of the people, maintain law and order, consult with elders, lead the army into battle, and act as mediator between ancestors and the clans (Busia, 1951). "Africa has had a long tradition of democracy based on the accountability of the rulers to the ruled … rulers were accountable to their people, to their ancestors, and to a regime of democratic principles" (Tandon, 1996, p. 296). Each king had a queen mother (biological mother or close relation) who watched the king's behaviour, gave advice and counsel to him, and was involved in marriage considerations (Obeng, 1988). Rattray (1929) describes the role of the queen mother as "the whisper behind the Stool" (p. 88).[2] She was the second-most important person in the traditional authority system. Her many roles within the community included community social welfare worker, distributor of local and governmental resources, liaison officer between people and the community support services, role model and care-giver for women and children, educationalist, guidance counsellor, and supervisor of puberty rites, to name a few (Boateng, 1982). She was and continues to be considered, along with the king, the keeper of culture and tradition. This traditional system evolved over many generations and brought stability to the different clans and communities.

These traditional social systems and mechanisms for social development already established were broken down with the colonization of Africa (Burke & Ngonyani, 2004; Kreitzer, 2004b). Colonization is a relationship between people, groups, or countries where there is a domination and oppression of one particular relationship over the other (Memmi, 1965). This oppression results in what Freire (1997) speaks of as the "culture of silence" in which a culture is so oppressed by another culture that it effectively silences the people of the oppressed culture. They no longer have a voice in the society or the world and are therefore of no importance. The effect of this invasion on Africa was a loss of identity and culture that greatly affected the psyche of the people of Africa. What is human and not human, what is civilized and primitive, were defined by European colonial discourse (Willinsky, 1998) and Africans were defined as non-human and primitive. The African continent has been a source of wealth for the growth of industrialized countries in the world (Busia, 1951; Hochschild, 1998; Sartre, 2001; Smith, 1999; Willinsky, 1998) and continues to be exploited by the more powerful countries and institutions of the present world. Through modernization, colonization favoured western expertise and attempted to 'civilize' Africa at the expense of its own knowledge and cultural practices (Kreitzer, 2004a; Mosha, 2000; Semali & Kincheloe, 2000; Smith, 1999; Willinsky, 1998). Today, the hegemony (a social condition in which all aspects of social reality are dominated by a certain powerful group; Mayo, 1990, p. 35) of western knowledge influences all aspects of African life. There is a strong desire to promote western knowledge, and to compete in a global world of universities that are on par with western/northern university systems (Ajayi, Goma, & Johnson, 1996). While seen as admirable, it often proceeds at the expense of traditional knowledge. Most African universities were established according to a European model and many Africans were trained in western universities in Europe, the United States, and Canada. On returning to Africa and assigned teaching positions, they "naturally emulated the practice established at the institutions where they conducted their studies" (van Wyk & Higgs, 2007, p. 68). This process promoted a dependency upon western written material and often undermined local knowledge and expertise.

While many African countries were seeking independence in the 1950s and 1960s, the new world economic order was established and Africa again became subject to colonization tactics. Borrowing money from western lenders and international financial institutions (IFIs), these countries experienced debts that devastated their chance for growth after independence (Boahen, 1975; Konadu-Agyemang, 2000; Rimmer, 1992). "These rigid fundamentalist policies did extraordinary damage to African economics from which they have yet to recover" (Lewis, 2005). By 2003, the total debt for all of Sub-Saharan Africa stood at US$218 billion (World Bank, 2005). After the Second World War, emerging development theory favoured a modernization approach to country growth. Modernization theory assumes that economic growth alone can alleviate poverty and that all countries of the world, through certain standard economic programs, would eventually have economic and social prosperity (Prigoff, 2000; So, 1990; Wilson & Whitmore, 2000). Along with modernization, the world is experiencing the phenomenon of globalization.

For some, globalization signifies interdependence, prosperity, and progress, while others see it as an advanced stage of colonization causing poverty, fragmentation, corruption, and marginalization (Lechner & Boli, 2000; Martin, 2000; Midgley, 2000). Wilson and Whitmore (2000) identify the present form of globalization, that of globalism (ideological orientation underlying the neo-liberal agenda[3]) as an orientation that supports the rich becoming richer and the poor becoming poorer. Countries in Africa continue to struggle to provide for their own people in their own land under globalism. Many countries in Africa still suffer from poverty, starvation, and famine, with millions of Africans dying of HIV/AIDS each year (Bar-On, 2001; Lewis, 2005). In 1996, out of fifty-nine countries listed in the World Bank low-income category, thirty-six countries were from Africa (World Bank, 2006). In 2010, twenty-nine African countries are still at the low-income level and eleven are at the lower-middle-income level (World Bank, 2010). Poverty in Africa is chronic and rising. Africa hosts only 10 per cent of the global population, yet it is home to 30 per cent of the world's poor (World Bank, 2007). In 2011 food insecurity is a main issue for many African countries with food riots organized to protest this trend (World Hunger, 2011), Aid has been questioned for some time now as an effective way to alleviate poverty (ASWEA, 1977; Mammo, 1999) and is now being criticized openly for its failure to alleviate poverty in Africa (Moyo, 2009). Neo-liberal economic policies have been tried and tested worldwide, and they have failed to achieve economic and social prosperity for many countries. This is still a future goal for these countries and only a concerted effort by African governments and the international community will change this situation.

The profession of social work's role in the world

The social work profession has been affected by all of these historical factors. Not only is it struggling to be a voice in countries of Africa, but social workers are struggling to empower clients and are fighting against the negative social effects of neo-liberal economic policies including cutbacks in health, education, and welfare (Prigoff, 2000; Sewpaul, 2006). The exportation of western social work theories and knowledge has helped introduce social work to many parts of the world with the assumption that its core theory and practice is universal and transferable and that a western social work curriculum is the best in the world.

Today, this exportation continues. A good example is in Asia where Australian Schools of Social Work are exporting their programs. Midgley

(2008) and Ife (2007) challenge this trend. Ife (2007) concludes that the exportation is done "regardless of the cultural, political and social differences involved and without any agonizing about the colonialist impacts of our international work" (p. 14). He continues by stating that if "there is a lack of any debate or analysis about the dangers of colonialism, there is nothing surer than that it will perpetuate such colonialism, and not be ultimately for the benefit of the countries concerned" (Ife, 2007, p. 14).

In Africa, from 1971 to 1986, there was debate concerning the relevance of western social work education in the context of the African reality. These debates were through the Association for Social Work Education in Africa (ASWEA). However, despite these debates, many social work educational programs have not critically reflected on the cultural relevance of their social work curriculum in relation to the social, political, economic, and spiritual aspects of its culture. Central to the theme of this book is why some countries have progressed more than others in changing their curriculua to their societal needs and factors that have affected producing culturally relevant social work in Africa and what are the possible ways forward in the future.

Overview of the book

Many of the ideas and thoughts that are presented in this book originated from a research project I facilitated from 2002 to 2003 concerning social work curriculum in Ghana. The research group consisted of ten people who had been involved in the social work curriculum over the years, plus a cultural advisor. We spent one year looking at the relevance of social work curriculum in Ghana, in light of the historical and current factors of colonization, modernization, and globalization as they relate to social work education and practice. The research methodology used for the project was Participatory Action Research (PAR). The reasons behind using PAR were: 1) only Ghanaians can critically look at and decide on a culturally appropriate curriculum for themselves; 2) Ghana is a society in which consensus was and is still used in decision-making processes (Gyekye, 1996; Sackey, 2001; Sutherland-Addy, 2003). PAR uses a dialogical consensus approach to generating knowledge; 3) African universities have isolated themselves from the needs of local society but are now recognizing the need to change (Tettey & Puplampu, 2000). Many African social workers have not had a part in the process of defining their professional and educational needs (Osei-Hwedie, 1993). This PAR project used social work practitioners, academics, students, and community persons interested in social work education; 4) PAR has been successful when examining situations of domination and exploitation (Fals Borda, 2001; Reason, 1994; Tandon, 1981). The domination of western social work knowledge was part of the attempt to modernize social work education in Africa and to promote the western way of knowing. This thinking is still predominant in many universities in Africa today; and 5) PAR is not new to the everyday life of Ghanaians. Many PAR examples can be found in the areas of agriculture (Dakubo, 2001; FAO, 2001), girls' education (Ministry of Education of Ghana, 2000), self-help activities in the informal sector (Schneider-Barthold, 1997), and gender studies (King & Oppong, 2001). However this type of participatory action research is not reflected in the university setting.

Dzobo (1981) identifies truth and knowledge as the key elements in indigenous African society. By examining the languages of two ethnic cultures in Ghana, Ewe and Akan, he identifies important aspects of acquiring knowledge. The four ways of knowing, in the Ewe language, are 1) Nyatsiname (oral tradition, knowledge passed down from generation to generation); 2) Susununya (the act of reflection, listening to others and reflecting on what others have said); 3) Nusronya (academic knowledge); and 4) Sidzedze (knowledge gained as a result of many years of living, self-awareness, wisdom, knowing yourself, how you interact with your environment and situations in life and your knowledge of your own past). These elements of knowledge-gathering, indigenous to Ghana, fit quite well within the philosophy and structure of PAR.

The original questions for the research were as follows: 1) how did the historical dominance of western knowledge and in particular western social work thinking emerge and how has it preserved itself? 2) how and to what extent has western social work thinking been replaced by indigenized approaches in social work in non-western countries? 3) how has the experience of the PAR process facilitated the creation of new knowledge? (Kreitzer, 2004a). These questions were presented to the research group at the initial stages of the process. Over time, two main topics emerging from these research questions were: 1) How did social work evolve in Africa; and 2) What is African culture? Through these two questions, the group was able to critically examine social work education and practice in Ghana. Our main data-collecting techniques were inviting appropriate people to dialogue with the group about a particular topic, group discussions, document analysis, and journal writing. Data analysis was a continual process through the group meetings and individual themizing. At the end of ten months, action plans were initiated that have played an important part in changing certain aspects of social work education in Ghana. For more details of this project, see Kreitzer (2004a), and Kreitzer, Abukari, Antonio, Mensah & Kwaku (2009).

The question of why an outsider had to come and do this project was discussed on various occasions. The group felt that sometimes someone from the outside is able to see things differently than insiders and can challenge them to think outside the box. Sometimes people need to be challenged to think about these issues, and a trigger can be used to do this. I was the trigger to the social work curriculum issue.

This book has been written with the hope that it will challenge African social workers and schools of social work to critically look at their curriculum and to continually evaluate this curriculum in light of the social, political, economic, and spiritual aspects of African life (Ife, 2007). It is time to cut the umbilical cord[4] with western theory and practice and create new theories and methods that are culturally relevant to the current African context. This book invites the reader to reflect on, explore, critically evaluate, and take action on the thoughts and ideas expressed here. My hope is that readers will take away new ideas and be challenged to think about the book's content; in other words, *explore* what has been written. To explore is to investigate, open up and discover new knowledge that challenges old assumptions. Foucault (1980) talks about the archaeology of knowledge as a way to get beneath the surface of an idea or structure. An archaeologist digs underneath the ground to find the layers of different eras in the world. Social archaeologists dig beneath the structures that we make in order to find out where they originate. In this case the structure is African education and in particular social work education. Questions that the research group contemplated were: 1) what is below the surface of education? 2) what are the circumstances or context behind the educational system? 3) whose perspectives or points of view influenced the educational system? 4) who is in control of the system; and 5) what are we actually trying to achieve by exposing the truths of these questions? In exploring ideas in this book I hope that new knowledge will be uncovered and questioned and that change will come about as a result of this exploration.

These chapters reflect the themes from this research as well as international, national, and local conferences, various articles read, and my own thinking and writing concerning African social work since the research.

- Chapter I provides an historical overview of influences, both foreign and local, that have made social work what it is today in Africa. This includes a brief history of the evolution of Sub-Saharan universities in Africa.

- Chapter II discusses the concept of cultural identity and its important influence on Africans and African social work in light of its current state in African society.

- Chapter III discusses the role that western knowledge has played in the development of Africa and in particular social work training. The role of traditional knowledge in this development is discussed.

- Chapter IV highlights the effect that neo-liberal thinking and economic systems have played in regards to social development and in turn the social work profession.

- Chapter V discusses development and aid in Africa and its influence on social development. Welfare institutions of the past are examined and questions surrounding who social workers are accountable to are discussed. The roles of professional associations are also discussed.

- Chapter VI offers practical ways to initiate a more culturally appropriate social work curriculum in Africa. Details of the research group findings and action plans will be elaborated upon. Suggestions for ways forward with social work curriculum will be discussed.

- Chapter VII offers concluding remarks concerning ways forward in creating African social work curricula that works for Africa.

There are five important issues concerning the content of this book.

1. Firstly, without the insights and critical thinking of the Ghanaian research group,[5] this book could not be written. I therefore, again acknowledge the research group, including the guest speakers, as the key contributors in this process. However, over the past years I have continued to develop some of the themes and tested them at various conferences against the different experiences of Africans at these conferences and have expanded them. Therefore, as much as I have tried to stay faithful to the reflections of the research group, it is important to acknowledge that some of the ideas I have developed may not be the ideas and reflections of the research group.

2. Secondly, the themes and questions in this book relate to the African context and in particular this work was focused in an anglophone West African country. To generalize for all of Africa would not be appropriate considering that the research was facilitated in a specific time, place, and cultural context. I am also aware of the different history that South Africa had in comparison with other African countries and the complexity of different ethnic groups there. However, I have used social work literature from other parts of Africa as well as my own experience of working in North America, Europe, Africa, and Armenia, to support different themes of the book so that some generalization can be made. Meredith (2006) points out that "although Africa is a continent of great diversity, African

states have much in common, not only their origins as colonial territories, but the similar hazards and difficulties they have faced" (p. 14). Particularly, other countries with a colonial history may find the concepts and ideas useful. Readers from outside Africa must judge how these issues relate to their own cultural and social realities. What is relevant should be considered and what is not applicable can be noted.

3. Thirdly, I am not a French speaker and therefore untranslated francophone African literature on social work education and practice has not been included.

4. Fourthly, students, practitioners, and academics from the western world will find this book useful in thinking about localizing their own curriculum. Faculty and students embarking on faculty and student exchanges in Africa will find the contents helpful.

5. Finally, when quoting from the research project using direct quotes from the participants I have kept to the original transcripts. Therefore, some of the wordings in the quotes are what people said and I have not changed the grammar or words. This causes some anxiety for people quoted as what we say may not be as grammatically accurate as we would like it to be. Some of the quotes were written into my PhD research thesis and in those instances I have referenced my thesis instead of the person.

Summary

There have been many historical and current factors that have influenced how the profession of social work has emerged in Africa. From a continent with a long and complex history made up of micro-nations (Maathai, 2009) to a continent that was colonized and is continuing to modernize, it has experienced more than its share of political, economic, and social challenges (Yimam, 1990). The profession of social work has been influenced by these factors, including a dependency on western social work education and practice. The challenge started back in the 1970s with the ASWEA conferences, to critically think through what social work education means in an African context and this was just the beginning. This issue continues today and is more relevant than ever. This book is written mainly for African social workers and academics in hopes that, through reading this book, a spark of revolutionary thinking is ignited as to what kind of social work education and practice would be most useful and practical for Africa in the twenty-first century. Mobilizing relevant people in order to go through this process of examining assumptions, critiquing and building culturally relevant social work curriculum is both difficult and creative. To remove one's self from western knowledge that has been deemed "the best," and held in high esteem, is to ask a culture to remove itself from its parent and start a new life on its own. Taking the best of the western theory and practice and balancing it with African indigenous knowledge and traditions is an important step in this process. This is the only way that African social work can be a creative and revolutionary force in Africa and in social work worldwide (ASWEA, 1974c, p. 32).

Prologue

In July 2007, I presented at an International Association of Schools of Social Work (IASSW) international symposium in Toronto, Canada. It was a one-day conference with participants from Africa, Asia, North America, and the Caribbean as well as students from the social work program at York University. I wanted to articulate some of the basic questions I have been asking about social work in Africa since my beginning days teaching at the University of Ghana, Legon. I asked participants to close their eyes, rid themselves of present thoughts and concerns, and open their minds to the following scenario.

> You are head of the only school of social work in a fictitious non-western medium-sized country. Your country was colonized but has been independent now for thirty years. You have been trained in a western country in social work and finished your training five years ago and have been head of this school of social work since then. You were recently told by your government that the social work curriculum and training does not meet the needs of your country. A new approach is needed as far as training people to help citizens of your country who are struggling with life circumstances. You are told to start fresh and get rid of western social work methods, theories, and knowledge altogether. You are challenged by this task as it goes against your western social work training but you are up to the challenge.

I then asked three questions: 1) How did it feel to be asked to delete all of your western social work training, including beliefs and values from your mind and start fresh; 2) Where would you begin? Who would you ask to help you in this task; and 3) what curriculum and training would you consider being appropriate and why?

For some there was a feeling of liberation, for others a feeling of fear and others realized how, even though they have lived in Africa all of their lives, western curriculum continues to dominate. Is the above task impossible? Other schools of social work have radically shifted their curriculua and training to meet the needs of their own country. Latin American countries are an example (Wilson, 1992). Why has this been slow to occur in Africa?

What would that curriculum look like? What knowledge, theories and practices would emerge from a fresh start? Would it even look like social work training and practice we have today? I also did this exercise in Durban, South Africa, at the 2008 IASSW workshop. In the short amount of time we had as a group, many of the ideas in this book were independently brought forward at the workshop as ways to make social work curriculum more African.

Doing an exercise like this highlights the complexity of social work education and practice. The reality is that countries today are living with many different worldwide influences, at the local, national, and international levels. These different influences challenge citizens concerning the cultural practices, values, and beliefs and challenges nations to work within the more powerful political and economic forces governing their world. Africans are embracing aspects of western culture as well as preserving their own traditional ways. For countries with a colonial history, Little Bear (2000) states: "No one has a pure worldview that is 100% Indigenous or Eurocentric; rather everyone has an integral mind ... a pre-colonized consciousness that flows into a colonized consciousness and back again ... colonization left a heritage of jagged worldviews" (p. 85). A country's or a people's cultural identity is affected by this push/pull factor and is strengthened and weakened by its own view of itself in relation to the past, present, and future world order (Sultany, Lavie, & Haimov, 2008).

Social work, throughout the developing world, is also challenged by this balancing act. In Africa, common themes surrounding social work keep re-emerging, through the years, as African social workers and academics try to promote the profession of social work as an important player in national development, including social development. The Association for Social Work Education in Africa (ASWEA) reflects this pattern of struggle in their twenty volumes of seminar documentation produced in the 1970s and 1980s. Mumeka (ASWEA, 1974c), speaking about rural development at one of these seminars, challenges African social workers and academics to this task of changing African social work and in particular using a more interdisciplinary approach to assessment and intervention.

> In my opinion the time has come for serious and critical re-examination of social work training in Africa.... Twentieth century Africa expects social work to be *creative* and *revolutionary*. In the context of the inter-disciplinary approach I see the profession of social work as a catalyst for the polarization of all shades of opinion relating to rural development. By virtue of their training, social workers should be able to make a positive contribution as members of inter-disciplinary development teams.... However, it is again necessary to reiterate my earlier concern that unless the *profession of social work is prepared to take a new path, social workers will for a long time to come remain ineffective in developing countries.* (p. 32)

Dr. Murapa (1977) speaking at a similar seminar four years later makes the strong and similar remark.

> African instructors, being from the most part products of Western education, have proved either incapable or unwilling to engage in *extensive* and *creative* revision of the existing textbooks, curricula and approaches to make them *relevant* to the social and other developmental problems and aspirations in Africa. (p. 32)

Since the 1980s, other African scholars have highlighted these same themes (Asamoah & Beverly, 1988; Bernstein & Gray, 1991; Brown, 1971; Drower, 2000; Gray, 1998; Gulati, 1974; Haug, 2005; Jacques, 1993; Kaseke, 2001; Midgley, 1981; Mupedziswa, 1996; Nagpaul, 1993; Nimmagadda & Cowger, 1999; Noyoo, 2000; Osei-Hwedie, 1990; Osei-Hwedie, 1993; Osei-Hwedie & Jacques, 2007; Rodenborg, 1986; Sewpaul, 2006; Shawky, 1972; van Hook, 1994; Venkataraman, 1996; Walton & Abo El Nasr, 1988). In 2003, similar themes were highlighted and questions asked through my research project in Ghana and when attending African social work conferences these themes are repeated.

Why has it been so difficult to cut the umbilical cord of western social work training and practice for a more culturally relevant social work education program for Africans? Why, after sixty years of social work in many countries in Africa is the profession still struggling and still on the periphery? Why has the re-examination of social work education in Africa, completed through the ASWEA conferences, been slow to take hold? Africa is re-emerging as an important force in the world order. Social work can play an important role in this re-identification process. However, in order to do this it first has to cleanse its own self from past indoctrination by others. Critical analysis of the curriculum in light of colonization and modernization and globalization is a possible next working step. Through these processes, the social work profession can create culturally relevant social work training and practice that fits its own needs as a continent. A new and creative curriculum will emerge when African social workers and academics question and take charge of their own training and practice, without the arbitrary constraints of western social work knowledge and practice. The time has come for Africans to have partners and not masters. This calls for a relationship of solidarity (Kreitzer & Wilson, 2010).

Social work academics and practitioners from around the world, in encouraging the development of a more culturally relevant social work curriculum in Africa, need to critically exam the approaches they have taken in the past when western curricula had been conveniently imported and used with little or no understanding of how this act supported colonization and an unhealthy dependency relationship. Sending western social work textbooks creates a climate of dependency whereby students have to adapt their learning to an African setting. Unfortunately, this exportation of western social work curricula continues today (Ife, 2007; Midgley, 2008). Western social work has to understand the complex interrelationship of history and present realities so that it can become more culturally sensitive to countries, particularly ones that have been colonized, when creating partnerships which may involve curriculum development. Therefore, an understanding of the past influences on African social work is worth an examination. Chapter I gives an historical account of influences affecting education in Africa and in particular social work education and practice in Sub-Saharan Africa.

I. Historical Context

In Ghana, the Adinkra symbol SANKƆFA is the bird looking back which means to "Go back and take" and it "signifies the importance of returning in time to bring to the present useful past cultural values, which are needed today. It is believed that progress is based on the right use of the positive contributions of the past." (Agbo, 1999, p. 3)

A. Historical influences affecting social work education in Africa

There are many historical influences that have affected the introduction and evolution of social work in Africa. The influences that shaped African universities, the institutions that influenced the importation of the profession into Africa and the institutions that struggled to define the professions place on the continent will be discussed. An example of how social work evolved in Ghana will finish the chapter.

1. Sub-Saharan African universities – Historical context

In my conversations with African social workers, I have come to realize that Sub-Saharan African university students are mainly taught the history and practice of social work from a European perspective with little attention paid to how social supports evolved in Africa. This Eurocentric approach to social work training and more broadly to African university education, is not surprising. Historically, many Sub-Saharan African universities were developed to meet the needs of the colonizer and the colonial institutions that were exported from the motherland (Ashby, 1964; Boateng, 1982; van Hook, 1994). The colonizer understood that controlling education, particularly in universities, was a way to control Africans. Curriculum could influence consciousness and awareness, and, if the colonizer's knowledge was taught, conflict with students would be minimized (Gaventa & Cornwell, 2001). There was a need to produce a class of Africans that were black on the outside but European on the inside to serve in these institutions (Ashby, 1964). Van Hook (1994) speaks about Zimbabwe's educational system as "designed to maintain the monopoly of power and resources by the whites" (p. 320). The British educational policies supported the following strategies: 1) control the pace and direction of social change; 2) maintain law and order and not foster social action; 3) discourage talk of racial equality; 4) educate African elites, who were fit, upright, and of good character and ability, to uphold the colonial administration; and 5) keep Africans in subserviant roles (Ashby, 1964; Austin, 1975; Maravanyika, 1990). These strategies helped the colonizers maintain their relationship of power over the local population (Amonoo-Neizer, 1998). These strategies were successful in that once independence was achieved many of the African intellectuals refused to support any progress towards the Africanization of universities.

Some resistance to this Eurocentric university education was promoted in the early years before independence through the activist work of James Johnson, Africanus Horton, and Edward Blyden (Ajayi et al., 1996).

Blyden saw missionary education as "slavery of the mind and worse than slavery of the body" (p. 19). Lebakeng (1997) describes the apartheid-colonial curriculum "with its reliance on scientific racism, as seeking to disprove the humanness of Africans and to prove both their inferiority and defective character as subhumans" (p. 5). This criticism of European education was not taken seriously by the early western developers of education. For example, missionaries had only to answer back to this criticism that, since "Africa has no past, how can race instincts be respected which either don't exist or are fatal and soul destroying to the Negro" (p. 22). These activists wanted a "secular African-controlled university" (Ajayi et al., 1996, p. 17).

Eventually, the colonial administration did take note and through a compromise created Fourah Bay College in Sierra Leone in 1826. Although not what many activists for African universities would have wanted, it was a start. It began as a college for the Christian Missionary Society and, eventually, in 1876, became a university institution. There were many conditions on which the college was created. It had to affiliate with an English university and this was the University of Durham. Courses were drawn up in Durham and most of the courses offered were courses needed to become a Church of England minister. One non-examining course was offered in Arabic and Islamic studies, but courses such as law, medicine, science, agriculture, economics, engineering, architecture, and African studies were missing. In other parts of Sub-Saharan Africa, universities were created from funding from Europe and course content was European. For example, the University College of Ghana, established in 1948 as an affiliate college of the University of London, was based on the Cambridge style of teaching, emphasizing the superiority of western curriculum and favouring European university format over practical African structures and African-centred curriculum (Ashby, 1964). In 1961, it was reorganized as the University of Ghana to award its own degrees. When walking through the University of Ghana, Legon, the distinctly Mediterranean (see book cover of the Balme Library) and British influence is everywhere, including the presence of senior common rooms, high tables in the old cafeterias, and the president and important people in the university housed on the top of the hill in the 'Ivory Tower.' In fighting long and hard for African-centred education, the universities became, for Africans, part of the "status symbols conferred on the new states in anticipation of the granting of political independence and international recognition" (Ajayi et al., 1996, p. 69). Ajayi et al. (1996) identify four areas of the colonial legacy in higher education that needed to be changed once African universities were under their own control:

- Educate people to uphold and respect traditional systems instead of training elites to uphold colonial administrations and in return exploiting their own people;

- Deliver African-centred curricula that address the needs of the country instead of keeping European curricula that don't address the needs of the developing country;

- Reduce the hierarchy of the university structures and management instead of keeping university structures and management as replicas of European universities;

- Provide education for all Africans instead of just the elites.

Once Sub-Saharan African universities were independent of direct European control, the issue of autonomy dominated the African university colleges in the 1960s and 1970s. Austin (1975) defined 'autonomy' as "a guarantee of and the protection of the freedom of thought and of speech, or reading and writing" (p. 244). It was thought that, through autonomy, progress could be made to reverse the influence of colonialism. This proved to be an idealistic view. Both international and national factors came into play that would challenge university autonomy and freedom. International factors contributing to the continual growth and westernization of the universities included the Cold War (many Africans were educated in Russia and Africans exploited Russian and U.S. rivalry to expand higher education); America's growing economic, political, and educational influence in the world and on African higher education; and the United Nations involvement and support of the internationalization of education. African university autonomy was also challenged at the national level by political groups and government control (Boateng,

1982). New governments realized that if they controlled the teaching and activities at the universities, this would help their political cause. This was certainly the case in Ghana (Austin, 1975). Kwame Nkrumah, first president of Ghana, used his position as chancellor and head of the university for political purposes by getting rid of expatriates and any Africans opposed to his political beliefs. "He was concerned that the university was in political opposition to his party" (p. 240).

2. Sub-Saharan African universities – Current state

The current state of Sub-Saharan African universities reflects many of these historical events which have hindered universities attempting to be African-centred, autonomous, and productive. "The euro-centric system of university education has hampered universities in these countries (non-western) in releasing endogenous creativity and seeking their cultural roots. There is thus a tension between the orientation toward indigenous values and problems, on the one hand, and addressing global problems, on the other hand, a tension that can only be alleviated or resolved by communication across cultural boundaries" (van Wyk & Higgs, 2007, p. 68). These authors distinguish between "the concept of an 'African university' as opposed to a 'university located in Africa'" (p. 61) and feel this distinction should be critically examined. The university located in Africa is usually a European university with the following characteristics:

> … a more or less sharp distinction between theory and practice; it has put a premium on autonomy and aloofness to the extent of complete irrelevance; it has been both socially and intellectually an elitist institution; and it has tried to be an 'ivory tower,' as an institution whose main purpose is to 'seek the truth.' (p. 65)

A former student at the University of Ghana, Legon, gave his own experience as an example. As part of their university education, they were made to take African studies. He and the other students were not interested in African studies and couldn't understand why this should be taken. Their education was mainly western and that was good enough. Van Wyck &

Higgs (2007) continue by describing an 'African university' as one that has an

> 1) African identity and vision; 2) providing an overarching education philosophy that is concordant with the culture of the majority, that is human rights, non-sexism, and non-racism that are critical to the promotion of citizenship; 3) representing a critical point of departure from the current colonial-christian-western identity that are no longer suitable nor compatible with our new dispensation; and 4) that creates a new paradigm that locates the African condition, knowledge, experiences, values, world-view and mindset at the centre of African scholarship and knowledge-seeking approach. (p. 68)

In order to achieve the above description of a true African university, understanding Africa's place and role in the world is needed and how these historical influences, colonization, modernization, and globalization have shaped the university's purpose. This includes content and style of teaching. It is here that the Brazilian educationalist, Paulo Freire, may be of some help. Freire (2007) offers a metaphor explaining traditional education as being like a bank machine in which a card is put into a slot; information is fed in and is received and then spat out at the end. Much of traditional education is like this machine whereby students are given information to memorize. They are given the information; they receive the information and then reproduce it on the exam at the end of term. "The scope of action allowed to the student extends only as far as receiving, filing, and storing the deposits" (Freire, 2007, p. 72). This type of education doesn't promote critical thinking; it is reproducing what was exactly, word for word, presented in the classroom and what has been deemed as important by the professor. He describes further the philosophical underpinnings of this type of education:

> Knowledge is a gift bestowed by those who consider themselves knowledgeable upon those whom they consider to know nothing. Projecting an absolute ignorance onto others, a characteristic of the ideology of oppression, negates education and

knowledge as processes of inquiry. The teacher presents himself to his students as their necessary opposite; by considering their ignorance absolute, he justifies his own existence. The students … accept their ignorance as justifying the teacher's existence … never realizing that they educate the teacher as well. (p. 72)

My initial experience as a teacher at the University of Ghana was similar to this metaphor of the bank machine. The lecture style teaching was used in the classroom and students wrote word for word what the lecturer was saying. However, this didn't work for me. When I began my teaching, I was told rather quickly that I spoke too fast and my accent could not be understood and therefore the students could not write word for word what I was saying. It was clear that the normal one-hour lecture by the professor was out of the question. So, I had to adapt to the situation. Instead of being the sole deliverer of knowledge as described above, I started each class with a ten-minute lecture and the rest of the time was devoted to adult education techniques that encouraged students to draw from their own life experiences and accumulated knowledge. Through creative group work, group projects and role-play they were encouraged to critically look at the topic through their own experiences and not the experiences of the lecturer. The problem came at exam time. The students panicked because they didn't have any notes from which to recite word for word the 'answers' on the exam. The exam I presented was a case study with questions in which they had to assess a problem and use an intervention. After the exam, the students complained that it was so hard because they didn't have the answers they thought I wanted them to reproduce in the exam. Although I had prepared them beforehand by telling them that the exam would be a case study that needed an assessment of the problem and an intervention, they found the exam difficult. The following year, the students were better able to cope with the exam because they understood that there was not necessarily a right answer and they would be graded on how they thought through the assessment and the intervention process rather than on what they could recite. In this case, students were empowered to think for themselves and were rewarded for this creativity instead of living under the assumption that they were absolutely ignorant and that the only right answer was the lecturer's answers. Freire (2007) offers a challenging statement to the bank machine type educational system. "The more students work at storing the deposits entrusted to them, the less they develop the critical consciousness which would result from their intervention in the world as transformers of that world" (p. 73).

In 2002/03, during my PhD research process, our research group invited Professor Glover, a well-known Ghanaian artist to talk with us about art and culture. His message was clear. In the present education institutions in Africa, people are being trained to carry on with the existing colonial culture. Things have become stale and the educational system does not provide an environment for creative thinking. Others in the group confirmed that current education is socializing students not to challenge the status quo. Glover went on to say that "We must train people who must be dreamers ... training people who can look at things and see something else other than what everybody sees" (Kreitzer, 2004a, p. 22). Part of seeing things differently is to disagree. "Disagreement brings about creative thinking. People must be nurtured within the educational system to begin to dream wild dreams ... if we are going to talk of development in any society in many situations then you must have dreamers" (p. 21).

In the past, the Association of African Universities (AAU), supported by the Organization of African Unity (OAU), tried to set up funds to create a more African-centred curriculum. They encouraged intercontinental contact between African universities and supported conferences and seminars looking at African higher education. Although, the AAU has been somewhat successful, it has been plagued by lack of funds and inadequate communication. The United Nations and the World Bank became less interested in educating people at the university level and international financial institutions imposed Structural Adjustment Programs (SAPs)[1] that have left vital money for university education unavailable (Sefa Dei, 2005). Their concern has been mainly with primary and secondary education, as can be seen by the Millennium Goals. Caffentzis (2000) links the policies of the World Bank and the IFI directly to the deterioration of African universities. "Structural Adjustment Programs (SAP's) conditionality's included the removal of subsidies to students for food and accommodation, a currency devaluation that inflated the cost of educational materials and cuts in government funding of education. But the most devastating impact was on the average family income, which made it difficult for parents to continue to send their children even to primary school" (p. 4). Federici (2000) goes further by stating that these policies are impacting African academia by promoting intellectual recolonization. "This means that conditions are being created whereby African academics cannot produce any intellectual work, much less be present in the world market of ideas, except at the service and under the control of international agencies" (p. 19). In order to turn this scenario around Sefa Dei (2008) argues that schooling

> ... should move beyond the traditional dichotomies of difference and look critically at how colonial relations get produced, reproduced and sustained in educational processes. It is important to recognise the legacy of colonial influence and historical context as they apply to African education and how groups, regions, and communities were pitted against each other relative to the differential allocation of resources and goods. (p. 234)

It is also important to critically look at what is influencing universities today. He offers important questions for educational institutions to ask of their departments: "1) How is politics mediating schooling in African contexts?; 2) How are the different bodies in schools acknowledged and validated?; 3) How does schooling promote, sustain or challenge dominant and colonial relations?; 4) How does schooling create possibilities for rupturing dominant forms of knowledge and thereby create pedagogical and curricular spaces for indigeneity?" (p. 234). Looking at power relations in the university setting is important so that the "dynamics of power as well as those oppressive patriarchal relations embedded in educational structures and systems" can be addressed (p. 242).

In 2009, the World Bank saw 'the light' and "the name of the game now is knowledge-intensive development" (p. xxxi). The World Bank report (2009a) highlights some of the problems with tertiary education and now asks that development include "a rebalancing of the relative attention given to primary, secondary and tertiary education in light of where countries are with respect to their primary education goals, the state of tertiary education and the anticipated role that knowledge and skills are expected to have in their future growth" (p. xxxii). This is good news;

however, there is little mention that past policies of the World Bank and the IMF that have contributed to the crisis in tertiary education, that in fact African universities have tried to keep up with the times but due to these international policies have seen the disintegration of universities and the brain drain of teachers. They offer six ways to help bolster the universities: 1) encourage private, public, and specialized training centres; 2) strengthen the governance and autonomy of institutions by creating competition between universities; 3) establish quality-based accreditation requirements, evaluation, and monitoring; 4) address low pay scales, hire retirement rates, and curriculum development; 5) increase research; and 6) support reforms consistently through funding from public budgetary sources. What is important to this topic in social work is the encouragement to

> ... offset impending retirement of a large fraction of faculty members in public institutions and to simultaneously begin augmenting the supply of instructors, as well as bolstering their caliber, through better pay scales and other professional incentives. This needs to be complemented by an overhaul of pedagogic practices, curricula, and access to libraries, laboratories and IT facilities. (p. xxxi)

An interesting advice from the report is the use of online teaching, particularly with Africans now teaching abroad. There is no fleshing this out as to the appropriateness of this online teaching to the African context. An African social work teacher in the UK may still be teaching western curriculum that may or may not be appropriate to the African setting. However, the goal of this change in emphasis towards tertiary education is to "establish education and training systems based on learning needs rather than on student age, and to replace information-based rote learning with educational practices that develop a learner's ability to learn, create, adapt and apply knowledge" (p. 110). Ife (2007) and Midgley (2008) both question this trend towards online teaching that continues to perpetuate a western curriculum.

The question is whether or not the World Bank will financially help these countries in updating and encouraging better tertiary education that is African-specific and meets the needs of African countries.

Some universities have critically looked at their structures, policies, and curriculum in light of the African context. An example is Makere University in Uganda, which has turned its university around from a depleted university to one that is less hierarchical, has more private investments, encourages autonomy, and is no longer in decline (Court, 1999). More universities need to change their ways of working in order to support and educate Africans who have pride in their continent and will increase its important place in the world today.

B. Institutions affecting social work education in Africa

The remnants of western teaching, the wish to be on par with European universities, and the desire to be black on the outside and European on the inside all resonate with the issues concerning African social work education. The contributions of African social work are often ignored within the African social work classrooms, and international social work books spend little time looking at African social work as an important part of social work development worldwide. There are many reasons for this, including: 1) the lack of exposure to African social work history; 2) language barriers between former anglophone and francophone colonial countries in regards to social work history; and 3) more generally, the lack of importance placed on African history as opposed to European and U.S. history throughout primary and secondary school systems. These perpetuate, often sub-consciously, the devaluing of the continent generally. No wonder African social work education reflects a Eurocentric perspective.

There have been several key organizations that have worked to introduce the social work profession to non-western countries. At the international level, the United Nations Surveys were one of the first and encouraged countries all over the world to incorporate social work training at a post-secondary level. The United Nations assumed that western social work curricula were transferable and appropriate to all countries. The United Nations Monographs looked at social welfare issues in the

African context. At the continental level, the Association for Social Work Education in Africa (ASWEA) seminars met to discuss ways that the profession could be integrated into the African context. An example of work at the national level was the Ghana Association of Social Workers (GASOW) seminars that discussed national changes taking place in the 1970s and how social work could respond to these changes.

I have taken the opportunity to explain some of the content of these documents for several reasons. Firstly, I have yet to see any of these documents thoroughly analyzed by Africans. If there is no in-depth analysis then the social work profession will not understand their contribution to the profession worldwide. (These documents are now available on-line at http://www.historicalpapers.wits.ac.za/inventory.php?iid=9014). Secondly, I hope that through a brief summary of their contents, researchers will be inspired to conduct a document analysis and write about them in the professional social work journals. Finally, between now and the time the analysis and writing happens, I have given academics and teachers a bit of information about the documents so they can use this information as a resource for teaching and research. The following provides a brief summary of these documents.

1. International level

United Nations Survey. The United Nations was supportive of exporting social work education worldwide (Healy K., 2001; Midgley, 1981), particularly as a way to address social concerns due to the effects of World War II and the various movements towards independence of colonized countries. They completed five surveys between 1950 and 1971 concerning social welfare training throughout the world. Titled "Training for Social Work," they laid out the state of the profession in hopes that it would grow and develop after independence. There was an assumption by the UN that social work was about assisting individuals, families, and groups, focusing on social ills and providing appropriate remedial and preventive services (Yimam, 1990). In fact, in the early stages of social work in Africa, nation-building and raising the standard of living conditions of the population were equally important (Yimam, 1990). The purpose of the UN's First International Survey was to "provide the Social Commission and the Economic and Social Council with a detailed description and analysis of the methods of training in educational institutions that have been evolved by the various countries for the professional preparation of social workers" (UN, 1950, p. iii). This came out of a concern and urgent need for staff of "competent men and women who possess the qualities of personality, the knowledge and the skill required for solving problems around social welfare" (p. 1). At the end of this survey, a table was produced, showing schools of social work and other educational institutions offering social work training. General characteristics of social work in all countries of the world were highlighted and country summaries of their own definitions of social work were given. Only four summaries were from African countries: Egypt, the Union of South Africa, Liberia, and Ethiopia. The report concluded that there had been an increased interest in the profession since the end of the war "as a means of raising the standards of living and thus promoting a greater measure of social and economic well-being for their peoples" (p. 87).

The Second International Survey, published in 1955, was a follow-up to the first survey but limited its research to the years 1950–1954. This survey was needed due to the "growing concern of Governments for a more rapid increase in the supply of social welfare personnel trained at different educational levels" (UN, 1955, p. 1). The survey identified "trends and problems that appear to be significant for the further development of training for social work … and described the curricular and non-curricular aspects of training programmes and identifiable trends in the countries in each region" (p. 2). The report concluded, in part, that it was the responsibility of international organizations (UN, International government agencies [IGO]) and international non-government agencies to "assist countries in establishing, coordinating, extending and improving training facilities and programmes in the field of social work" (p. 160). Interestingly, Ghana was left out of the first and second surveys, even though social work training has been available there since 1945.

In 1958, a Third International Survey was published with the purpose of

> … reviewing problems of social work training and to set out
> in some detail for the use of government agencies, schools of

social work, voluntary social agencies and others, the range of subject matter and the educational method, which is coming to be considered desirable at the present stage in the development of training for social work. (UN, 1958, p. 2)

The report was extensive and covered all aspects of the social work profession, including current trends, the nature of social work, the field of social work, community development and social work, the historical background, and current trends in training for social work. The training section covered non-professional training of auxiliary workers, the content of training for professional social workers and the educational method of training for social work practice, including curriculum planning, course content, and fieldwork. One of the issues identified in this survey was the universal lack of local textbooks, as well as published reports of research projects, case records, and films. "It is recognized that western social work training texts are helpful as background and historical teaching ... but they do not suffice for teaching courses on social problems of Asian countries and for the appropriate use of methods of dealing with such problems" (p. 17).

Forty-six years later, this issue continues to be a problem in many parts of the world, including Africa.

The Fourth International Survey, completed in 1964, was "designed to identify significant developments and trends in training for social work at all educational levels" (UN, 1964a, p. 1) and relates to the years 1954 to 1962. It is interesting to note that the African section on Social Policy and Social Services refers only to Uganda, Tanganyika, Morocco, Kenya, and Ivory Coast. The survey contains cursory references to social work training in different parts of the world and information on objectives and patterns of training. In light of the significant number of surveys during the period between 1950 and 1962, it is surprising that many African countries like Ghana were not mentioned or assessed.

The Fifth International Survey (UN, 1971a) "drew attention to the unintended consequences of development and the critical role that social welfare personnel must play in ensuring that the social objectives of national development are kept in focus" (Asamoah, 1995, p. 227).

After these surveys were published, it was decided that many ex-colonial countries needed the profession of social work in their countries. Therefore, the United Nations sent many western consultants to non-western countries in order to help create social work curricula. As Kendall (1995) suggests, these consultants went with the understanding that western social work knowledge was transferable to other cultures. Thus, it was believed that duplication of the western curriculum would lead other countries to acquire this same knowledge that would create excellent, prestigious social work programs. "The implicit assumption was that developing countries were incapable of finding their own models ... and were inferior to Western social work knowledge and practice" (Gray, 2005, p. 235). Through the setting up of new social work programs in many non-western countries, experts promoted western social work theories and methodologies, with little understanding of the relevance of these theories to those countries (Midgley, 1981; Rodenborg, 1986). Faculties of western social work institutions also helped set up social work programs in non-western countries and continue to do so today (Asadourian, 2000; Driedger, 2004; Ife, 2007; Midgley, 2008).

One of the first official challenges to the universality of western social work knowledge was made at the United Nations Fifth Conference on Social Work Education (UN, 1971). Ten years later Midgley's (1981) seminal book *Professional imperialism: Social work in the Third World* challenged the social work profession worldwide in its assumption that the profession is transferable to all countries of the world and that western social work education and practice is appropriate to developing countries (Gray, Coates, & Yellow Bird, 2008). Subsequent articles and books have continued this debate.

United Nations Monographs. Along with the surveys, the United Nations published monographs between 1964 and 1971 concerning various issues related to social welfare in Africa. These monographs give an historical account of this period of time when the profession was evolving in African society. The first was a *Directory of social welfare activities in Africa* and a second edition came out in 1967. The purpose of the first edition was to "compile significant steps towards meeting the ever-growing need for regular exchange of information and available resources in social welfare" (UN, 1967a, p. v). Forty-eight countries of Africa were included and it was hoped that the revised edition "would give an indication of what experience is already available within the region itself and what is available outside" (p. vi). The document is divided into two parts: 1) country reports; and 2) the Economic and Social Council resolutions concerning the following: i) ESC's role in social development of developing countries; and ii) social welfare services, including social policy and development, training for social work, rural life and community action, social defence, establishing an expert committee on social development, campaign against illiteracy, mobilization of youth for national development, and co-operation between the United Nations High Commissioner for Refugees (UNHCR) and the economic commission of Africa. The document ends with a comprehensive list of the activities of the social development section of the Economic Commission for Africa, and a list of international voluntary organizations in the field of social welfare. What is most interesting about this forty-year-old document, are the priority actions it identified for the coming years:

> 1) Establishment of minimum standards for schools of social work including professional requirements, curricula, practical field work and textbooks; 2) operational research evaluating teaching content and methods to suit Africa; 3) establishing an Association of social work education to help with the implementation of recommendations; 4) production of indigenous teaching materials; 5) arrangement of ad hoc training courses and seminars for staff; 6) exchange of professors and teachers and 7) development of sub-regional training centers. (p. 95)

Some of these goals were reached over the years but many have still not been achieved.

The second monograph, entitled *Patterns of social welfare organizations and administration in Africa,* includes a clear identification of the lack of local culturally relevant structure and services:

In the tradition of little or no consultation with indigenous elements, the resulting administrative structures for social welfare services were a direct imitation of those services already provided in the home countries.... The social services to be found throughout Africa accordingly reflect the differences in structure, traditions, intellectual values, and concepts of the colonizing countries and not of the indigenous African societies. (UN, 1964b, No. 2, p. 7)

Ghana, Ivory Coast, and the United Arab Republic were highlighted concerning their administrative structures. The third monograph concentrated on *Training for social work in Africa*. It describes the various types of training programs and in-services training then happening in different countries concerning social welfare. Over fourteen African countries produced information concerning the history of their schools of social work curriculum (UN, 1964c, No. 3).

The fourth monograph, *Social reconstruction in the newly-independent countries of East Africa* (UN, 1965) looks at trends in social reconstruction in East Africa. Researching six East African countries, the researcher set out to

... explore and examine the peculiar features of rapid social change and adjustment resulting from the quick political transformation in that sub-region; how these have evolved, the problems and tensions which have followed the change-over from colonial administration to national sovereignty, and the various efforts of the individual national governments, both to achieve satisfactory readjustments and to transform their economic and social systems. (p. 1)

The four areas that came up as concerns were: 1) desegregation (the crumbling of racial barriers and banning legal discrimination); 2) rectification (equalizing living standards between town and country and of bridging the gulf that separates rich from poor. It is about restoring a just balance between the rural areas and the urban areas.); 3) the racial pyramid (non-Africans earn ten times as much as Africans, and variables to consider are social class, educational level, life expectancy at birth, occupation, and residential location. These all produce a race-linkage pyramid.); and 4) the new order (it's attributes being national, nationalist, planned, non-racial, nation-wide one-party solidarity, co-operation, and re-development of human resources).

In 1966 the *Family, child and youth welfare services in Africa* monograph was published emphasizing the mother and the family, health problems, food and nutrition, and social welfare for children and youth, including the rural exodus of youth (UN, 1966, No. 5). In 1967, *The status and role of women in East Africa* was published looking at all aspects of women's issues, including education, family life, work, community development, legal and political rights of women, and the participation of women in community life (UN, 1967b, No. 6). *Youth employment and national development in Africa* was the next monograph, and it concentrated on the problems of youth unemployment and youth training schemes (UN, 1969, No. 7). In 1971, *Integrated approach to rural development in Africa* was published, documenting factors influencing rural development, problems of rural development, present strategies for rural development, and an integrated approach to rural development (UN, 1971b, No. 8). These monographs are important in documenting the social development of African countries and the important dialogue that took place concerning social work education. They are indigenous to the African continent and are thus important to the historical understanding of the evolution of social work and social services in Africa. It is unknown whether these documents are used in social work history courses in African Schools of Social Work. They should be. Possible reasons they may not be used are that these monographs are not available in many parts of Africa and ordering them through the UN is expensive. However, they are important documents to critically analyze as part of the history of social work in Africa.

2. Continental level

Association for Social Work Education in Africa. The social work profession came nearest to being accepted by Ghanaian society during the era of Kwame Nkrumah (1951–66). One pioneer of social work in Ghana, Dr. Blavo, recalls those years:

The aim of the country at that time was a welfare state. So they tried to recognize social work as a profession. And for the first time in the whole of West Africa, a meeting was held in these same premises [the University of Ghana] concerning social work.... But even then it [the welfare state] was not done because the man [Kwame Nkrumah] was ousted and we went back to square one. (Kreitzer, 2004a, pp. 49–50)

The conference mentioned above was preceded by other conferences concerning urbanization and industrialization and their effect on African social issues. They were held in various places in West Africa. The first was held in Abidjan, Ivory Coast, in 1954; another took place in 1961. Still others were held in Accra–1960, the Congo–1961, Abidjan–1962, and Dar-es-Salaam–1962 (Drake & Omari, 1962).

In 1962, a conference was held at the University of Ghana, Legon, entitled "Social Work in West Africa." The president of Ghana, Kwame Nkrumah, asked the Ministry of Labour and Social Welfare "to explore the possibility of convening a conference in collaboration with the Department of Sociology of the University of Ghana for the purpose of discussing problems confronting social workers throughout West Africa" (Drake & Omari, 1962, p. 2). Fifty-three delegates came from five West African countries: Ghana, Guinea, Nigeria, Sierra Leone, Togo, and Ivory Coast. The purpose of the conference was to "a) discuss present methods of social work, particularly in West African countries, b) make concrete proposals for improved methods of social work and c) foster inter-territorial co-operation" (p. 3). The introductory comments spelled out the situation in West Africa at that time:

With the recent changes in political and economic structures in West Africa, it seems timely to consider the attendant social problems, their causes and what solutions we have for them. The African Way is no less relevant in the field of Social Welfare than in other areas, but it should conform to the internationally accepted principles and practice of social work and we do not wish to be found wanting in this respect. (p. 3)

Recommendations were made in the areas of creating a journal of social work, professional training, the professional status of social work, appropriate legislation concerning social issues, research and different areas of vulnerability in society.

In 1963, an important conference was held in Lusaka, Zambia, on social work training in Africa (ASWEA, Doc. 6, 1974c) that "created a number of chain reactions and several developments took place in connection with social work education" (p. 17). This conference instigated the monographs described above and focussed on preventive rather than remedial practice. The common problems of social work education were identified: "a) general shortage of trained social workers at all levels, including teaching staff, b) lack of adequate local literature for teaching purposes, lack of adequate financial backing to improve and expand training facilities and c) problems of determining curricular content" (p. 17). The main concern expressed at this conference was that social work and social work education was not working for Africa because of its western origins and there was a need to redevelop African social work for Africa. Other issues identified in this conference were the differences between anglophone and francophone countries concerning social welfare and the need to "concentrate more on the preventative than the remedial.... Social welfare programs should be concerned more with developmental or educational activities of the community in order to raise the standard of living of the total population instead of special groups" (ASWEA, Doc. 6, 1974c, p. 18).

Creation of ASWEA. The above conference set the stage for a further conference in Alexandria, Egypt, in 1965. Sixteen African schools of social work were represented, and the purpose was to "examine the content of training programs and syllabuses and to make a critical survey of existing trends in training for social work" (p. 18). In 1969, the Expert Working Group of Social Work Educators met to further discuss the issue of social work training in West Africa. The Second Expert Working Group met in the same year with the intent of establishing the Association for Social Work Education in Africa (ASWEA). The Third Expert Working Group, in 1971, formally established ASWEA (Asamoah, 1995). The purpose of the organization was to "serve, among many other functions, as a forum where social work educators will discuss and resolve common problems that face Schools of Social Work in Africa" (p. 20). From the first United Nations Surveys to the monographs and these earlier conferences, the stage was set to create an organization that would bring African social workers and academics together to discuss issues surrounding the evolution of social work education in Africa. One pioneer of social work in Ghana, Dr. Blavo, explained to the research group the importance of the ASWEA seminars:

> We were attending ASWEA seminars and the reports from these conferences were being used as teaching material. ASWEA motivated or got money to get a casework booklet, collected caseworks from the whole of Africa, which we were using ... so indigenous teaching materials had long been started in 1960s here to the 1970s in ASWEA where the United Nations Economic Commission (UNEC) started and are doing all these things to help social work to be accepted by the society. (Kreitzer, 2004a, p. 52)

From 1971 to 1989, ASWEA produced an impressive twenty-one documents. A social work journal was established in 1974 and eight issues were published. ASWEA offered the institutional backup to put the issue of social development on the agenda in Africa (ASWEA, 1986). The momentum of the 1960s to the 1980s offered a good start to an effective organization to bring social work into the forefront of African issues.

Details of the documents. The first five ASWEA documents were published in 1972 and only one is still available. They are as follows: 1) An effort in community development in the Lakota Sub; 2) Community services, Lakota Project Methodology; 3) The important role of supervision in social welfare organizations; 4) The use of films in social development education; and 5) Guidelines for making contact with young people in informal groups in urban areas. The only one available is document number 3 (ASWEA, Doc. 3, 1972), and this document laid out the important part that supervision can play in "promoting continuous and progressive learning" (p. 8). It included the process of supervision, the structure of supervision, and the qualifications of a supervisor. Special reference was made to the importance of the supervisor in fieldwork.

Following the above documents, compilations of case studies in social development were completed; one from West Africa and one from East Africa (ASWEA, Vol. 1, 1973; ASWEA, Vol. 2, 1974a). Funded and supported by the United Nations Children's Fund (UNICEF) and the United Nations Economic Commission for Africa (UNECA), the case studies project was launched and seven East African countries were selected to develop case studies. These countries were Ethiopia, Kenya, Malawi, Mauritius, Tanzania, Uganda, and Zambia (ASWEA, 1973). "From each country, a set of ten cases in group work and community development activities were compiled" (p. ii) because there were no African case studies available and social work students and teachers continued to rely on western case studies that didn't always fit within an African context. There was an urgent need to compile these for classroom use. "These cases are believed to be more realistic and comprehensible to the African students than the ones they are used to in most cases – excerpts from western written textbooks" (p. iii). Analysis of each case study and questions for classroom use are provided after each scenario. In 1974, a similar compilation was completed for West Africa that included the countries of Ghana (English), Sierra Leone (English), Maurice (French), Togo (French), Ethiopia (French), Madagascar (French), Malawi (French), Uganda (French), and Zambia (French) with French translations. These documents provide a wonderful and rich teaching resource for social work classrooms in Africa.

In 1973, the General Assembly for ASWEA was convened in Togo and looked at the *Relationship between social work education and national social development plan* (ASWEA, Doc. 6, 1974c). Four papers were given, including one from Dr. Shawky, in which the complacency of social work educators and practitioners regarding influencing the development of social policy was highlighted. One of the major discussions at this conference and throughout all future conferences was the use of the terms 'social development' and 'social welfare.' There was a strong move to replace the term 'social welfare' with 'social development' and as a result social welfare workers were encouraged to call themselves 'social development workers.' This debate reflected the tension between the emerging capitalist/socialist trends in Africa and the need for solid social policy that was developmental as well as the need for social development workers to advocate for social development. The traditional social welfare role of remedial social work was too dominant on the continent and the need for social development workers for the whole country was paramount. The influence of western curriculum, complacency of educators to change the curriculum, and the imbalance of financial support for urban development at the expense of rural development were also highlighted.

The next document published was *Curricula of schools of social work and community development training centres in Africa* (ASWEA, Doc. 7, 1974b). This was a comparative study of the curricula of relevant schools and training centres (nineteen countries were represented) so that a "cross-referencing of training curricula" could be used in order to "later, modify and strengthen curricula so that the training would be in harmony with the over-all objectives the respective National Development Plan" (p. i). It highlighted the need for a good exchange of information and sharing of experience among African countries.

The *Directory of social welfare activities in Africa* (3rd ed.; ASWEA, Doc. 8, 1975a) provided a list of activities and projects of national social welfare agencies in forty-one different African countries. The purpose was to: 1) promote the exchange of information related to social work/development; 2) establish a better flow of information between ASWEA and other social welfare agencies; 3) provide information on existing resources and experiences already available within and outside the region; and 4) serve as reference material for Schools of Social Work and training centres. Following the country-specific activities of these countries, the United Nations activities were listed followed by international voluntary organizations and professional organizations in social welfare. The document finished by including a chart listing basic information on schools of social work and community development training centres in Africa.

In 1974, a workshop in Ethiopia was held concerning the *Techniques of teaching and method of field work evaluation* (ASWEA, Doc. 9, 1975b), with ten African countries represented. The aim was to divert from the same lecture style of teaching and to bring creative styles of learning to the workshop. Techniques of teaching included: 1) relationships between teachers and students; 2) use of case studies; 3) use of role playing; 4) using media for developing ideas; and 5) planning the teaching process. The second half of the workshop looked at methods for fieldwork evaluation. A similar workshop was held the following year for French speakers in Cameroon (ASWEA, Doc. 10, 1976b).

In 1976, *Realities and aspirations of social work education in Africa* was the theme for the third ASWEA conference in Ethiopia (ASWEA, Doc. 11, 1976a). This conference was marked by the support of the International Association of Schools of Social Work (IASSW) and followed the theme of the XVIII IASSW conference in Puerto Rico. This support brought Africa into the international professional arena. Forty-three representatives from fourteen African countries attended. Five issues were highlighted by the rapporteur's report: 1) the involvement of schools of social work are crucial to national development; 2) social work services need to be indigenized and foreign models of service provision need to be changed so that services meet the needs of Africans; 3) research should be an important part of understanding what is needed in Africa and a regional research and training centre should be established for local social work educators; 4) family planning needs to be a core part of social work curriculum; and 5) national governments need to support the work of the schools of social work. The debate concerning a social development approach to social work progressed during this conference.

A regional workshop was also held after the ASWEA conference with the theme of *The role of social development education in Africa's struggle for political and economic independence* (ASWEA, Doc. 12, 1977). Four main objectives were: 1) to broaden the teaching skills of African teachers, instructors, educators and supervisors of schools of social work and community development courses; 2) to identify common problems of social work and community development training and reflect on how to minimize these problems and how to indigenize training methods and materials; 3) to acquaint participants with the role, objectives, and programs of ASWEA; 4) to strengthen professional associations; and 5) to "acquaint the participants with the objectives of the Organization of African Unity (OAU), instil the idea of pan-African solidarity, and encourage them to propagate the idea in their respective institutions" (p. 12). Dr. Tesfaye's address highlighted the following issues with curriculum:

The dearth of teaching materials related to the particular culture of the respective countries of the continent had been a chronic problem. As basic social service materials adapted for classroom teaching are in short supply, there has been a heavy reliance on books and other materials produced in the industrialized countries in the West. (p. 52)

Why are schools of social work in Africa so shy in radically reorganizing their curricula? Is the problem within or outside the schools? ... Social welfare training in Africa draws its objectives and strategies from the socio-economic needs of African peoples and also from the development strategies adopted by African Governments. In order to develop sound social welfare curricula, social welfare policies in African countries must be clearly spelled [out]. (p. 53)

Revolutionizing social work training and practice was suggested as far back as the 1970s.

The next two documents published were from the ASWEA Expert Group meeting in Addis Ababa in 1978. Unique to this workshop was the presentation of country statements concerning *Guidelines for the development of a training curriculum in family welfare*, the title of the conference. Ghana was one of six countries to make statements concerning training they had developed in family welfare (ASWEA, Doc. 13, 1978b). The five areas of interest around the topic were as follows: "1) basic demographic situation of African countries; 2) health aspects of family welfare problems; 3) policies and programmes on population and family welfare in Africa; 4) social development programmes and family welfare; and 5) the role of social development and social welfare workers in population and family welfare and incorporation of these questions in social development education" (p. 21). Two main discussions centred on national policies with regard to population and family welfare and social work curriculum, social theory, and practice. In 1978, a similar workshop was held in Addis Ababa for francophone countries (ASWEA, Doc. 14, 1978a).

The next ASWEA seminar in Lusaka, Zambia, highlighted the work of the expert groups with the topic *Guidelines for the development of a training curriculum in family welfare* (ASWEA, Doc. 15, 1978c). The seminar was a follow-up to the previous seminars concerning family welfare. The purpose of the seminar was to give the opportunity for ASWEA member institutions 1) to evaluate their experiences and programs in regards to family welfare; 2) conduct an examination of relevant materials, country statements, and resource papers to see if family planning was effective; 3) review curriculum, and 4) make appropriate recommendations about the incorporation of the proposed curricula into the existing curricula of social development training institutions. An extensive curriculum on family welfare and planning was designed for use in African schools of social work courses. In Lome, Togo, the following year, a francophone seminar was held on the topic of *Principes directeurs pour l'établissement d'un programme d'étude destine à la formation aux disciplines de la protection de la famille* (ASWEA, Doc. 16, 1979).

The fourth ASWEA conference was held in Ethiopia in 1981. Eighteen African countries were represented to look at the theme *Social development training in Africa: Experiences of the 1970s and emerging trends of the 1980s* (ASWEA, Doc. 17, 1981). The objectives of the conference were to

> ... examine and discuss social development in the continent and its potential role in the promotion of social development programmes ... examine country statements to determine the impact of social work education in the overall development strategy of Africa, and to identify resources, opportunities, limitations and constraints and make appropriate recommendations for the indigenization of social development concepts and approaches. (p. 7)

There was concern about the "neglect of the social dimensions of development both in the colonial and post-colonial eras" (p. 24). These social dimensions were: 1) demographic characteristics of African populations; 2) deficiencies in the formal educational system; 3) low rate of female participation in the labour force; 4) plight of physically disabled persons in Africa who have to fend for themselves through begging; and 5) displaced persons like refugees, victims of man-made and natural disasters. The conference recommended: 1) pushing governments to promote the role of social planners and to support a more highly trained workforce in social development; 2) that curricula be more specific to the needs of Africans in different countries and that teaching materials be produced to help in the curricula development; 3) that research capabilities be intensified; and 4) international cooperation be promoted and in particular ASWEA representatives need to sit on United Nations, government, and OAU meetings and projects. In 1982 another *Survey of curricula of social development training institutions in Africa* (ASWEA, Doc. 18, 1982b) was produced with twenty-eight countries providing information about their social work programmes. The objectives of the seminar was: 1) to show similarities and differences between the curricula of the anglophone and francophone training programs; 2) to show what courses are being taught at the intermediate and higher levels of training; 3) to assess courses to their effectiveness and appropriateness for African realities; 4) to evaluate teaching material and methods; and 5) to stimulate further discussion about social development training.

An ASWEA seminar was held in Egypt with the theme *Organization and delivery of social services to rural areas in Africa* (ASWEA, Doc. 19, 1982a). In highlighting the issues of rural development, it examined course content of rural development and the opportunity for the exchange of ideas and recommendations concerning rural development. In particular, the role of women in rural development was discussed. Recommendations included: 1) making structural and infrastructural changes to social development; 2) taking a multi-disciplinary approach to rural development using research as a guide; 3) making rural development a component of national planning, including rural development in social work education; and 4) recognizing the role of women in rural development. The fifth ASWEA conference was held in Ethiopia in 1985. The theme was *Training for social development: Methods of intervention to improve people's participation in rural transformation in Africa with special emphasis on women* (ASWEA, Doc. 20, 1985). Six areas were examined, including: 1) community participation; 2) research; 3) curriculum; 4) women and development; and 5) population and regional cooperation. "About 80% of the African population lives in rural areas where social services are either inadequate or totally non-existent. It is therefore recommended that African governments give top priority to Rural Development" (p. 9). A curriculum for rural development was created for social work courses.

The final document was a selection of readings (ASWEA, Doc. 21, 1989) from the previous conference. The readings included issues around: 1) giving faculty the chance to examine operational implications of the concepts of social development and integrated rural development for practice; 2) identifying areas of activities that social service agencies are involved in; 3) examining the content in existing curricula and seeing what needs to be added; 4) exploring training in research and evaluation methods in social development curricula; and 5) examining staff development and training and teaching material to see if it is adequate to the task. Concerning curricula, guidelines should be developed in the areas of "rural development, women in development and child survival and development" (p. iii). By the fifth conference, "ASWEA had a membership of about 55 Social Development Training Institutions and 150 social work educators from 33 African countries" (Tesfaye, 1985, p. 17). From these conferences and workshops two culturally relevant course outlines were developed in family planning and rural development.

The sad fact is that few African social work students and academics are aware of these documents and little analysis has been completed on them. Whether these documents were buried for political reasons or lost due to wars, the destruction of infrastructure and the closing of the School of Social Work in Addis Abba are unknown but these documents contribute to a knowledge base that needs to form part of the emerging identity of social work in Africa and international social work. Midgley (1981), Asamoah (1995), and Yimam (1990) are exceptions to the above statement and have mentioned these in their writings. Most of these documents are in the United States and a 2009/2010 joint Association of Schools of Social Work in Africa (ASSWA)/International Association of Schools of Social Work (IASSW) and the University of Calgary, Faculty of Social Work, project brought these documents back to Africa. Students, practitioners, and academics can analyze them and use them for teaching in the classroom. These documents are crucial to understanding the history of social work in Africa.

The African Centre for Applied Research and Training in Social Development (ACARTSOD). The United Nations Surveys, the monographs, and the ASWEA conferences were instrumental in engaging the continent in developing the profession of social work. Other conferences emerged that continued this engagement. One was the Conference of Ministers that was first was held in 1968 (Asamoah, 1995). "This conference challenged the international social work community to pursue a dynamic agenda that would put social work out front on issues of development and make it, as a profession, more relevant to current realities" (p. 225). The second conference, now called the Conference of African Ministers of Social Affairs, was held in 1977; the third in 1980. They "continued to press the issue of reorienting social welfare services to a developmental model and training key personnel accordingly" (p. 226). The African Centre for Applied Research and Training in Social Development (ACARTSOD) was formed out of these conferences, and together ASWEA and ACARTSOD highlighted issues concerning social work practice and training through their work and publications.

> A systematic study of the gradual development of social work
> education in Africa indicates that certain amount of dynamism
> has been generated since the early 1960s. The various national
> and international seminars, conferences and expert group
> meetings on social work education and practice that have been
> taking place throughout the continent are good testimony.
> (Tesfaye, 1973, p. 16)

The above gives an overall picture of the kinds of activities that took place between the 1960s and the 1980s in North, East, and West Africa. Many of the issues raised through the literature and social work conferences are still being debated today. This raises the question as to why progress has been so slow (Asamoah, 1995). A fourth set of documents conclude this section on historical documents relating to social work in Africa. These are national documents from seminars organized by the Ghana Association of Social Workers and paralleled the ASWEA seminars. The seminars are progressive for their time, practical to the situation in Ghana, and come from grassroots issues confronting social work and Ghanaian national development.

3. National level

Ghana Association of Social Workers. The Ghana Association of
Social Workers (GASOW) was established in 1971. Members active in
planning their own seminars and publishing these seminars as part of
indigenous education material for teachers and students. The purpose of
GASOW was to

> a) promote activities that strengthen and unify the social work
> profession as a whole, b) stimulate sound and continuous
> development of the various areas of social work practice as a
> contribution to meeting human needs and c) contribute effect-
> ively to the improvement of social conditions in the country.
> (GASOW, 1972, p. v)

Mrs. Nana Apt, secretary of GASW was instrumental in organizing these
seminars and publishing their content. The first seminar was in 1972, ten
years after the conference on Social Work in West Africa encouraged by
Kwame Nkrumah and after over twenty-five years of organized western
professional social work in Ghana (GASOW, 1972). This first seminar was
held at the University of Ghana, Legon, and the theme was *Social welfare
education and practice in developing countries.* Sponsored by the Friedrich-Ebert
Foundation, the seminar featured Mr. Walter Karberg, the Director of
Information, ASWEA, and Dr. Jona Rosenfeld of the Hebrew University
School of Social Work. "It was felt that Ghana could learn from Israel's
experience in development" (p. vi). The speaker from ASWEA spoke
of changing the term 'social welfare' to 'social development' in order to
"highlight the future perspective of social welfare in Africa" (p. 11). The
seminar identified several sources of social workers' discontent, including
discontent with the profession, social conditions, and national priorities.
Recommendations were made and are very interesting:

> a) the name social welfare be replaced with social development,
> b) the term social worker be replaced with social development
> officer, c) investigate the basis of differential treatment ac-
> corded to social workers in different areas of work, d) GASOW

be the voice of social protest through professional publications etc. (pp. 66–67)

The second GASOW seminar was held in 1973 with the theme *Social planning in national development* (GASOW, 1973). This conference addressed many of the national issues facing social planning in Ghana, including the resettling of over 80,000 people displaced by the Akosombo Dam on the Volta River and the planning of the new town of Tema, created as a result of the building of Tema Harbour. A wider question of the conference spoke to the need to collaborate with other countries; this point came from guest speakers from Tanzania and Mali.

> The Ghana Association of Social Workers support the views of our foreign guests in hoping that in the not too distant future, social workers in Africa, East, West and Central shall get together in mutual co-operation to develop social welfare practice in the total African context, and thereby transcend any political and other boundaries that now appear to separate us. (p. ix)

In 1974, the third GASOW seminar was held with the theme *The role of agriculture and rural technology in national development*. It observed "the realization that social workers in a developing country like Ghana ought to break away from traditional welfare practices and be more involved in the economic development of the nation, is gradually catching on" (GASOW, 1974, p. 5). The purpose of this seminar was to

> a) bring together an interdisciplinary group of social workers, community development workers, specialists in the field of agriculture and rural technology and social and economic planners to look at agriculture and rural technology, b) to review research in these areas and c) to develop guidelines for social workers which will enable them to play their role as rural animators and initiators of social change efficiently (pp. 5–6).

Representatives from ten different African countries were present, as well as professionals from other faculties within the University of Ghana at Legon and the University of Science and Technology in Kumasi.

The fourth seminar, held in 1975, concerned *Popular participation and the new local government system* (GASOW, 1975). The objectives of this seminar continued to be very relevant to the local situation in Ghana and the role of social work in this ever-changing society.

> The objectives were to a) bring together social workers and local government officials from Ghana and other West African countries to examine the structure and functions of the new local government system in Ghana, b) to develop practical guidelines for greater participation and effective utilization of local resources in development and c) to consider the Treaty establishing the Economic Community for West African States (ECOWAS) and its implications for social work and social services. (p. 5)

These seminars were impressive examples of the energy and commitment by GASOW to develop the profession of social work and give it an important voice to the Government of Ghana. The seminars also exemplified the continual attempt to intertwine social work and the important issues facing Ghana in the 1970s. I was not able to find any more publications of GASOW after the fourth seminar. One of the reasons for this was the untimely car accident that the secretary endured, requiring her to go to Germany for a year to recover. No one was able to do the things she had done and GASOW seminars lapsed. Since that time the professional association has had its ups and downs and more recently has not represented the profession of social work effectively. This was part of the action plans for the research project that will be explained in chapter VI.

4. Summary

This section on the United Nations surveys, the United Nations monographs, the creation of the ASWEA and its role, through the seminars, of addressing social issues in Africa, the influence of ACARTSOD and

GASOW seminars highlight the amount of work that was completed in a twenty-year period concerning social work development in Africa. Added to these documents concerning the growth of the social work profession in Africa are the country-specific stories of how social work was developed in those countries and a critical analysis of each country's success with the profession. If the feelings of social workers in countries that I have had contact with through my research, conferences, and personal contact are a reflection of what is happening in other parts of Africa, then the profession is still struggling to find its identity throughout the continent. A case in point is Ghana. The following is a brief summary of how social work emerged in a country influenced by the British but was also at the heart of Pan-Africanism through its first president Kwame Nkrumah.

C. History of social work in Ghana

1. Introduction

The history of the profession of social work in Ghana coincides with the development of a colonial social welfare system. However, according to a pioneer of social work in Ghana, Dr. Blavo, social work "has been in existence from time immemorial in Ghana because we all have problems … long ago, before colonialism, social work was in practice but it was being performed by a different group of people". Another pioneer in social work, Professor Apt, agrees:

> Before colonialism, social problems were solved within the context of a traditional system, which had always been an integral part of social life of the indigenous people. This traditional system was a social institution of extended families characterized by strong family ties, which assured the security of its members. The system dictated its social norms, safeguarded its moral values and conserved its economic base. (Apt & Blavo, 1997, p. 320)

Asamoah (1995) explains that "African social work has historical roots which are value based, indigenous and imported" (p. 223).

2. Colonial period

The need for professional social workers increased with the breakdown of the family institutions. Dr. Blavo explained:

> When Ghana was colonized our extended family system and the power of the chiefs broke down and this also came with its problems so the colonists brought in what they call "social work" to help solve the problems due to the capitalist economy and the broken down extended family.

Before these times, "religious missions to the Gold Coast, working closely with ethnic societies, provided various charities for families in need" (Apt & Blavo, 1997, p. 320).

> In Africa organized social services owes much to the activities of missionaries who pioneered in the medical services, in education and in the care of needy children and mothers ... the missionaries were involved in literacy ... they did much to bring home to colonial administrations the need to concern themselves with the social welfare of their subjects. (UN, 1964, No. 2, p. 7)

On June 22, 1939, an earthquake with a magnitude of 6.5 on the Richter scale struck the Gold Coast (Amponsah, 2003) and many people lost their homes. Shortly thereafter, veterans from the Second World War began returning to Ghana and families were experiencing problems related to separation due to war. Both of these factors influenced the government to take action to help affected individuals and families. In 1929, the British government passed the first Colonial Development Act (Wicker, 1958). This led to the Colonial Development and Welfare Act of 1940. Social development projects were requested by the colonial administration that "maximized co-operation of the local peoples in the initiation and execution of projects" (p. 182). In the 1940s, a Secretary of Social Services was appointed and given the task of coordinating all existing welfare activities in the country. In 1946, the Department of Social Welfare and Housing was created. Other changes followed. "A social development branch of this department was set up in 1948, which has now become the Community Development Department. In 1951, social welfare separated from housing and a Ministry of Education and Social Welfare was created" (Apt & Blavo, 1997, p. 320). The Department of Social Welfare and Community Development was created in 1952. Due to the many changes between ministries and departments during this time, it was becoming increasingly important to have trained social workers. The first recruits in Ghana for the profession were volunteers and experienced people who had acquired some knowledge of human beings. They recruited experienced and mature people to do the work especially teachers and people who had worked in the villages. The required training was short because these experienced volunteers had the background knowledge of human behaviour, and all they needed was the social work theory and methods subjects.

In the 1940s, in Ghana, both expatriate and indigenous social workers were all trained overseas. A classic example was a well-known social worker and head of the Social Welfare Department in Accra, whom I met when I was volunteering in Ghana. "David was one of seven teachers selected by the new Department of Social Welfare to proceed to the London School of Economics and Political Science to undertake a two-year course leading to the Social Science Certificate in 1945" (Hill House newsletter, 2004, No. 1). These new practitioners formed the nucleus of the administration of social welfare.

In 1948, an indigenous initiative took place in Ghana that used the skills of professional social workers. This was the community development movement (Sautoy, 1958), which grew "during the 1950s as one of the most important factors in the social and economic development of the country" (Abloh & Ameyaw, 1997). More importantly, community development depended upon inspired voluntary leaders (Sautoy, 1958) and traditional local leaders who contributed through their knowledge and skills in the area of village development (Abloh & Ameyaw, 1997). Community development provided "adult literacy, home economics, self-help village projects, extension campaign (teaching locals how to improve their lifestyle) and training" (pp. 282–83). Much of the success of community development was due to financial backing from the colonial government and the rise of nationalism. The rise of nationalism not only helped community development; it also helped the profession of social work become public. As one pioneer of social work, Dr. Blavo, explained:

> Social work practice in Ghana, and I am saying we were lucky to be more or less the first to try and start in Africa what we now call professional social work. Because by that time we were free … we had been liberated but the other parts were still fighting for their liberation.

Between 1945 and 57, the Colonial Development and Welfare Act was revised to include greater funding and commitments to social sciences; including education, medical and health services, housing, nutrition, water supplies, broadcasting, and welfare. Britain set up a welfare system "that reflected both the ideology and basic structures of the system in the United Kingdom" (Asamoah & Nortey, 1987, p. 22). These structures used primarily a remedial model in which clients problems were identified and immediate needs were sought to solve the problem. Preventive measures, structural changes, and social developmental social services were not addressed. Attention was given to physical and mental rehabilitation, with special attention to homeless children, the disabled, women, and migrants. Asamoah & Beverly (1988) point out the short-sightedness of the colonial welfare policy as: "(a) failure to take a holistic view of the human condition, (b) an overriding importance of political considerations, (c) minimization of the positive effects of traditional structures, and (d) emphasis on economic expediency or advantage for the colonial power instead of benefiting the colonies" (p. 178).

3. Social work training in Ghana

The School of Social Work in Osu, established in 1946, offered a "nine-month certificate course" (Apt & Blavo, 1997, p. 328). One of the important figures during this time was Dr. Gardiner. "He actually started the

School of Social Work and he was then the Director of Social Welfare and Community Development.... [T]hen the University of Ghana came together with the Department of Social Welfare and they moved the program to the University" (Kreitzer, 2004a, p. 27). The University of Ghana, Legon, began social work training in 1956.

> Since 1956 the University of Ghana has taken responsibility for training of social workers at higher levels. A two-year diploma course in social administration was designed for experienced trained social workers who were products of the certificate course ... a 10-week mandatory field experience was included. (Apt & Blavo, 1997, p. 328)

Dr. Apt, head of the social work unit for many years, explained the different types of people who enrolled in this diploma course.

> There were the beginnings of a whole lot of interest from different spheres: education, social security, even firms, textile firms. Telephone companies where they would be sending people to come and take the social work course.... I found a whole spectrum of institutions interested to send their workers/employees to come and take the diploma course.

She went on to say that as the social work profession progressed in Ghana, the training requirements became more comprehensive.

> If the university was to recognize a particular study they also had requirements. The training should be scientific and there should be a lot of research. We had to pump into the curriculum research knowledge ... and then the profession had international standards that required background subjects, knowledge of man and society ... for a trained social worker, theory should match with practice. This was the requirement by the international Association to recognize as a professional training that we should have a strong fieldwork practice.

Thus, fieldwork began with student placements in local and national agencies, with the added task of organizing supervisors for the students. This new undertaking challenged the already-depleted financial support.

In 1989, a three-year undergraduate course in social work was established at the University of Ghana, Legon. Yvonne Asamoah, together with others like Nana Apt, developed a bachelor's program. To date, Mrs. Asamoah is one of the few authors in the western world to publish articles and book chapters, particularly in Ghana and West Africa, which document the history of social work in parts of Africa (Asamoah & Nortey, 1987; Asamoah & Beverly, 1988; Asamoah, 1995).

In 2000, the social work unit separated from the sociology department and became the Department of Social Work. In 2001, the bachelor's curriculum was revised and the master's program was created. In 2003, the first master's program was started, with fifteen students enrolled. In 2004, the revised bachelor's program began, with our project's recommendations contributing to this revision.

The profession of social work was most dynamic during the initial independence years when the government spent time and money on health, education, and social welfare. Since the 1980s, the profession has suffered from the political, economic, and social problems due to many countries plagued by world debt, coups, and general instability. When asked why social work seemed to have collapsed, Professor Apt, a pioneer in social work in Ghana, stated that continual government withdrawal of funding as well as a change in attitude towards how social services should be administered were factors.

> When the Department of Social Welfare and Community Development was set up part of the problem was that in Ghana they seemed to think that if you work in social welfare and this person also works in community development and another in rehabilitation, you who are in welfare can never work in community development. If you are in welfare you can work with youth or family but somebody in community development can never work with youth or family.... I believe that everybody who has gone through a bachelor's degree ought to have the

competence to work with individuals, groups and communities. (Kreitzer, 2004a, p. 30)

This separation continues today. Community workers have their own educational training facilities, and there continues to be a Department of Social Welfare and a Department of Community Development. Maybe this is why social work continues to struggle to find its proper place in Ghanaian society.

D. Conclusion of chapter

In this chapter I have given an overview of how African education at the post-secondary level has been influenced by colonization and how this has created universities that continue to teach from a Eurocentric worldview. This situation influenced how social work training in many parts of Africa continued during colonialism. With the independence of colonized countries and the entrance into the global economy, international institutions such as the United Nations saw the need for the profession of social work to be introduced to these countries. They were introduced by experts from western countries with the assumption that western social work education and practice was transferable. Continental, national, and local organizations tried to take this western profession and integrate it into the African context. The documentation of these organizations like ASWEA and GASOW were summarized in an effort to conscientize readers as to the important contribution African has made to the social work profession worldwide. As Maathai (2009) states: "What Africans need to do, as much as they can, is recapture a feeling for their pasts that is not solely filtered through the prism of the colonialists" (p. 182). These documents are the work of Africans concerning social work education. A theme throughout these documents and emerging through African social work writings and in my research is that western social work education and practice has not worked well for Africa. Yes, it provided social work training that upheld the colonial social welfare institutions that were needed when capitalism broke down traditional society. It grew and developed through the above local and national seminars. These documents highlight the same themes over and over again, and there seems to have been little forward movement. These themes are that 1) social work remains on the periphery[2] in Africa; 2) social work education and practice continues to be Eurocentric and not ideally suited to the African social, cultural, and economic context; and 3) attempts to change training and practice have been slow in coming (ASWEA, Doc.12, 1977; ASWEA, Doc. 17, 1981). In summarizing the themes of one ASWEA conference, Dr. Murapa (ASWEA, Doc. 12, 1977), in his rapporteur's report stated:

> A major observation made was the fact that there exists, in the field of social work education and training, a disturbing paucity of innovative teaching methodology and materials. Most of the fields, African instructors, being from the most part products of Western education, have proved either incapable or unwilling to engage in extensive and creative revision of the existing text books, curricula and approaches to make them relevant to the social and other developmental problems and aspirations in Africa. There is a need for social work educators to be original and innovative in developing new and appropriate conceptual framework, which, in turn, would produce relevant social education theories. With the problem and goal pointed out, the question arose as to how to produce the desired type of teacher, curricula and approach. No exhaustive panacea was found there than urging that action be taken both individually and collectively. (p. 32)

Understanding the reasons for this slow pace of change is essential for the design and implementation of future social work education and practice. The lack of a critical analysis as to whether the profession, in its present state, should even remain the same continues.

Williams (1987) speaks to the necessity of the liberation of the African mind from thousands of years of oppression by many different forces in the world. Concerning Africans, he says the following: "Dependence has become comfortable; it frees them from the initiative, responsibility and planning required of independent free men and women. 'Leave it to the white folks' has become their unspoken creed" (p. 317). Continuing a dependency on western social work education and practice may have something to do with the lack of pride in the profession. A lack of pride in the profession may result from a foreign system intruding upon society. "Social work as it is known today is an *'adopted child'* in the African context" (ASWEA, Doc. 11, 1976a, p. 28). If something is not indigenous but comes from an outside source, there is a feeling that it is not quite right and does not support the culture that it has been placed into, which causes it to be on the periphery of society. This causes a crisis of identity and herein lies one of the key challenges facing social work and social workers in Africa; the loss of cultural identity. As Kofi Annan (Annan 2007) states: "Our narratives have become our prison." How will Africans reshape their narrative in order to break the mental bondages of western imperialism? The president of the Ivory Coast, Laurent Gbagbo, forcefully stated one critical necessity when speaking of the 2007 Ivorian Crisis: "The Ivorian Crisis revealed to me that Africans underestimate themselves and do not have confidence in themselves. Time has come for Africans to have confidence in themselves, to take their destiny into their own hands. Time has come for Africans to have partners and not masters" (Tete, 2007, p. 46). The social work profession reflects the state of the society in which it operates. This crisis of identity is, therefore, directly linked to the success of social work in Africa.

II. Cultural Identity

Disunity and noncooperation have been characteristics of black society. And this fact, more than anything else, helps in understanding not only why the Blacks eventually lost their battles with the whites, but also why even today they are still unable to deal with the white world. This situation of antagonism, self-hatred and attending disunity in the race is a matter of grave concern (Williams, 1987).[1]

A. African culture and identity

In William's book (1987) on the destruction of black civilization, he links disunity of the race as a result of a loss of cultural identity in a world where the dominant culture has not been African. This identity crisis has historical roots reinforced through colonization and exploitation. The consequences are a continent of people still trying to find their way in a global world dominated by western influences. From early on, the continent has been an unknown entity with western writers and scholars ignoring it, fearing it, intrigued by it, devaluing it, and speaking about it as the "heart of darkness" (Conrad, 1995). G.W.F. Hegel (1956) simplified African culture when he wrote:

> Africa is no historical part of the world; it has no movements or development to exhibit. Historical movements in it – that is in its northern part – belong to the Asiatic or European World.... [W]hat we properly understand by Africa, is the unhistorical, undeveloped spirit, still involved in the conditions of mere nature and which had to be present here only as on the threshold of the World's History. (p. 99)

Willinsky (1998) comments on Hegel's attitude towards Africa: "The radical historical consequence of this Hegelian progression of consciousness is a world divided among people who live inside and outside history.... Hegel constructed his philosophy of history on this principle of inequitable participation in History, which is not a given of human experience; it is a privileged mode of being in the world" (p. 119). As Kuykendall (1993) states: "Hegel's Philosophy of History is a philosophical treatise that disrespects Africa's contribution to civilization.... [T]raditional African culture is very complex, and Hegel's use of facts is not only questionable but shallow as well" (p. 580). A more accurate view of Africa is that it is one of the most vibrant continents with its history dating back to Nowe and Egypt (Williams, 1987). Despite what was believed and taught in the past through history lessons that were mainly Eurocentric, Africa had a complex and organized culture. It was a continent with many different micro-nations "brought together in a single entity, or macro-nation, by the colonial powers" (Maathai, 2009, p. 184). In her own personal journey of discovering her African identity and culture, Maathai (2009) learned that, unlike what she was taught in her African classroom, "much of what occurred in Africa before colonialism was good" (p. 161). She goes on to say the "people carried their cultural practices, stories and sense of the world around them in their oral traditions, which were rich and meaningful. They lived in harmony with the other species and the natural environment, and they protected that world" (pp. 161–62). Knowing ones culture and being proud of that culture is essential to a positive cultural identity.

1. Understanding culture

UNESCO World Conference on Cultural Policies (1982) defines culture as:

> ... the whole complex of distinctive spiritual, material, intellectual and emotional features that characterize a society or social groups. It includes not only the arts and letters, but also modes of life, the fundamental rights of human beings, value systems, traditions and beliefs.... [I]t is through culture that man expresses himself, becomes aware of himself, recognizes his incompleteness, questions his own achievements, seeks untiringly for new meanings and creates works through which he transcends his limitations. (p. 1)

McKenzie & Morrissette (2003) define culture as "ways of life, shared behaviour, social institutions, systems of norms, beliefs, values and world views that allow people to locate themselves within the universe and that give meaning to their personal and collective experience" (p. 259). Some people describe it simply as a people's way of life, a collective way of thinking, feeling, and believing. It binds people together through a shared belief, customs, and values. Others see it as traditional customs and taboos, knowledge, morals and religion, etc. Professor Awedoba, a professor at the Institute of African Studies, University of Ghana, stated that culture can also be the "customary usages, which have been institutionalized and acceptable to the majority of people, perhaps not everyone, but the majority of people."

Culture is about the past, present, and future (Mammo, 1999). It is not about absolute uniformity. It doesn't mean that all people of an ethnic group will behave exactly the same. It is learned and does not come to people automatically.

> Culture is dialogue, the exchange of ideas and experiences and the appreciation of other values and traditions; it withers and dies in isolation.... [T]he universal cannot be postulated in the abstract by any single culture; it emerges from the experience of all the world's peoples as each affirms its own identity. Cultural identity and cultural diversity are inseparable. (UNESCO, 1982, p. 2)

Within any cultural group there are intercultural variations in the details of a particular cultural activity depending on gender, occupation, location, and groupings. In other words, the transmission, from one generation to another, of a cultural activity does not necessarily mean that it will be transmitted in the same way. Once transmitted, the cultural activity can change as groups copy, reject, or use it accordingly. In particular this is true with indigenous knowledge and practice. "Practices are handed over and through such that a process each generation adds some new and meaningful knowledge to the previous store and this new addition demonstrates the adaptability or modernity of tradition" (Mammo, 1999, p. 181).Culture shapes and is shaped by history. Culture can influence our perception of the world around us. Culture is also intangible and often can't be pinpointed in tangible terms. Maathai (2009) describes culture as something that

> ... gives a people self-identity and character. It allows them to be in harmony with their physical and spiritual environment, to form the basis for their sense of self-fulfillment and personal peace. It enhances their ability to guide themselves, make their own decisions, and protect their interests. It is their reference point to the past and their antennae to the future. Conversely, without culture, a community loses self-awareness and guidance, and grows weak and vulnerable. It disintegrates from within as it suffers a lack of identity, dignity, self-respect, and a sense of destiny. (pp. 160–61)

Culture and identity are intricately linked to each other.

2. Understanding Identity

Identity is the means by which a person, group, nation, or continent defines themselves in terms of their individuality and difference to others. It is the way that a person, group, nation, and continent sees themselves in relation to those around them and what makes them unique from others. An African sense of identity is holistic and encompasses not only ones body, soul/mind, and inner head but the whole cosmos (Adeofe, 2004; Venter, 2004). A sense of identity is often developed through the communities in which people are raised. Graham (1999) identifies four different principles and values that underpin African-centred worldview and identity:

Interconnectedness of all things. All of the elements of the universe are interconnected from the atom to the human. There is no separation between the material and the spiritual worlds. "To become aware of the cultural self is an important process that connects a person spiritually to others within a culture" (p. 259).

The spiritual nature of human beings. This requires a shift in thinking "towards valuing human beings above the social and economic status which has been assigned to them. Personhood comes through your relationship with community" (p. 259).

Collective/individual identity. The collective nature of identity is intertwined with others. "I am, because we are; and since we are, therefore I am" is an African proverb that speaks to this belief. The collective nature of identity entails a collective responsibility for what happens to other people.

Oneness of mind, body, and spirit. The mind, body, and spirit have equal value and are interrelated. "The African-centred worldview includes the concept of balance. The task of all living things is to maintain balance in the face of adverse external forces. When this inner peace is compromised, the psychological, social and physical well-being of a person is threatened" (p. 263).

Venter (2004) enforces the idea that community is fundamental to African identity. "Community and belonging to a community is part of the essence of traditional African life" (p. 151). "In the African view, it is the community which defines the person as a person, not some isolated static quality of rationality, will or memory" (p. 154) (Menkiti, 1979, as cited in Venter, 2004).

All of these beliefs and values were undermined by the colonizers. Once the colonizers came, the African way of life was deemed 'backward,' 'satanic,' and 'primitive,' and with this labelling the identity of Africans was destroyed. Not only were practices considered 'uncivilized' but the names of people were changed from African names to western names, thus imposing a foreign identity onto Africans. Maathai (2009) explains that this loss of identity has been the reason why many African leaders have failed to put their nation's interest first. "Both African leaders and ordinary citizens, facilitated the exploitation of their countries and peoples. Without culture, they'd lost their knowledge of who they were and what their destiny should be" (pp. 166–67). A positive identity is important for the growth of any individual, group, community, nation, or continent. Part of regaining a positive identity after generations of negativity is to rediscover ones personal heritage, recognize that what was taught was inaccurate, and reclaim the positive aspects of culture. This will open the door for positive identity.

3. Understanding cultural identity

Cultural identity, according to UNESCO (1982) has many facets but includes:

> ... a unique and irreplaceable body of values since each people's traditions and forms of expression are its most effective means of demonstrating its presence in the world.... [T]he assertion of cultural identity therefore contributes to the liberation of

peoples. Conversely, any form of domination constitutes a denial or an impairment of that identity. (p. 1)

To locate ones culture within the universe is crucial to the way in which a culture progresses in this world. If a culture is identified as a positive contributor to the world by the dominant group, then progress within that dominant world will take place. If it is seen as a negative contributor or a burden to the world or gets in the way of modern progress, then it is seen as primitive and in need of modernizing or being eliminated. With that in mind, it is concerning that Africa, with its many problems, is consistently branded as the 'hopeless continent' (Heron, 2007; Ray, 2008). The western world portrays Africa as no more than "a tragic continent whose only hope lies in the pockets of Western consumers" (Ray, 2008, p. 18). It seems as though the "only thing going for Africa is the West" (p. 18), and this is suspiciously like a repackaging of colonization. Heron (2007) explains further.

> The 'Third World' or 'developing countries' are presented...
> as places of 'suffering, starvation and bloodshed' via persistent
> magazine and newspaper articles, television programs and news
> clips, as well as direct-mail and TV fundraising drives by many
> development organizations ... these images have the effect of
> (re-)establishing the idea that the South in general and Africa
> in particular are in need of Northern...interventions. (pp. 2–3)

Africa, considered by the United Nations as part of the worldwide indigenous community, is "all too often ... defined by the social and health problems they experience. This deficit orientation and perspective by the majority culture becomes pervasive and generalized into negative stereotyping of indigenous peoples or other minority groups and their cultures" (Bradshaw & Graham, 2007, p. 101).
This perception of Africa is truly simplistic and one-sided as many positive developments are happening in Africa today. The task of Africans is in changing the perception of their cultures from a perceived idea that its cultures are negative and western-dependent, to a positive contributor to the world. In changing the perception of a continent, western

development organizations will have to change their own perceptions of Africa as a continent to 'help.' In other words, re-establishing a positive attitude towards Africa, by Africans and westerners, requires a change of self-perception, a country's perception of itself with other African countries and how each continent perceives itself in the world. Baylis (2003) speaks to her own identity as an African with white skin. "Racial identity is a fairly stable aspect of an individual's personality, it is a developmental process influenced by environmental and personal factors. My own view is that lived experience inexorably shapes racial identity. Who I am is both a function of how I live in the world and how I engage with others" (p. 143). She goes on to say that "the development of personal identity and the maintenance of personal integrity are dependent upon interpersonal relations with others" (p. 144). Ross (2008) agrees. "Culture goes to the very heart of how people define themselves and is intrinsic in the construction of human identity" (p. 384). Baylis (2003) suggests that "we are both who we say we are (based on our own interpretation and reconstruction of personal stories) and who others will let us be (as mediated through historical, social, cultural, political, religious and other contexts)" (p. 149).

There are many reasons why the cultural identity of Africans is being defined by the western dominant sector of the world. Maathai (2009) challenges Africans to re-educate themselves to a more accurate understanding of African history, to reconnect with this past in order to develop politically, spiritually, economically, and socially. Williams (1987), disturbed by the fact that his own education of world history in the United States portrayed Africa as having a primitive and negative history, also wanted to set the record straight concerning Africa's positive history and why it became such a negative African history. In doing so, the highs and lows of African history will be presented, according to Williams (1987), and how this has affected the continent and its identity in the world.

B. How Africa's history has influenced African cultural identity

Williams (1987), in trying to understand how a great people could be destroyed through the ages, identifies the different periods of black civilization and the high points of achievement to the points of destruction. The first period was before written history and centred on Lower Egypt (then Northeastern Ethiopia or Chem). The second period was from the conquest of Lower Egypt in 3100 B.C. to the end of the Sixth Dynasty, 2181 B.C. This era was the "Golden Age in the history of the Blacks, the age in which they reached the pinnacle of a glory so dazzling in achievements" (p. 39). The third period was from "2181 B.C. with tragic periods of internal turmoil and white invasion. The fourth period from 1786–1233 B.C., the great Eighteenth, 1567–1320 to the Age of Ramses to 1330–730" (p. 40). The fifth period was the last of the black pharaohs, 703 B.C. to the fifth century A.D. The sixth period was the "re-emergence of the successor black states in the 5th century A.D. to their final destruction by the Arabs in the thirteenth century" (p. 40). The seventh period was a period of wandering and migration, "a race that tried to outdistance famine, disease, slavery and death" (p. 40). The eighth period was the "re-emergence of African kingdoms and empires, by regions between the tenth and nineteenth centuries.... [H] owever the ultimate fall of the black states, first under Islamic and then under European Christian blows, closed this period with the triumph of colonialism" (p. 41). Meredith (2005) creates a picture of this last colonial carving up of Africa by stating that

> when marking out the boundaries of their [Europe's] new territories, European negotiators frequently resorted to drawing straight lines on the map, taking little or no account of the myriad of traditional monarchies, chiefdoms and other African societies that existed on the ground.... In all, the new boundaries cut through some 190 culture groups ... by the time the Scramble for Africa was over, some 10,000 African polities had been amalgamated into forty European colonies and protectorates. (pp. 1–2)

The final period is the Black Revolution "that ended the political colonialism with the rise of politically independent states" (p. 41). And yet most history books, even those in Africa, do not tell the African story (Foucault, 1980; Williams, 1987; Willinsky, 1998). It is subjugated knowledge that

Foucault (1980) describes as "historical contents that have been buried and disguised in a functionalist coherence or formal systemization" (p. 81). It is also "a whole set of knowledges that have been disqualified as inadequate to their task or insufficiently elaborated: naïve knowledges, located low down on the hierarchy, beneath the required level of cognition or scientificity" (pp. 81–82). This type of knowledge is buried because it concerns itself with "a historical knowledge of struggles" (p. 83). Willinsky (1998) speaks to this burying of unpopular knowledge: "Our history lessons have plotted the progress of freedom and nationhood as a Western rite of passage; modernity has been set against the primitive and despotic ways of the rest of the world. The West has defined a single path to modernity, civilization, and the idea of a fully developed nation" (p. 121). So much of African history, written by Europeans, does not give a balanced understanding of African history. Yet, this exclusion of the positive aspects of black civilization has had a marked influence on the psyche of African people disregarded by the world as unimportant.

These various episodes of history where Africa has been conquered by other forces, including the slave trade, have caused the destruction of the African people and culture. The more recent colonization of Africa by Europe led to a mass slaughter of millions of Africans in places like the Congo (Hochschild, 1998). Freire (2007) defines the process of dehumanization as "an historical distortion of the vocation of being human that leads to despair" (p. 44). A culture of silence permeates the colonized. He identifies four mechanisms of control that form a culture of silence: (a) conquest, (b) divide and rule, (c) manipulation, and (d) cultural invasion. Conquest refers to the conquering of a culture through any means using relations of subordination and domination. The aim of the conquest is to leave the people conquered dispossessed of their word, culture, and expressiveness through myths and oral action (Freire, 2007; Morrow & Torres, 2001). In order to keep the oppressed suppressed, a divide and rule mechanism keeps the oppressed from uniting and maintains the power of the oppressor. Unity is a threat to the oppressor, and in order to keep the oppressed from uniting, the oppressor localizes problems and prevents the identification of the wider problems of social structures. Bribes, promotions, threats, penalties, and benefits are used to manipulate the oppressed into staying suppressed. This strategy is often hidden behind the social structures supporting the oppressive society (Freire, 2007). Manipulation, through non-dialogical agreements, tries to manipulate the oppressed to conform to the oppressor's objectives. It teaches people not to think critically but to accept their oppression. Finally, cultural invasion "penetrates the cultural contexts of groups, imposing a view of the world that deprives subordinate groups of any sense of their 'alternative' possibilities" (Morrow & Torres, 2001, p. 103). This invasion is an act of violence; it moulds and shapes the oppressed into conforming to the oppressor's objectives. The oppressed have to be convinced of their inferiority and the oppressors' superiority. Many Africans became colonized not just intellectually, but psychologically and socially. Ndura (2006) describes this further.

> Africans experience the kind of cultural confusion ... have lost a sense of their cultural identity and as a result become alienated from their own cultural groups.... As victims of the self-fulfilling prophecy that is propagated through Western-bound educational philosophies and practices, they associate whatever is good and desirable with the West and denigrate the products, values, and traditions of their African motherland and culture. They become psychological captives who buy into the stereotypes of Africans as inferior and unsophisticated and Westerners as superior and civilized. (pp. 93–94)

The colonizers did their part portraying the continent as in need of Europe's civilizing and Christianizing. Not only did they redefine territories convenient to them but they also defined particular ethnic groups within a country by what is known as racial identity. "The arbitrary division of Africa's ethnic groups by colonialism arrested the process of nation formation in Africa for centuries" (Mammo, 1999, p. 72). Race doctrine came to fruition in the writings of Comte Arthur de Gobineau (Mamdani, 2001; Willinsky, 1998). The idea became an increasing fascination to Europeans. "Race became the marker dividing humanity into a few superhuman and the rest less than human, the former civilized, the latter putty for a civilizational project" (Mamdani, 2001, p. 77). This interest in race continued into the scientific world, after the Emancipation

Act of 1833, "shedding what had earlier appeared to be a humanistic and egalitarian disposition, in favour of dissecting human racial differences" (Willinsky, 1998, p. 162). As race ideology developed, it was clear that Africans were considered the uncivilized or less than human race.

However, a problem arose. As Europeans explored Africa, they could not comprehend that Egyptian civilization could have been developed by the negroid. To justify this impossible reality and to face the fact that "they were confronted with, and had to explain, growing evidence of organized life on the continent before the encounter with Europe" (p. 79), they established a theory concerning a certain type of African that was Caucasian inside and black on the outside. Thus the Hamitic Hypothesis was developed. This Hamitic Hypothesis traces its origins to the Biblical story of Noah, in which the descendents of Ham were cursed by being black (Mamdani, 2001). However, the hypothesis was reinvented in order to explain why negroids could not have been part of the Egyptian civilization. Thus, the Hamites became something other than negroid. A second reinvention of this hypothesis further justified, through Biblical interpretation, how Egyptians were not cursed after all. What is important here is to understand that certain African groups, those in North Africa, were deemed Caucasian on the inside and black on the outside and therefore could have created the great civilization of Egypt. This further confirmed the idea that negroid people were not intelligent or civilized.

An example of how devastating a hypothesis like this can be is in the case of Rwanda. The Tutsi's came from the North and were considered 'more superior' than other ethnic groups in the area of Rwanda. This hypothesis fuelled the Belgian authorities to institutionalize racial ideology. "Race policy became such a preoccupation with the colonial power that from 1925 on, annual colonial administration reports included an extensive description of the 'races' in a chapter called 'race policy'" (p. 88). Race policies, taken from race ideology, included practical implementation through five particular areas: 1) race education (gave Tutsi's a superior education); 2) state administration (weaken the role of chiefs and the *mwami*, make administration less accountable to the community and racialize the local authority); 3) taxation (heavy taxation to non-Tutsis; 4) religion (converting to Christianity by taking away the power of the *mwami*, thus perpetuating the colonial agenda); and 5) classification (classifying people into Tutsi, Hutu, and Twa through means of head size, information from the church and ownership of cows). Throughout the Belgians' control in the area of Rwanda, they established Tutsis as the privileged group. This racial classification has had enormous ramifications for that part of Africa, culminating in the Rwanda genocide. "It could be argued that the lack of clarified ethnic identity is one of the primary causes of the continuing conflicts between the Tutsis and Hutus in Burundi and Rwanda, and to a great extent in the Democratic Republic of Congo" (Ndura, 2006, p. 97).

Adding to the cultural dislocation caused by colonialism was the impact of modernization. Parton & O'Byrne (2000) define modernity as "a cluster of social, economic and political systems which emerged in the West with the Enlightenment in the late eighteenth century" (p. 19) that relied on science to give answers of truth. Western concepts of modernity were seen to be: "the understanding of history as having a definite and progressive direction; the attempt to develop universal categories of experience; the idea that reason can provide a basis for all activities; and that the nation state could coordinate and advance such developments for the whole society" (p. 19). In reality modernization was a way to civilize the world into a western way of living in the world. For Africa this included becoming independent and entering into the world economic order. It has been suggested that modernization was an extension of colonization and this modernity has not been beneficial to Africa and pushed aside African traditions and cultural heritage (Mammo, 1999). Sachs (2005) sums up the exploitation of Africa after colonization: "As soon as the colonial period ended, Africa became a pawn in the cold war: Western cold warriors, and the operatives in the CIA and counterpart agencies in Europe, opposed African leaders who preached nationalism, sought aid from the Soviet Union, or demanded better terms on Western investments in African mineral and energy deposits" (p. 189). This modernization trend tended to devalue traditional knowledge and practice, deeming it to be 'primitive.'

From modernization the world has entered a period of globalization. Many see globalization as a continuation of colonialism and modernization. Through the neo-liberal policies of present-day globalization, Africa continues to be exploited and this in turn affects the identity of Africa.

Exploitation is strong, deep, and seductive. It takes on many shapes and sizes but the exploitation of Africa continues and will get worse as global natural resources become increasingly scarce. For example, recently, Simon Mann and his mercenaries were sent to prison for organizing an "invasion of Equatorial Guinea to overthrow its government and replace it with one which would share the country's oil resources among a group of European businessmen who financed the coup" (Duodu, 2008, p. 10). Another example was the veto by Russia and China of the UN Security Council resolution supporting sanctions against Zimbabwe, tying this veto to the effect it would have on Chinese and Russian weapons exporters (Elliott, 2008b). More recently, world tobacco companies are taking advantage of child labour, against ILO regulations, in Malawi (Palitza, 2011). It takes time and resources to stop these types of exploitations that hinder the growth of Africa. It also takes a rethinking by African leaders of who they are and what their destiny should be. Instead of exploiting their countries, they should be protecting them and keeping Africa's best interests in the forefront (Maathai, 2009). Speaking about globalization, Robertson (2003) gives a warning: "Actions that seek to marginalize human agency and creativity, and undermine democratic gains, will also deny humans the mass global dynamism they now need to address problems that exist in global proportions" (p. 6). In short, colonialism, modernization, and globalization have not benefited Africa like they have other parts of the world.

C. African cultural identity today

Understanding one's own cultural identity through knowing and understanding history is crucial to understanding the place Africa has in the world today. Culture, like an onion, has many layers, and confirms the complexity of culture. Within African countries, one finds cultural differences, but underlying these differences are certain core principles. "Some parallels and commonalities are cultural and epistemic.... Others are a consequence of the homogenizing effects of imperialism" (Heron, 2007, p. 15). The research group looked at the different layers of colonization, westernization, traditions, history, ethnic diversity, gender, age, sex, etc., in order to understand the core culture. What was found in this process was that Ghana's culture is a dynamic mixture of African tradition, western technology, traditional and western beliefs, and different religious influences. It is a society that embraces many cultures and traditions. The group identified four Ghanaian cultural traits, each of which is found in other cultures: 1) a consensus society; 2) saving face; 3) externalization of feelings and emotions, and 4) hospitality. As generations have gone by and Ghanaian culture has evolved, these distinctions have been blurred, and it is difficult to identify entirely indigenous cultural components. As Ross (2008) states: "In view of the coexistence of cultures in pluralistic societies such as South Africa, there is likely to be a degree of cultural assimilation or melding of cultures to enable them to survive" (p. 384).

It is here where it would be helpful to comment on the dynamic of culture itself. It is easy to look back at the past and idealize African culture and to assume that it has not changed in the past five hundred years. But we know that it has been affected by colonization and westernization. It is also easy to assume that the traditional cultures before colonialism were perfect, equitable, and democratic. This is not altogether true either. In light of human rights, traditional culture can be destructive to certain people, including women and children. Mammo (1999) argues that many peoples in Africa relied on traditional knowledge and practice to survive during colonialism. There are many traditional practices that were the forerunners for modern technology and these should be acknowledged. Culture is not static. It is dynamic and a crisis often produces change. Along with the change in culture comes the re-identification of identity. New ideas come in, people begin to reconsider their traditional ways of doing things, and people borrow ideas from each other. "Cultural identity is a treasure that vitalizes mankind's possibilities of self-fulfilment by moving every people and every group to seek to nurture in its past, to welcome contributions from outside that are compatible with its own characteristics and so to continue the process of its own creation" (UNESCO, 1982, p. 1). Laws also change cultural practices. In fact the Ghanaian constitution speaks to the prohibition of customary practices that are injurious to the physical and mental health of a person (Government of Ghana, 1992). When culture changes or expands, it require people to be involved in agreeing to that change, participating in developing alternatives to those changes or the law will be ineffective.

One afternoon I was swimming in a pool near Accra. Inlaid in one of the walls of the pool, underneath the diving board, were two pictures; one of the first president of Ghana, Kwame Nkrumah, and the other of Queen Elizabeth II, positioned side by side. This is what cultural identity entails. A working out of one's own identity that is strong and true and using that strength to live in the different worlds that are demanded of people in countries like Ghana to survive in the global world. Ghanaians are taking the best of the many different identities and using them in parallel with each other. Two examples of these parallel systems can be seen in law and religion. The first concerns the British legal system and a traditional chieftaincy system. In Ghana, the chiefs and queen mothers have legal responsibility as does the Government of Ghana. Each has a role to play in working out legalities appropriate to the issue at hand, whether this is carried out in a traditional manner or in the courts. Both systems work in the same country, side by side, but not always agreeing. A second example concerns religion. I was riding a minibus in Accra and there was a preacher on the radio talking about Christianity and traditional religion. He was accusing Ghanaians of being hypocritical because they worshipped a Christian god (portrayed by wearing western suits) and yet they wore their traditional beads next to their skin, and on special occasions their traditional cloth. The preacher claimed that this was un–Christian and one can't worship both religions; it was either one or the other. People on the bus laughed when they heard this, but these are the pressures in a society trying to live in many different worlds.

This concept of living in many different worlds is described by Sultany et al., (2008) as two forces pulling in opposite directions. It is a "the push towards greater modernization and westernization and the pull of traditional values" (p. 398). An example of the push-pull effect is exiled Rwandans, returning to Rwanda and entering into a culture that has changed since they left. Returnees to Rwanda say that "they felt they belonged neither to the host country nor to Rwanda: That they seemed to occupy an in-between space … getting a job and Rwandan national identity was not easy" (Kabeera & Sewpaul, 2008, p. 328). Many African societies have tried to balance these worlds by compromising so that both can exist together, as in the case of Ghana, or have refused to do this balancing act, as in the case of Zimbabwe. Is this blurring of cultures a form of colonization, where eventually the dominant western culture will prevail and a traditional culture will be lost? Or can different cultures work side by side? Does the blurring of cultures strengthen or weaken cultural identity? Does it make a difference if one is accepted as an equal in the world or as primitive, or "less than the other"? Does cultural blurring allow for the fact that culture is dynamic and ever-changing? Maathai (2009) asks these questions as well:

> African communities have been attempting to reconcile their traditional way of life with the foreign cultures that condemned their own and encouraged them to abandon it. What are people to do when everything they believe in – and everything that makes them who they are – has been called "Satanic" or "primitive" or "witchcraft" or "sorcery"? What do they turn to? What wisdom do they call upon? What can be done to resist? And when, as is usually the case, this heritage is solely oral, how can they rediscover and reclaim its positive aspects? (p. 173)

Indigenous peoples around the world have experienced oppression, assimilation, and attempts to destroy their societies. And yet some indigenous cultures, like the Maori of New Zealand, the Sammi of the Arctic, and the First Nations, Metis, and Inuit of Canada, are re-emerging as strong cultures. This re-emergence is due in part to a resurgence of lost history, retelling of history and identifying, acknowledging, and being proud of their culture along with modernity. This process of cultural re-emergence also benefits from the acknowledgment of past wrongs and reparations of those wrongs. "The postcolonial struggle is not merely about political or economic independence; it is about having these other voices and world views heard and validated, and about questioning the comfortable consensus on which the privileged colonial world is based" (Ife, 2007, p. 13).

I see Africans and African nations working to regain their identity in the world. However, there are perceptions that need to be changed. A process of decolonization is necessary to change this identity crisis.

There have been many suggestions as to how peoples and countries should continue the process of decolonization. Laenui (2000) speaks of five stages to this process. These stages are not linear but are circular, happening over and over again. The stages are as follows: 1) rediscovery and recovery (This phase of rediscoverying one's history and recovering one's culture, language, identity is fundamental to the movement of decolonization); 2) mourning (when a people or country feels victimized and a time of mourning occurs and can include putting up statues, creating museums, or creating public memorial services); 3) dreaming (a time where people can explore their own cultures, experience their own aspirations for their future, and consider their own structures of government and social order to encompass and express their hopes); 4) commitment (moving forward together as a people or country); and 5) action (take action that is proactive and based on the consensus of the people). Weenie (2000) speaks to the notion of resistance in the decolonizing process. It starts with "unlearning what we have been taught about ourselves and learning to value ourselves" (p. 65). She goes on to say that resistance involves "the study of the constructed images of East and West and the essentialist notion of self" (p. 69). Decolonization allows for the re-emergence of culture and tradition, strengthening its importance in the modern world as well as balancing this tradition with modern culture. It is also appropriate when looking at ways to decolonize social work education in Africa.

D. Cultural identity and social work

The above discussion of cultural identity is important in the context of social work in Africa. As Gray (2005) explains: "Given that culture is central to indigenising, universalising and imperialising processes, we need to examine the definition of culture we are using in the context of these paradoxical processes.... Our understanding of culture affects the way in which we view universalising trends within social work" (p. 234). Smith (2008) further explains this link. "Internalized oppression and the power of hegemonic paradigms and language continue to influence the preparation of social workers" (p. 375). There are three main areas of social work that are influenced by cultural identity: 1) professional identity; 2) professional training; and 3) professional practice.

1. Professional identity

If the people of Africa are going through an identity crisis, then this is reflected in the organizations and institutions of society. As Mafile'O (2004) states in her research concerning Tongan social work, "social work theory and practice is socially constructed and culture is a key factor in that construction" (p. 254). Knowing one's own culture and identifying strongly with that culture will strengthen appropriate social work practice. If one is confused, uncertain, and torn between a western culture and traditional culture, chances are the resulting social work practice will reflect that confusion and ultimately end up reflecting the dominant beliefs. Interestingly, one of the main themes emerging from my PhD research was that social work is on the periphery in Ghana. Concerned about the reputation of social work, one research group member asked the following questions: "Why is social work on the periphery and how do we change the stereotypes of social workers and broaden the scope especially in regards to our role as social workers"?

Insights into these questions came out in various ways. During the research process, one of the pioneers of social work in Ghana, Dr. Blavo, felt that social work has not been accepted in Africa at all, and there is a continual struggle to keep its professional identity alive. The apathy and lack of involvement seen in professional association meetings, practitioners refusing to admit to being a social worker in public, being shy about the profession, and the lack of advocating for the profession are all reasons why social work is still on the periphery in Ghana. He continues: "I am telling you in Ghana, the enemies of social work are the social workers themselves." "Self-reflection and action must occur about how social work practice is shaped by society's assumptions and power dynamics" (Smith, 2008, p. 376). Gavin and Seabury (1997, as cited in Smith, 2008) state that "we must each delve into our own positionality and explore how we have been conditioned by the master discourses of our culture and reject that which is founded on oppression and stereotypes" (p. 376). If this critical reflection is not encouraged at the education level, then social work practice will continue to be ineffective to meet the needs of the community and society. "One must not cease to ask questions, or breed complacency along well-worn paths, or worse still to rest one's levels [sic]

... there is good reason to make continual revisions and adaptations, to keep abreast of new trends and possibilities" (ASWEA, 1977, p. 74).

During the ASWEA conferences, particularly in the 1970s, there was a concerted effort to encourage professional associations to be involved in African unity (ASWEA, 1977, pp. 34–36). Mmatli (2008) explains: "Social workers have been systematically excluded from the broader social policy formulation responsibilities. Instead, they are confined to the administration and supervision of ill-defined and inadequately funded welfare programs, community development projects and self-help activities.... [I]nstead professional groups, politicians, economists and bureaucrats, predominantly define the social work agenda" (p. 299). Ife (2007) considers this part of our role. In many situations,

> ... social workers have not been high-profile, and have been see by others as marginal ... this is nothing new ... it is social work's lot to be always struggling for recognition, and that is only to be expected; after all social work represents the views of the vulnerable, of the marginalized, of those whose voices are not readily heard, and so social work will always be unfashionable and will threaten the agendas of the powerful. (pp. 1–2)

Although Ife's words ring true, there are other forces at work that support the fact that social work continues to be on the periphery. One group member asks the question: "Why is it that often social workers are the ones that people turn to as a last resort and when they arrive they are feeling hopeless and worthless"? There are many factors to consider in answering these questions. My own feeling is that this is an example of modernization, in which a western model was encouraged to grow and develop in places where that model may not have been appropriate. Instead of questioning the value of the western model of social work, the curricula remained western with social workers having to try to adapt this model to a traditional culture. As Dr. Shawky explained:

> Social welfare programmes designed to solve urban problems of highly industrialized countries were transplanted into

African societies without serious examination of local priority needs and local approaches to problems and with little attempt towards their adaptation. As a result, the dynamic role of the social work method was overlooked. African social workers were led to believe that there is a certain set of legitimate and unchangeable fields where the social work methods can be utilized. This orthodox attitude towards social work, and social welfare in turn, reflected on social work education. Trained social workers in Africa keep on using the term social welfare referring to individualized attention to persons under strain of stress or in need for special care. They forget that there are millions of Africans living in rural and peri-urban areas. They keep on emphasizing remedial services, forgetting that Africa needs more of the preventive and developmental. (ASWEA, 1974, p. 53)

Like forcing a square peg into a round hole, the western social work model keeps being forced into a culture to make it fit. If we stop and ask the question 'why are we forcing the square peg in the round hole,' a different critical perception would emerge.

2. Professional training

"Critical consciousness," likened by Freire (1997) to 'decolonizing of minds' is imperative for social work training. At the start of my PhD research, genuine questions were asked about the social work curriculum in Ghana. It came out that changing curriculum to be more culturally appropriate was not something that either the department as a whole or the faculty or students had contemplated. However, a group of faculty and community people interested in social work training (representatives from government and non-government organizations) and others met two years before my research project and had already made some changes to the curriculum. What was still missing was a critique of the curricula in light of colonization, modernization, and globalization. A group member explains:

We have been raised in a society that does not allow one to challenge the status quo. We are discouraged from critically looking at an existing system, whether it is an institution or training. That is why this kind of project had to come from an outsider. We are too frightened to criticize a system or challenge a teacher at University.

One of the first statements and questions asked by a research group member was that she could understand why a place like South Africa, due to apartheid, needed a whole change in curriculum but what were the reasons why others changed their curriculum? Was the curriculum adapted or did they start from the beginning again? As the research progressed a question emerged: "Is there a body of knowledge and material that could be drawn from that was particularly pre-colonial, and that could provide the basis for this change of curriculum?" What these questions revealed to me was the lack of communication between African states concerning social work curriculum. The work completed in the 1970s and 1980s with the Association for Social Work Education in Africa (ASWEA) also asked these and other important questions and had debates concerning the curriculum but the work and ideas seem to have been forgotten. For the research group, there was also a lack of awareness of the many influences that affected the social work curricula in Ghana. However as conscientization took hold of the group, one group member stated that we have to ask the questions: 1) "who has taught us"; 2) "what have we been taught"; 3) "how this has affected our way of thinking"; and 4) "how is this curriculum been influenced by outside or inside influences"? Once these were answered then the group needed to ask: 1) "where do we start from in order to make social work training more African"; and 2) "how do we do this?" Another group member asked the question: "If colonialism had not taken place in our system, could we have strengthened our traditional institutions, taking into consideration advancement in technology, increased migration and economic independence"? Some of these answers will be explored in chapter VI.

Is it possible to develop curricula that are culturally relevant for a country in which there are many different ethnic groups? Where do modernity and tradition meet? Are there commonalities that can form the basis for universal curricula but have the flexibility for adapting to the different cultures in which people are working? Social work international bodies have worked on universal guidelines for curricula worldwide (IFSW, 2004). Within these guidelines is there flexibility to be culturally specific (Williams & Sewpaul, 2004)? Or, as Gray & Coates (2008) suggest, standardizing social work curricula may not be that helpful to the majority of social workers in the world. "We argue that the evidence would point strongly to the majority of social workers being locally-based workers trying to do their best with limited resources to respond to their local contexts advocating wherever possible, with local, municipal or national context for policy change. The global stage stands at odds with local practice" (p. 24). At my own university, the University of Calgary, there has been an attempt to merge different worlds together. Social work training developed specifically for rural and Aboriginal communities has been adapted to the needs of people working in those communities (Bodor, Zuk, Feehan, Badry, Kreitzer, & Zapf, 2009). The basics of social work education and practice are taught, as well as pertinent issues relating to rural practice and the colonization of Aboriginal peoples. This adaptation appears not to be occurring in Ghana specifically, or in Africa generally. One research group member expressed frustration of things not changing. "How come we are still the same? ... it looks like we haven't moved forward ... it is still the same ... it means we actually need to plan how we are going to tackle the new problems that have arrived like AIDs and even with childcare." It feels like African social work has been in a time warp.

3. Professional practice

It is not surprising, with a social worker's own confusion of identity and the profession's feeling of being on the periphery, that social work practice will reflect that confusion as well. Throughout the 1970s and the 1980s, there was confusion as to the role of social workers in relation to national planning, i.e., a social developmental role or a social welfare role (ASWEA, 1976; ASWEA, 1977; ASWEA, 1982). This cultural identity crisis seen in social work in Africa affects the way social workers are able to respond to the confusion of individuals, groups, and communities concerning cultural change in society. Ideally, social workers are change agents and pioneers of change, and their practice should be culturally appropriate to the culture in which they are working. "Social workers should specifically play an important role in identifying problems related to development, setting up priorities, defining the different approaches to be used and involving themselves in overcoming these problems" (ASWEA, Doc. 6, 1974, p. 13). The research group talked about both of these issues in relation to social work practice in Ghana.

Understanding transitional change. For people of any culture, cultural change is frightening, and people are not always able to make a transition from one cultural practice to another. According to Bridges (1991), transition is "the psychological process people go through to come to terms with the new situation. Change is external, transition is internal" (p. 3). He goes on to say that "unless transition occurs, change will not work … transition starts with an ending … it begins with letting go of something" (pp. 3–4). He offers three stages of transition that are useful here. The first is letting go of the old ways. The second is being in a neutral zone in which a person is in "no-man's-land between the old reality and the new. It is a time when the old way is gone and the new doesn't feel comfortable yet" (p. 5). The third stage is getting past the neutral zone when change happens and there is a new beginning, belief, or practice. In order to help others with this change, social workers need to have worked through this transition in their own lives. Conscientization needs to begin at an individual level and move on to social work practice. Through reflective critical education, this is possible.

In relation to their critique of social work curricula, it was necessary for the research group to see that there are other ways of training social workers than in the present western curricula currently used in Ghana. In order to be critical thinkers, they had to be open to other ways of training that may be more culturally appropriate to their setting. As this awareness grew, one group member summarized: "Just because things are different, doesn't necessarily mean that they are wrong … we should be ready to adapt new ideas and new ways of looking at things."

The rural community in Ghana has seen changes in recent times due to the migration of youth to the cities, the loss of traditional family and community supports, a growing dependency upon outside help, and the continuation of poverty. Is it the job of the social workers to revive this lost cultural activity or to negotiate a balance between western influences and traditional culture? Should they walk alongside their clients as they work through the transition of cultural changes? Here are a few examples that I have seen that show the complexity of cultural change:

Female genital mutilation (FGM) is one part of a traditional puberty right or a ceremony of initiation. This right gives respect and honour to the girls in their society. Now deemed as unhealthy and inappropriate, many African countries have banned this part of the ceremony. But it is difficult to change behavioural practices in which there is an important historical ritual that seems to need to be preserved. The puberty right ritual itself is important to keep, and therefore a healthy, safe alternative to FGM that will satisfy the culture and keep the ritual seems appropriate. However, achieving this change entails education, dialogue, and the community coming together to find an alternative that works for everyone.

Two other examples are the *trokosi* system in Ghana and the witches villages. Both are practices that affect women particularly in a negative way. *Trokosi* is when daughters are given over to priests and priestesses in order to appease the ancestors for a crime which the family did against the deities. Usually this includes sexual favours, and they are treated like slaves. Once the daughter has left the system, it is very unlikely for her to obtain a husband in mainstream society. If an alternative to whom or what is sacrificed could be agreed upon, then practice could be changed. To change the *trokosi* system, the deeper issues of the rights of women and freedom over their own bodies as well as religious beliefs also need to be discussed.

The issue of witches is also important. If bad things happen in a village, there is usually a witch hunt to find out who has brought this bad omen to the village. It is usually a woman and once she has been found, she is sent to a witch's village (Palmer, 2010). If she returns to the home village, after rehabilitation, the village tends not to accept her back. This is a gender issue and one of human rights. Education, dialogue, and discussion around the reasons why bad things happen as well as gender issues, with a discussion of alternatives, might shift this cultural practice. In all of these examples, social workers could play an important mediation role.

4. Culturally relevant social work practice

As situations change, it is an opportunity for social workers to identify these changes, whether it is the home, family lineage, or authority figures in society, and to offer alternatives to this shifting sand. This is where it is crucial for social workers to have a skill in culturally relevant social work theories and methodologies. Without an Africa-specific curriculum, these cultural issues cannot be addressed in an appropriate way. Urban Chicago case studies from western textbooks given to Schools of Social Work in Africa cannot address these issues, and it is imperative that culturally relevant articles, case studies, and textbooks be available for students. Part of social work involves helping people resolve cultural issues that involve a different value set. Culture does change slowly over time. It could be a change in the economy, political situation, social impact, or a particular leader introducing something that affects culture that may result in a cultural practice becoming obsolete. People may want to alter or eliminate a practice for various reasons, and it is possible to introduce alternatives to these cultural practices, only with the right set of knowledge and skills. An assumption can't be made that the practice is bad just because some people don't like it. Others may like it. Many of these cultural practices are about cleansing, starting a new life, starting afresh.

The more important point is that if people want to abandon an idea, they can either be persuaded to try something different or be forced into an alternative. Abolishing a cultural practice via the law can be effective or ineffective, depending on how it is completed. Passing a law doesn't change cultural behaviours if the people are not behind the law. They will continue with the cultural practice. However, if the people are taught about the practice, its history, positives and negatives, and are persuaded through dialogue that something needs to change, then chances are the cultural behaviour will change. If people don't understand why the law has changed, they will continue the cultural practice in question. If people are brought together, educated about the issue, and asked to come up with an alternative or better practice, they might shift in what they are doing. The transition period is important and time-consuming in order for people to accept change in a positive way. This is not always easy but social workers have the skills and knowledge to do this type of intervention.

Social workers are often faced with centuries of history, entrenched ways of doing things, and dealing with people's perceptions and beliefs. That is why it is very important to understand tradition, culture, and people's ways of interpreting that tradition. Knowing a culture also gives an opportunity to question that cultural practice, particularly if it is not acceptable but meets a need. A social worker needs to know this difference.

> Community development has an important contribution in bringing about change and growth. First, it awakens people and initiates them into conditions and methods of achieving progress. While doing so it avoids the breakdown of basic and traditional values.... [C]ommunity development provides a mutual link of co-operation and understanding between the government and the people and thus reduces social conflict and tension. (ASWEA, Doc. 6, 1974, p. 29)

People are living in an increasingly pluralistic, modern society. They are trying to hang on to tradition while tradition is changing and moving in directions people may not wish to go. People are juggling many different worlds and are challenged by the differences and conflicts, and often it is difficult to keep a balance within these different worlds. A point of reference is sometimes difficult to find and life may seem chaotic. However, the job of a social worker is to be a point of reference and with the help of traditional leaders and the community a way forward can be found.

One group member asks: "How do we decide what culture we keep and what culture we take away? And who decides?" Another group member asks: "So where do we start? We have our traditional system and we have our formal western system. How are we going to integrate these things ... to make social work more practical....? How are we going to use the positive side, use the positive things from our traditional system and blend it so that we make social work more suitable to the condition in which we find ourselves? How do we practice culturally appropriate social work in a world where many different cultures are influencing life at a rural and urban level?" The answers to these questions will influence how social work is taught in Africa.

E. Conclusion of chapter

National and international forces have been at work, for many centuries, in destabilizing the African continent, most recently through colonization, modernization, and globalization. These forces have played a role in exploiting Africa and keeping it on the periphery of the global community. The way in which Africa views itself in the world, the way countries view themselves within the continent, and the way African people view themselves as individuals in the world all need to be acknowledged and addressed at the individual, national, and international levels. The continent continues to change. Culture is changing and social workers have the opportunity to be on the cutting edge of new and appropriate responses to people who are vulnerable in society as well as in the development of their country. And yet, social work in Africa reflects this identity crisis and has much work to do in creating a positive professional identity whereby it is recognized as an important service to the people of Africa. "To become a modern society, we must fully understand our conditions. As social workers we are the people that could act as trustees because only when we have the background, that is the background of our culture and people that we are dealing with, then we will be able to apply remedial, corrective or preventive measures, which are necessary for society to strive" (Drake & Omari, 1962, p. 1). Written in 1962 at the Seminar of Social Work in West Africa conference, these words, from the pro-vice chancellor, still ring true today. "Through education individuals can reaffirm their cultural identity as well as their rights and responsibilities as citizens of nations and a world that celebrates and values ethnic and cultural diversity" (Ndura, 2006, p. 99).

This reaffirmation has to take place at the individual psychological and emotional level, at the community level, at the national level, and at the international level. A shift in thinking has to take place. Culturally relevant curriculum has the potential of creating this shift and developing a positive identity in African social work. For change to take place, a decolonizing process that includes a critical reflection and evaluation of a student's own understanding of the historical influences that affect social work education and practice, working through their own cultural identity issues, re-learning their own African history, and critically evaluating their curriculum has to take place in the classroom. It also has to happen at the association level. As can be seen, this work was started with the seminars of the ASWEA and GASOW. Unfortunately, this growth seemed to stop and progress has been slow in creating a revolutionary social work profession specific to the African context. ASWEA recommended a radical transformation of curriculum in the 1970s and this has yet to take place. However, positive signs are appearing in various parts of Africa, including South Africa where the social development model is being practised, and the curriculum is changing to meet the needs of the national social policy agenda (Patel, 2005). The 2008 IASSW conference in Durban has also helped social work to be seen as an important profession in the transition of that country.

What is the role of social work in African society? How is it viewed by society? Why is it still on the periphery? How do we change unhelpful stereotypes of social workers and broaden people's views of the role of the social worker in society? How do we educate social workers to be highly skilled to deal with cultural issues? How do we educate people to appreciate the work social workers are doing? How do we maintain the good reputation social work education has with many organizations that now ask for that qualification for employment? How do we change old institutions and make them more relevant to society? These are the questions African social workers need to ask about their own profession in their own country. On a continent where people are struggling to find a strong cultural identity, the profession must change its training and practice to be more culturally relevant, meeting the new and challenging needs of its own people.

Bob Marley says it quite well in his "Redemption Song."

Old pirates, yes, they rob I; Sold I to the merchant ships, Minutes after they took I from the bottomless pit. But my hand was made strong by the hand of the Almighty. We forward in this generation triumphantly. Won't you help to sing these songs of freedom? – Cause all I ever have; Redemption song; redemption songs.

Emancipate yourselves from mental slavery; None but ourselves can free our minds. Have no fear for atomic energy,

Cause none of them can stop the time. How long shall they kill our prophets, while we stand aside and look? Ooh! Some say it's just part of it: We've got to fulfill de book. Won't you help to sing these songs of freedom; Cause all I ever have, Redemption song; These songs of freedom, songs of freedom.

Maathai (2009) challenges Africans to reconnect with their cultural history. "I call for Africans to rediscover and embrace their linguistic, cultural, and ethnic diversity, not only so their nation-states can move forward politically and economically, but so that they may heal a psyche wounded by denial of who they really are" (p. 6). The question is then asked: Why does Africa continue to embrace this western social work training and practice and is it relevant for today? Another mental slavery that affects social work training and practice in Africa is the undying belief that what is western is civilized and the best and that traditional knowledge and practice is primitive and bad. This is the topic of the next chapter.

III. Hegemony of Western Knowledge[1]

Western social work knowledge is the best knowledge and we deserve the best knowledge, therefore we want western social work taught to us. If we learn western social work knowledge then it will give us the opportunity to go to the U.K., USA and Canada to practice social work. (Comments from social work students when asked if they wish to Africanize their social work curriculum)

A. Imperialism and education

The above statement is an underlying theme among African social workers when I have visited and have spoken to faculty and practitioners at different social work conferences. Is this attitude a deeply engrained colonial idea, civilized versus primitive, which continues to permeate the African continent? Is it a sad reflection of the state of social work in Africa that people want to move away and work in the western world? Is it an inevitable by-product of westernization? As can be seen in the previous chapters, colonization, modernization, and globalization have affected the identity of a continent both positively and negatively. Deep down there appears to be a continued belief, by Africans and non-Africans, that African traditional knowledge is primitive and western knowledge is civilized.

> The secret that Europeans discovered early in their history is that culture carries rules for thinking, and that if you could impose your culture on your victims you could limit the creativity of their vision, destroying their ability to act with will and intent and in their own interest. The truth is that we are all "intellectuals," all potential visionaries. (Ani, 1994, p. 1)

> Westernization, connoting modernization ... pushed aside African traditions, cultural heritage, accumulated knowledge, indigenous practices and the use of their local institutions. Westernization appears not to promote the sense of self-dependency and in short is a process of self-denial. (Mammo, 1999, p. 17)

Ndura (2006), speaking about education in Rwanda, states: "the entire educational system, from the boarding schools to the curriculum, was set up to bring shame to native cultures and aspiration for and honour to European or Western culture" (p. 91). He goes on to say: "Dominant groups have always used education as a major tool for assimilating and even subjugating dominated populations" (p. 99). Willinsky (1998) and Ndura (2006) speak of the absolute importance behind consolidating the European empire through education, noting that some former colonized countries are still working through this today. "We need to learn again how five centuries of studying, classifying, and ordering humanity within an imperial context gave rise to peculiar and powerful ideas of race, culture, and nation that were, in effect, conceptual instruments that the West used both to divide up and to educate the world" (Willinsky, 1998, pp. 2–3). Following the understanding that what is taught in the past affects the future mentality of a continent, Ndura (2006) states that western-bound education "produces at best graduates who hold a truncated and distorted vision of themselves and of their place in their respective African communities. It has produced isolated African educated elites that lack a global perspective" (p. 96). Concerning Africans going to the West for educational training and practice van Wyk & Higgs (2007) observed that "graduates from other continents were sent to Europe and the United States for advanced degrees in order to provide indigenous faculty to replace expatriate ones. Those who studied abroad and were assigned teaching positions after the completion of their studies quite naturally emulated the practices established at the institutions where they conducted their studies" (p. 68). This cycle of western-educated teachers has had a socializing affect on African students. There seems to be a barrier in allowing the freedom to creatively and proudly teach African history, culture, philosophy, and traditional knowledge and practice. There is a fear that if anything other than western books is used and western knowledge is taught that somehow the educational experience will be less than what the western student has received. The importance of traditional knowledge and practice is often ignored.

B. Hegemony of knowledge

Gramsci defines hegemony as "a social condition in which all aspects of social reality are dominated by a certain powerful group" (Mayo, 1990, p. 35). This includes knowledge-making. "Knowledge-making cannot be neutral and disinterested but is a political process in the service of particular purposes, and one which has been institutionalized in favour of the privileged (Reason & Bradbury, 2001, p. 6). There is an intimate relationship between power and knowledge and "knowledge-making supported by various cultural and political forms creates a reality which favours those who hold power" (Reason & Bradbury, 2001, p. 6). Willinsky (1998) highlights the way in which Europe set out to civilize Africa through education and religion. The African educated in western ways fed the system of colonialism and also perpetuated the idea that African knowledge was primitive and western knowledge was civilized. Colonialism, modernization, and globalization have all had a part in taking forward the idea that western knowledge is the best and have also had a part in repressing indigenous ways of knowing and discouraging people from making use of their own traditional knowledge in everyday life and in a higher education setting (Bamgbose, 1983; Mammo, 1999; Mosha, 2000; Smith,

1999; Venkataraman, 1996). Edward Said (1991) speaks of the effect his western education had on his own psyche:

> There was a tremendous spiritual wound felt by many of us because of the sustained presence in our midst of domineering foreigners who taught us to respect distant norms and values more than our own. Our culture was felt to be of a lower grade, perhaps even congenitally inferior and something of which to be ashamed. (pp. 8–9)

The recognition that 'other ways of knowing' are as valid as western knowledge is increasing with different indigenous peoples and ethnic groups speaking out about their own knowledge and practices. The post-colonial literature challenges a western biased knowledge base and encourages the 'other' voices to be heard. As Ani (1994) states, "You have to teach Pan-African studies alongside European studies so people will understand the assumptions behind each. This is demanded by an African-centred view because we are Africans and because the future towards which Europe leads us is genocidal" (p. 2). What was this western education really about? Ndura (2006) sums up his thoughts on his own educational experience in Rwanda:

> What did we learn from this lesson that was imported from our colonial master? ... [W]e learned that the White man was the supreme symbol of civilization. We learned to accept the superiority of the White man and his products and the inferiority of Blacks and their products. We learned that our worth was determined by our closeness to the White man's ideals and way of life. We learned to be ashamed of our ancestors, our customs, our history and ourselves. (p. 93)

Willinsky (1998) speaks of imperialism as an educational venture. "Imperialism was an educational venture that captured and captivated the imagination of the West. From its interests in tourism to interior design, the West still lives within the spell of the imperium" (p. 19). He finishes by asking the question "How then can we distance ourselves from the spell?" (p. 20).

Education is a socializing process and it is assumed that this knowledge will be passed down from generation to generation. It is, therefore, understandable that western education continues to be the dominant form of education in Africa, due to its past colonization process. This imbalance between traditional and western knowledge can also be seen in social work in Africa. The impacts of colonialism, modernization, and globalization are reflected in the spread of western social work knowledge (Asamoah & Nortey, 1987; Haug, 2005; Osei-Hwedie, 1990; Torczyner, 2000; Venkataraman, 1996). The honouring of indigenous ways of knowing in social work has, until recently, been virtually ignored (Ani, 1994; Durst, 1992; Midgley, 1981; Smith, 1999; Venkataraman, 1996).

C. Western knowledge and social work education

The social work profession, including the development of its values, theories, and ideologies, originated in Europe and the United States (Healy L.M., 2001; Kendall, 1995; Midgley, 1981). By the early 1900s, the profession had been established and educational facilities had been created to train social workers in these countries. As Nagpaul (1993) notes, social work educational values "were and still are dominated by ideologies of capitalism, Social Darwinism, the Protestant Ethic and individualism" (p. 214). The early social welfare policies, from mainly European countries, were the basis for the social welfare policies of their colonized territories. According to Kendall (1995) and Midgley (1981), a combination of different influences moved social work into developing countries. As seen in chapter II, the spread of western social work knowledge worldwide had its beginnings with the United Nations, who felt the need for the increase of this profession after the Second World War and who assumed this knowledge was universal and transferable. The United Nations sent western consultants to non-western countries in order to help create social work curricula. As Kendall (1995) suggests, these consultants went with the understanding that western social work knowledge was superior to local knowledge. It was believed that duplication of the western curriculum would lead other countries to acquire this same knowledge and have excellent, prestigious social work programs thus alleviating some of the social problems created through entering the new world economic order. From the 1960s onward, experts set up new social work programs in non-western countries and promoted western social work theories and methodologies, with little understanding of the relevance of these theories to those countries (Midgley, 1981; Rodenborg, 1986). Faculties of western social work institutions also helped in this process and continue to do so today (Asadourian, 2000; Driedger, 2004; Midgley, 2008). Bradsaw & Graham (2007) noted that, "the social work profession is heavily imbued with Northern culture and ways of knowing. Many countries have relied on Northern social work educators for the design of the content and structure of their social work curriculum" (p. 99).

One of the first official challenges to the universality of western social work knowledge was made at the United Nations Fifth Conference on Social Work Education (UN, 1971a). Others challenged this universality as well. Brown (1971) discusses the compatibility of western social work in Zambia; Gulati (1974) discusses western social work's role in traditional societies and questions the assumption of universality. Midgley's *Professional imperialism: Social work in the Third World* (1981) brought this subject to the forefront and challenged the exportation of western social work knowledge to developing countries. More recently, social work colleagues and academics from the non-western world have questioned western social work knowledge and its appropriateness in solving problems confronting non-western countries (Walton & Abo El Nasr, 1988; Lebakeng, 1997; Noyoo, 2000; Osei-Hwedie & Jacques, 2007; Gray et al., 2008; Osei-Hwedie & Rankopo, 2008). The traditional values of western social work stem from a Judeo-Christian background and the methods used arise mainly from a medical model. Those values and methods seemed to be inadequate and inappropriate for dealing with the consequences of colonialism, poverty, government corruption, religious practices, and other philosophical orientations. Social workers in non-western countries learned theories and methodologies alien to their cultures and had the added burden of filtering the parts that worked from the parts that did not work in their own social work practice (Midgley, 1981; Nimmagadda & Cowger, 1999; Venkataraman, 1996). Osei-Hwedie (1993) stated that African social workers had no part in defining their profession with government and non-government organizations dictating much of their education. American and British textbooks continue to be used and translated into different languages. These textbooks promote American and British values and use case examples from urban western cultures. Osei-Hwedie (1993) found, in Africa, that there was a strong social science knowledge base that had no reference to Africa. To promote indigenous ways of knowing went against the trend of modernization. Lauer (2004) states: "Underdevelopment is not due to traditional knowledge or folk knowledge. Modern scientific tradition itself is a failure in the successful integration of modern and traditional knowledge" (p. 2).

Unlike other countries that have discarded western social work knowledge and theories, Africa has been slow to do so. Osei-Hwedie & Rankopo (2008) give an example of attempts to make African curriculum less western in Botswana. This was not as easy as they thought it would be due to pressures by the university authorities to keep up the international competition and recognition with western universities and to keep the student's degrees internationally marketable. Senior academics were uncompromising in the faculty's struggle with localizing curriculum and were adamant that "there was only one social work and it was Western" (p. 214). For the Botswana social work faculty "the challenge was to blend local and international content and in the process avoid Western domination" (p. 214). This critical process has not been encouraged by schools of social work from the western world either in the past or today. "In Australia it is sad to see social work schools seeking to export their programmes to Asia, and to recruit aggressively students from overseas to study social work in Australia, regardless of the cultural, political and social differences involved, and without any agonizing about the colonialist impacts of our international work" (Ife, 2007, p. 14). Midgley (2008) suggests that the increasing online approach to social work education continues the imperialism of the profession over the culturally relevant training and practice. "Students in the recipient country do not actually attend the provider university but are taught at a local site. They receive exactly the same curriculum as their counterparts in the Western country and little, if any, effort is made to include local cultural or other appropriate curriculum content" (p. 40).

There is a growing awareness that in this "multicultural and global context in which we live and work there is an increasing understanding that exclusively Northern approaches are ineffective for many communities" (Bradshaw & Graham, 2007, p. 94). The authors point out that in the thirty-five years since this issue was highlighted the profession has been slow and sporadic in changing this hegemony. A recent book, *Indigenous social work around the world* (Gray et al., 2008), brings this to light. However, this is not a one-way process. Many non-western countries, including Africa, also accepted a western curriculum at face value even though throughout the ASWEA seminars of the 1970s and 1980s there was a recurring theme that curriculum needed to be changed and was too western. And yet there seems to be a lack of critical thinking concerning what kind of social work would be appropriate to Africa. As one group member stated: "I believe we have learned from the western way but it has also inhibited us in just a way that we sort of can't do things on our own. Because after independence, barely 40 years, we are still hanging on to all that they brought. We haven't moved away."

Ndura (2006) lays out important questions concerning African education that African social worker educators and students should be continually asking:

Why is Western literature elevated to the center stage of the educational experience while African languages and literatures remain under-explored? Why is Western financial assistance used to hire Western expatriates instead of preparing local educators for local schools? Why are most school textbooks imported from Western nations? Why do Western institutions deny so many African academic credentials when they were educated under Western philosophies and standards? (pp. 98–99)

More specifically to social work, other questions need to be asked as well: Who do social workers in Africa serve? Is the training appropriate for the important task of serving clients? We all know that social workers can be change agents as well as agents of social control. What does the social work curriculum encourage, a critical understanding and action or conforming to the role the government has assigned to the social work profession?

Concerning culturally appropriate interventions, Demmer & Burghart (2008) suggest that "interventions should be developed that are more compatible with the issues and concerns of individuals in their context, mindful of each country's resources" (p. 368). Mwansa (2010) suggests that the traditional case work approach may not be the best interventions for Africans. Cham (2008) gives an example of the difficulties in transferring interventions from one culture to the other: "Not much is known about the interventions or models of care that are available for street children and orphans of HIVAID ... and determining which models or interventions are working best is often difficult" (p. 411). Although community-based interventions seem the best approach for street children and orphans, little research has been completed on the fostering of street children and orphans as opposed to institutional care. "Orphans and street children have a voice about how they can interpret these practices and their voices should be incorporated into the structure of these models" (p. 414).

Transferring and replicating interventions from other countries is often not the best approach. "We can compare experiences, share expertise and resources in a manner that is sensitive to each culture and context, and we can promote indigenous responses that aim to help individuals affected by AIDS-related deaths" (p. 368). Ross (2008) suggests that "social workers need to revisit the issue of formulating African models of social work practice that do not rely exclusively on British, European or American models but which draw on indigenous best practices, knowledge and culture from the African continent. We need to understand, appreciate and engage the cosmological, ontological and epistemological differences that separate Euro-American and African medical and cultural approaches" (p. 392). This attempt will improve people's acceptance of appropriate interventions. "If interventions make sense to the client, a greater likelihood exists that the client will be invested in applying the intervention" (Hodge, 2006, p. 163). These interventions need to take into account the contextual aspects of society. Ross (2008) and Mensah (Kreitzer, 2004a) advocate for the collaboration of social workers and traditional healers to provide new approaches to counselling that incorporate an African approach to healing. "Students need to understand the psychology of indigenous ways of knowing and be encouraged to construct intervention models that address the needs of most Africans in culturally appropriate ways" (Ross, 2008, p. 393).

This hegemony of western knowledge has created a number of critical issues in African social work:

1. There is a lack of critical process to redefine social work in Africa.

2. There is a lack of recognition of western dominance of knowledge in social work education and with this lack of recognition little is being done to create a culturally appropriate curriculum for Africa.

3. There is a lack of knowledge and understanding concerning the history of social work in Africa. This is partly due to the difficulties of accessing appropriate documents, many of which are in the western world or published in western journals.

4. There is a fear of breaking away from the colonizer's educational knowledge and institutions because it may not be as good as the west. Who defines good social work education? Why is looking at culturally appropriate social work education so difficult to do?

5. There is a lack of creativity in producing social work theory and practice based on traditional knowledge and practice, African philosophy, and traditional lifestyles. One group member asked an appropriate question:

If colonialism had not taken place in our system, could we have strengthened our traditional institutions, taking into consideration advancement in technology, increased migration, and economic independence? ... Now we have our traditional system and our formal system. How are we going to integrate these things? Where do we start from? We need to use the positive things from our traditional system and blend it so that we make social work more suitable to the condition in which we find ourselves.

6. There are greater financial opportunities to work in Europe, the United States, and Canada due to poor salaries practitioners are paid as professional social workers in Africa. This causes a brain drain[2] that continually undermines the profession.

7. When Africans return to Africa, they tend to be distanced from the culture and teach and practice in a western way that may or may not be appropriate to the setting.

8. Africa consists of oral societies and yet research continues to be quantitative and non-oral. Qualitative research needs to become an accepted research in African universities. It naturally works with the Africa-centred worldview and the social work profession.

The ASWEA documents recorded a critical debate and showed attempts at steering away from a western curriculum and had some success with curriculum development in family welfare and planning and community development. Osei-Hwedie & Jacques (2007) also points out that it should not be assumed that every western-educated African is uncritical of their western training: "Western educated Africans have been critical of Western knowledge and theories and have been in the forefront of the fight against domination, such as was the case with colonialism and Apartheid" (p. 32). The fact that there have been debates is a positive sign that critical thinking is happening, and the challenge is to see this thinking play out in teaching, research and practice in social work training centres in Africa.

1. Ethics and values

Another aspect of social work education that has been neglected is a critical look at social work values and ethics in relation to culturally relevant curriculum. Kreitzer (2006) discusses the issue of social work values and whether or not they are universal. This debate of the universality of social work values has been documented through social work literature (Abbott, 1999; Bogo & Herington, 1986; Cox, 1995; Gray, 1995; Taylor, 2000). The debate has somewhat been negated by the "IFSW/IASSW Ethics in Social Work: Statement of Principles," which identifies two universal ethical social work principles at the broader level (IFSW/IASSW, 2008). These are: 1) human rights and human dignity; and 2) social justice. What I have found is that, beyond these two universal ethical values, the more culturally specific ethical values may or may not be appropriate to a particular culture. One of the main value differences is usually accentuated by cultures that are traditionally communal as opposed to cultures that are individual oriented. For example, confidentiality and self-determination may be important in all cultures but the way they are manifested in each culture may be very different. Many countries have as their code of ethics the American Code of Ethics. Ramsay (1999) found this to be true in India. He challenged the Indian social work profession to rewrite their code of ethics to reflect the cultures of India. After many drafts, a more Indian value system and ethical practice became the new code of ethics. The preamble states the following: "The declaration is rooted in the contemporary social reality which has a historical background and in the framework of humanistic values, based on the intrinsic worth of all human and non-human life" (TISS, 1997, p. 1). Including the Indian ideologies of Sarvodaya, Swarajya, and Lokniti,[3] as well as Ghandian[4] principles, shows that a Code of Ethics has been created that reflects that society.

In Ghana, discussion centred on the fact that their code of ethics was drawn directly from the National Association of Social Work (NASW) Code of Ethics and that work should be completed on rewriting it to reflect a more African/Ghanaian value and belief system. But of course this involves critical awareness of African philosophy, values, and beliefs in order to begin this process. In 1993 the New Zealand Association of Social Workers re-wrote their code of ethics to reflect the trend toward a culturally appropriate curriculum. It took into account the importance of the Maori in New Zealand culture. It "affirms the right of independence for the Maori people and represents the active commitment to the promotion of an indigenous identity for social work in Aotearoa[5] New Zealand" (ANZASW, 1994, p. 16). As the first bicultural code of ethics, "it recognizes that at the moment, the European has the power over resources and decision-making and social work needs to address this power regularly at an individual and institutional level" (Kreitzer, 2006, p. 9). It "attempts to accommodate difference and diversity in an emancipatory and social justice sense which, in turn, offers some direction of change" (Briskman & Noble, 1999, p. 65). All national professional associations around the world should go through this critical process of re-writing their codes of ethics to reflect their own culture and its diversity. As Osei-Hwedie & Jacques (2007) explains: "If foreign values predominate, then the practice derived from them will be of little relevance to the people to whom these values are alien" (p. 32).

D. Conclusion of chapter

The influence of western knowledge, used as a tool of European imperialism, has shaped the way in which Africans view western knowledge and how they view their own knowledge, traditions, and history. It is just as easy to idolize African traditional knowledge and practices, some of which are harmful and based on unsubstantiated evidence. This is equally unhelpful when looking at African social work education. The idealism of western knowledge can also be seen in social work education and practice. In my experience, African social workers now seem to find it difficult to think about a more African curriculum. It seems easier and safer to assume that western training, which has been tried and tested (in the western world mainly), is somehow appropriate to their situation. My point is that there needs to be a critical examination of all knowledge, and what is being addressed here is the imbalance of the use of western knowledge over African knowledge. There is a need in African social work to shed the clothes of colonial social welfare and western social work knowledge and radically shift its curriculum in a fresh, creative, and revolutionary way. When one has "let go of preconceptions, frameworks, models, theories, intervention strategies, our assumptions and skills, beliefs, materialism …

then we will open ourselves up to other possibilities, other wisdoms and other world views. It is only by letting go that we can enter into dialogue, learn from rather than about other people and cultures" (Ife, 2007, 14–15). We can then shed the colonial ideas of where Africans are in the world and grow in traditional knowledge and practices, which in turn will have a radical effect on social work education in Africa. This involves a decolonization process of re-education of the history of Africa, rediscovering the history of social work in Africa, and creating new theories and practices that reflect African culture. Cutting the umbilical cord of western social work curriculum, then creating culturally relevant knowledge and interventions, and then seeing what portion of western social work knowledge and theories fit within the new curricula is a starting point.

> Much of the knowledge achieved through conquest and colonization was understood to legitimate the political and cultural domination of imperialism. The resulting perspective on the world formed an educational legacy that we have now to reconsider. We cannot readily sort through and discard the colonial tainted understandings we carry, without devoting attention to how our view of the world has been shaped by imperialism's educational project, which included fostering a science and geography of race; renaming a good part of the world in homage to its adventurers' homesick sense of place and imposing languages and literatures on the colonized in an effort to teach them why they were subservient to a born-to-rule civilization. (Willinsky, 1998, pp. 3–4)

An example of the process above concerns naming the curricula. When I was asked to teach two courses at the University of Ghana in 1994, I was asked to teach "Framework for social diagnosis and "Framework for planned change." These terms were straight out of Social Diagnosis (Richmond, 1965) and Social Diagnosis in Case Work (Sainsbury, 1970). I asked myself if they were still teaching 1950s social work. Looking at the American social work books in the library I think they were. No course had a name that would indicate it was a social work course that reflected African society. I believe that the social work program would take on a very different mindset if the courses were named and associated with African concepts. Understanding the history of these names, renaming the courses to be African names, and adding western names when appropriate would be a great start to the process of decolonization. Once this is completed, owning one's own curricula by making it culturally appropriate will complete the process. Language is so important to cultural identity and doing a simple task like renaming the courses is important. Like an onion, the layers of colonialism need to be peeled away so that there is an understanding of where words originate and why they are used in social work education.

The following story sums up my own thinking concerning the relationship between western social work education and practice in the African context. This story was in a tenth grade reading book in Burundi:

> Mecca was a very fortunate West African man. He had a job that drew envy from his fellow villagers. He worked for a White man who was very generous. Indeed, the White boss was so nice to Mecca that he gave him a special gift: a pair of used shoes. Mecca was very excited. This was his very first pair of shoes. The shoes had a little problem, though. They were too tight to fit Mecca's untamed feet. But, he was still determined to wear them. So, he drilled holes in the corners of the shoes such that his pinky toes would stick out as he walked. He was very proud. He marched through the village showing off his new acquisition to friends and neighbours and praising the White man for his infinite goodness. (Ndura, 2006, pp. 92–93)

Why is African social work still running around with a curriculum that doesn't fit but still showing it off, adapting it, and grateful for western schools of social work for providing them with used texts to study it? Let's get a new pair of shoes that fit. This calls for critical reflection on how social work came to Africa, influences like colonization, modernization, and globalization on the evolution of social work and present issues of power and inequality. "Unless there is critical engagement with the stark past and present realities of structural and social relations of power, privilege, inequality and oppression, social workers in South Africa will deserve the past label of being upholders of the status quo" (Smith, 2008, p. 374).

Buying a new pair of shoes is not always easy when after years of working a person still doesn't have enough money to buy them. Financial backing is needed to buy these shoes. The present world economic order does not favour African countries when it comes to economic and social development. This in turn affects the growth of the social work profession, its associations, and the pay and conditions of social workers and academics. Even more importantly it affects the communities and people served by social workers who continue to work harder and harder and can't seem to get out of poverty. This is the theme of the next chapter.

IV. Neo-Liberal Policies

As it stands, the economic climate is certainly not in Africa's favour; and there is enough reason to believe that it has been one of the major contributing factors impeding Africa's economic effort.... African states have repeatedly demanded that the existing International Economic Order be re-examined in the best interests of world peace and mutual cooperation, but this has not been heeded because Africans are not negotiating from a position of strength. (Yimam, 1990, pp. 15–16)

A. The rise of international financial institutions

The above statement, written twenty-one years ago, still holds true today for Africa. Progress has been made in countries like Ghana, but the lowest countries on the Human Development Index continue to be African. The African continent has an abundance of natural and human resources that are valuable both to Africans and to the world. Unfortunately, during the colonial era and since the time of independence, the present world

economic order has prevented Africans from benefiting from these resources. "Neo-liberal economic policies have exacerbated poverty levels"
(Smith, 2008, p. 372) and have not improved poverty statistics of the
world (UNDP, 2007). In fact, the gap between the rich and the poor
is wider than it has ever been. Many would say that colonization never
stopped in Africa, it just shifted to economic domination by the most
powerful countries in the world.

According to Wilson & Whitmore (2000), the neo-liberal agenda
is, "an ideology that makes the market central in governing economic,
social, and political life.... At the international level, this is expressed
through advocacy of 'free trade' in goods and services, free circulation
of capital and freedom of investment" (p. 14). Born out of the United
Nations Monetary and Financial Conference held at Bretton Woods,
New Hampshire, in 1944, with the task of supporting European countries after the Second World War, the international financial institutions[1]
(IFIs, including the International Monetary Fund [IMF], the World Bank
[WB] and the General Agreement on Tariffs and Trade [GATT]) grew
to control the world financial economic order (Black, 2001; Hancock,
1997; Prigoff, 2000; Wilson & Whitmore, 2000). When the IMF and the
World Bank were created, only three African countries were represented,
thus continuing the domination of western thought concerning Africa's
non-importance to the world. This created an imbalance of power that
has remained to this day (Faiola, 2008).

From an African historical context, the IFIs have had an important
controlling influence on Africa. After colonization, many countries were
left in a weakened position. Sachs (2005) explains:

> Three centuries of slave trade, from around 1500 to the early
> 1800's, were followed by a century of brutal colonial rule. Far
> from lifting Africa economically, the colonial era left Africa
> bereft of educated citizens and leaders, basic infrastructure, and
> public health facilities. The borders of the newly independ-
> ent states followed the arbitrary lines of the former empires,
> dividing ethnic groups, ecosystems, watersheds, and resource
> deposits in arbitrary ways. (p. 189)

The critical need for development money led many African countries to borrow money from the IFIs to help them develop after colonization. As a result, "Africa was left in dreadful shape by the departing colonial powers, and was subsequently whip-sawed between ideological factions in the Cold War. But rather more decisive, it was also delivered to the depredations of the so-called IFIs – the collection of International Financial Institutions dominated by the World Bank and the International Monetary Fund, and including the African Development Bank and other regional development banks" (Lewis, 2005, pp. 4–5). These financial institutions, encouraged developing countries to borrow money for economic and social development projects (Midgley, 1995) with lax rules on paying the money back. However, in the late 1970s interest rates soared and borrowing money became expensive, and the world prices of raw materials dropped to record lows. Debts grew, and due to these interest rates many countries could not meet their payments to the IMF. As a result, countries borrowed more money to pay off their debts and the IMF tightened its economic and social control of these countries by introducing Structural Adjustment Programs[2] (SAPs) (Chossudovsky, 1997; Mammo, 1999; Prigoff, 2000).

These neo-liberal programs were meant to help countries pay off their debts through requiring countries, who were in debt, to cut government spending, promote exports, privatize public enterprises, devalue currency, keep interest rates high, strictly control credit and money supply, remove controls on trade and exchange and deregulate wages and prices (ECEJ, 1990; Prigoff, 2000). The negative effects of these programs are the continual cuts in health, education, and government-funded social programs. "The result of the IFIs' destructive power over Africa was to compromise the social sectors, particularly the health and education sectors of the continent to this day" (Lewis, 2005, p. 5). A good example is Ghana's experience with SAPs. By the end of Kwame Nkrumah's presidency, the nation had a large debt (Boahen, 1975). The IMF granted a loan to Ghana, and with the world economic recession in the 1980s this debt increased. In 1983, an IMF Economic Recovery Program was implemented to help repay the debts. Structural adjustment programs were implemented. These programs helped the economic reform but it was clear that these programs "did not take into account social objectives and excluded many forms of protection for the poor" (Jeong, 1996, p. 66).

In order to alleviate the effects of SAPs on the poor, the Program of Action to Mitigate the Social Costs of Adjustment (PAMSCAD) was introduced as an answer to the social side effects of SAPs. Critiques of PAMSCAD state that the program did not help alleviate poverty because it was grossly underfunded, there were administrative problems, and the money was used for political purposes (Herbst, 1993; Hutchful, 1997; Joeng, 1996; Ninsin, 1991). Prigoff (2000) suggests that the original intent of SAPs was to make "the nation competitive in a global market" (p. 122), but this has not been the case. These policies "result instead in the destabilization of long-established, self-sufficient communities.... [T]hey encourage private – often foreign – exploitation of natural resources on which vulnerable populations depend for survival in nations around the world.... [I]t has failed to address the needs of women, families and communities and has led to markedly sharper class stratification in the nations" (p. 122). Prigoff goes on to list several negative effects to nations due to these programs, including: 1) increased migration locally, nationally, and internationally; 2) declining levels of income and assets for the majority of people, especially the more vulnerable in society; and 3) loss of hope for many people to live healthy happy lives. A combination of these effects can be seen daily with the increase of migrants from Africa to Europe coming by boats in which many are killed along the way (Keeley & Hooper, 2008).

B. Present economic issues in Africa

Africa continues to have the largest share of the world's absolute poor (Mmatli, 2008). Plagued with poverty, pandemics, civil wars, and corruption, it continues to be at the bottom of the human development reports. The UNDP Human Development Report (2010) still shows many African nations at the low human development index while most of the rest of the world is shown in the high and medium development indexes. Since 1975 there has been little economic and social change in these countries in the low human development index. Sewpaul (2006) believes that colonization continued under these unfair trade and economic policies.

Most African countries are suppliers of raw materials and, at the same time, recipients of development aid. "That means that it [African countries] could be a victim of an unhealthy international economic arrangement on both grounds" (Yimam, 1990, p. 15). African countries continue to "suffer from worsening terms of trade with industrial countries, severe balance of payments crisis, and high interest rates on foreign debts" (p. 15). Goods are sold at a cheap price through exports and then resold at a much higher price; sometimes back to the same country, as can be seen with Kenyan tea in which Kenyans buy their tea at inflated prices. Unfair trade laws are perpetuated by neo-liberal policies. Lewis (2005) would agree. "As things now stand, there's simply no way for Africa profitably to export its own primary agricultural commodities" (p. 17). He goes on to state that "these rigid fundamental policies did extraordinary damage to African economies from which they have yet to recover" (p. 5). Western countries have been slow to open their markets to African products and this one-way system of trade hurts many poorer countries in the world. Yunus (2007) visualizes this imbalance and inconsistency within the present economic structures. "Unfettered markets in their current form are not meant to solve social problems and instead may actually exacerbate poverty, disease, pollution, corruption, crime and inequality" (p. 5). He describes the present global trade:

> Global trade is like a hundred-lane highway criss-crossing the world. If it is a free-for-all highway, with no stoplights, speed limits, size restrictions, or even lane markers, its surface will be taken over by the giant trucks from the world's most powerful economies. Small vehicles — a farmer's pickup truck or Bangladesh's bullock carts and human-powered rickshaws — will be forced off the highway. (p. 5)

He describes a fairer road with traffic laws, signals, and police by stating that "the rule of 'the strongest takes all' must be replaced by rules that ensure that the poorest have a place on the highway. Otherwise the global free market falls under the control of financial imperialism ... in the same way, local, regional, and national markets need reasonable rules and controls to protect the interests of the poor" (p. 5).

Many African countries still struggle under these economic plans laid out by the IFIs. In fact, a new index of heavily indebted poor countries

(HIPC) was established in 1996 to "ensure that no poor country faces a debt burden it cannot manage" (IMF, 2010, p. 1). Interestingly, twenty-nine out of the thirty-five countries in this new index were from Africa.[3] "Structural adjustment is not dead; it's just morphed into other forms. The imposition of conditionality is still alive and well; fashioned now more often by the IMF as it continues to impose macroeconomic frameworks on impoverished African countries" (Lewis, 2005, p. 14). Lewis (2005) gives a summary of debts incurred by African nations:

> Between 1970 and 2002, Africa acquired $294 billion of debt. Much of the debt was assumed by military dictators who profited beyond the dreams of avarice, and left for the people of their countries, the crushing burden of payment. Over the same period, it paid back $260 billion mostly in interest. At the end of it all, Africa continued to owe upwards of $230 billion in debt. Surly that is the definition of international economic obscenity. Here you have the poorest continent in the world paying off its debt, again and again, and forever being grotesquely in hock. (p. 22)

Many countries in Africa, "remain on the margins of the world economy with little prospect of integration for years to come ... and will go largely unnoticed by the mainstream international public" (Holscher & Berhane, 2008, p. 319).

C. Consequences of neo-liberal policies

Prigoff (2000) suggests that the present global domination of neo-liberal economics has affected many people in the world in a negative way. "Globalization of economic markets and international agreements that promote 'free trade' now are changing the economic and social environments of all nations in ways that have profound impact on individuals, families and communities.... [I]t results in the exclusion of poor people from access to resources which have been essential for their survival" (p. 1). Organizations like the World Bank, claiming to try and eliminate poverty, have not done so well. They are slow-moving and often self-serving. "Like nonprofits, they are chronically underfunded, difficult to rely upon and often inconsistent in their policies. As a result, the hundreds of billions of dollars they have invested over the past several decades have been largely ineffective – especially when measured against the goal of alleviating problems like global poverty" (Yunus, 2007, p. 11). They continue to believe that large-scale economic growth, at the expense of social development, is the way to end poverty. In spite of demonstrated failures, they are slow to change their policies. Although they have modified their programs in more recent times, due to critiques of their programs, they remain convinced that through neo-liberal policies, countries will eventually become industrialized and wealthy like western countries. Little value is given to the capacity of people to think for themselves and solve their own problems. "They cannot see the poor as independent actors. They worry about the health, the education, and the jobs of the poor. They cannot see that the poor people can be actors themselves. The poor can be self-employed entrepreneurs and create jobs for others" (Yunus, 2007, p. 12).

These neo-liberal policies have had a profound negative impact on African education, health, and social welfare. "Cutbacks in social investments, the privatization of social programmes, the abandonment of social planning and similar policy developments which accompanied the rise of the Radical Right have resulted in a significant increase in unmet social need" (Midgley, 1995). "Under structural adjustment, sub-Sahara African countries have had to cut back on social spending, lessen financial regulation and adopt exchange rates that are favourable to the North" (Heron, 2007, p. 783). In Africa, these programs have not benefited the people and have made things worse. Heron states that:

> As of 2005 almost a whole generation of Africans has grown up under the structures of structural adjustment. For some countries, the failure to achieve economic growth through this approach has resulted in political destabilization; for many more, corruption, a burgeoning underground economy, strained gender relations and widespread theft at all levels of society are now common as people struggle to cope with chronic unemployment and fast-rising costs of living. (p. 787)

Structural adjustment programs have also damaged the educational systems in Africa. "The state has significantly reduced recurrent expenditures on staff, staff training, and textbooks. User fees for school services, equipment and laboratories, parent-teacher association fees and room and board charges for institutions of higher learning have been introduced" (Sefa Dei, 2005, p. 230).

As the negative impact of structural adjustment programs were exposed, the next decade of 2000 saw two more United Nations and IMF programs imposed onto developing countries. The Millennium Development Goals (MDG) were developed through the United Nations and include eight goals: 1) end poverty and hunger; 2) obtain universal education; 3) obtain gender equality; 4) increase child health; 5) provide universal maternal health; 6) combat HIV/AIDS; 7) promote environmental sustainability; and 8) develop global partnerships (UNMDG, 2010). Part of the agreement signed by 189 nations gave special reference to helping Africa meet these goals (UN General Assembly, 2000). "We will support the consolidation of democracy in Africa and assist Africans in their struggle for lasting peace, poverty eradication and sustainable development, thereby bringing Africa into the mainstream of the world economy" (Article 27). The MDGs have had mixed results for Africa (UNMDG, 2011).

Although great strides have taken place in many parts of the world, Africa has had its share of challenges in reaching its goals. The poorest people live in Sub-Saharan Africa with 58 per cent still living on less than US$1.25 a day (p. 6). Unless neo-liberal economics change to support Africa in meeting these goals, little will change in regards to the majority of African countries. The other programs initiated by the IMF were the Poverty Reduction Strategy Programs (PRSP) (Allen & Leipziger, 2005). According to Levinsohn (2003) "the Bank and the Fund laid out a process that very poor countries would need to follow if they wished to make use of various concessionary lending facilities" (p. 1). This was the process by which the Bank and the IMF were to implement their Comprehensive Development Framework, which meant country-specific plans for poverty reduction. Although these plans encourage civil society participation and involvement of different departments of the government, there is lack of analysis as to whether or not this process has alleviated poverty

(Levinsohn, 2003) and there are mixed findings as to their effectiveness in reducing poverty (Aryeetey & Peretz, 2005; Zaman, 2002). Mouelhi & Ruckert (2007) critique the Poverty Reduction Strategy Program (PRSP). Responding to the growing resentment of the affect of SAPs on countries, the IMF endorsed this program because it "placed greater emphasis on poverty reduction and on 'pro-poor' policies, as well as on country ownership of policy reforms, involving civil society participation in the formulation of national poverty reduction strategies" (p. 178). Recognizing this to be a significant policy shift, the authors found, however, that the IMF was still wedded to neo-liberal structural reforms and this approach "has yet to demonstrate that it is delivering on its promise of real country ownership, the notion that developing countries are not in the driver's seat steering the PRSP process and ultimately their development agendas" (pp. 278–79).

Recent events in the world are showing signs that the IFIs are losing their power over their economic empire. Countries like Venezuela, Brazil, Argentina, Ghana, Uganda, Nigeria, and Tanzania have either paid off their loans early and are not interested in borrowing again or "have adopted new policy support instruments" (Faiola, 2008, p. 44) and moved away from IMF cash. Changing the IMF's role to that of advisor may decrease the devastating affect that SAPs have had on some countries. "It heralds the fund's diminishing importance in a world where developing nations have more lending options than ever before" (p. 44). Particularly China and India are lending money to African countries in exchange for African oil and minerals with no fiscal restraint or free-market reforms. As developing countries gain power, they are demanding to be part of the decisions made by the IFIs and the G8.[4] The 2008 world trade talks collapsed because of India's insistence that "developing countries must be able to protect their agricultural sector against sudden surges of subsidised imports from the US and EU" (Stewart, 2008, p. 46). This is supported by over a hundred countries, representing a billion subsistence farmers. Voices are slowly being heard and the "emerging powers of the East are not longer prepared to be pushed around" (p. 46).

Another trend away from neo-liberal promotion of privatization can be seen in New Zealand. There is revival in public ownership, due to the "wider disillusionment with the neoliberal experience of the past decade.... New Zealand has at least helped break the spell that privatisation is somehow the natural order of things in this modern world" (Milne, 2008, p. 21). Sachs (2005) believes that Africa's issues are solvable with practical and proven technologies. "A combination of investments well attuned to local needs and conditions can enable African economies to break out of the poverty trap" (p. 208). An understanding that we are all affected by each other's policies is slowly becoming a reality. With the increase in food prices and the rising demand of food "in the long-term the stability of every country in the world will require energy security, action on climate change and the spread of economic prosperity to the billions living on or below the breadline" (Elliott, 2008a, p. 18). It is a well-known fact that, once people are lifted out of poverty, the population will decrease over time. Social workers can be in the forefront in linking poverty and economic issues, advocating for fairer trade rules and global economic policies. It is, therefore, important that economics be included as a required component of African social work curricula.

D. Social work and neo-liberal policies

Social workers in Africa are caught between many different economic, political, and social ideologies over which they have little control. Poverty alleviation programs, pursued in many African countries, can do only so much when the national policies are up against the global IFIs and their policies. "The structural nature of social problems besieging Africa ... means that such problems are beyond the scope of social casework to resolve. Confronted with such situations, social workers become the cooling agents, as it were, in attempting to help people to cope with the persisting problems" (Mmatli, 2008, p. 300). According to the IFSW and IASSW (2008) code of ethics, "Social workers have a duty to bring to the attention of their employers, policy makers, politicians and the general public situations where resources are inadequate or where distribution of resources, policies, or practices are oppressive, unfair or harmful.... [T]hey have an obligation to challenge social conditions that contribute to social exclusion, stigmatization or subjugation, and to work towards an inclusive society" (p. 10). Is this task feasible for social workers in Africa? Prigoff (2000) believes that social workers should understand the economics of the time: "The profession of social work has a unique opportunity to help local communities respond effectively to the challenge of economic globalization ... to provide leadership on economic issues; social workers need skills in organizing and in political action; knowledge of the economic profile of communities ... and knowledge of tools, methods and limitations of economic theory and practice. The values of economics and the values of social work are profoundly different" (p. 2). A profession that seeks to "enhance the social functioning and health of individuals, families and communities" (p. 2) should be concerned that "ninety-four percent of the world income goes to 40 percent of the people while the other 60 percent must live on only 6 percent of world income. Half of the world lives on two dollars a day or less, while almost a billion people live on less than one dollar a day" (Yunus, 2007, p. 3).

Understanding the economic situations that African countries and their people face is an important element in social work education. Understanding neo-liberal policies and why so many African countries are still in the HIPC index, is crucial for the student's own understanding of social policy and the difficulties faced by their clients and communities (Ife, 2007). For example, one research group member explained the power the IFIs have on Ghana: "Even when they are giving you loans, they decide how it should be used, irrespective of need. And that goes a long way to affect our economy." An awareness of how these policies affect social welfare and the continual decrease in money allocated to the Department of Social Welfare and the Department of Community Development needs to be critically looked at in the university social work classroom. Cutting health, education, and social welfare funding has been felt throughout the different levels of education from primary school to post-secondary institutions. Governments, using a purely economic development plan, see these areas as unworthy of financial help because they are not directly producing income. It is short-sighted to assume that the social development of people is not profitable financially and is therefore not worth supporting. As one guest speaker in the research project put it:

> The improvement that you have brought to the person's life
> is not something that can be seen or touched. But when the
> government comes and builds roads and puts up nice buildings,

you can see those things and then next time you vote for them.... I don't think we value people as much as we should.... [I]f we want development we have to develop the people who will bring about development.

These cutbacks affect teacher retention and promote a depressing atmosphere on university campuses. I saw the consequences of these policies while in Ghana. Indeed, I was part of the effects of these policies. While I was teaching at the university, from 1994 to 1996, two teachers' strikes occurred at the university due to low pay and poor working conditions. The lack of finances to pay teachers and lecturers meant that students had to have five years of university education in order to obtain a four-year degree. Teachers often had two jobs (e.g., teaching and a consultancy job) to make ends meet. In addition to these labour issues, it was simply difficult to find qualified Ghanaians willing to teach social work. Many were in Europe, the United States, or Canada studying for their MSW and PhD (no MSW was offered at the University of Ghana until recently) or working as social workers. I was asked, along with two Peace Corp volunteers, to come and teach at the university in the social work unit. Through these voluntary organizations, we were asked to teach, with the commitment that the University of Ghana would provide accommodation and Voluntary Services Overseas would provide a daily stipend. The lack of consistent university staff, the introduction of new western lecturers from different countries, and the high turnover rate resulted in ongoing inconsistency in teaching style and material. Even if a course outline was available, the new lecturer did not necessarily have the knowledge to teach that subject. One group member explained:

The problem is that we don't have permanent lecturers here. Some come and teach but if a lecturer is gone someone must teach the course. And so they give the outline to another lecturer, and maybe when that lecturer looks at the content, he may not have total control of things on the outline. He had to go and find it and find things that he can teach very well and leave the ones he cannot.

Another group member stated: "We all appreciate the fact of the lack of full-time lecturers at the department. It is kind of hampering effective work at the department in even teaching and supervision of students and their fieldwork and the rest." When an institution has little funding, it limits the resources (teaching equipment and books) available for teaching. Two examples given by the research group described a course, in which there was one book for fifty students, and that one book was checked out by one student and often the recommended reading pages had been torn out. Many libraries, including social work libraries, are dependent on western textbooks and have little money to upgrade their services electronically. These examples highlight how western education continues to dominate simply because of a lack of financial support by the governments of these countries to publish their own textbooks. Thus the dependency cycle continues and this, in turn, upholds the neo-liberal policies that have not favoured educational needs. What I found over time was that a lack of motivation and apathy sets in and lecturers do what is necessary and then go home to a second job. If a lecturer or professor stays on, it is out of commitment and love for the job in spite of poor pay and conditions. For example, one lecturer told us that one year's salary at the university equalled one month's salary as a case manager in the United States. The only reason she remained as a tutor was that her motivation and good will was stronger than money. This low morale is not only evident with teachers but also with the professional association and social work practitioners. This depression feeds off of each area of social work, whether it be teaching, practising, or running an organization, and produces a profession that is on the periphery and is not proud of its achievements. Lecturers come and find inadequate resources with which to teach. This becomes very discouraging after a while. Some use their own precious money to buy essential resources and materials for their classes. Students also have many hurdles to cross just to get a degree from a university, including lack of books and resources, teachers' strikes, and residential accommodation that was built for two people but often holds five or six in a room.

In many countries in Africa, getting a social work education opens the door to work overseas. Engelbrecht (2006) researched the trend of South African social workers leaving South Africa and going to the UK to work. His study shows the increasing number of practising South Africans looking for a better lifestyle and pay in the west. He identifies the reasons for South Africans leaving to go to Europe to practice social work as being "low pay; risk of violence; staff shortages; high caseloads; administrative burdens; inadequate supervision; an imbalance between the salary offered and the job demands; a negative public image; a lack of funds; secondary trauma; compassion fatigue; burnout; and lack of job satisfaction" (p. 130). His conclusion is that the migration of social workers can be "ascribed mainly to less-than-favourable remuneration and less-than-favourable working conditions" (p. 143). His research showed that "the migration of South African social workers is largely driven by financial reasons (100%), to some extent by working conditions (82%), and insignificantly by personal reasons (3%)" (p. 138). Lack of appropriate pay and conditions in order to work effectively as a social worker or educator in Africa also limits the ability of colleagues to network and share ideas. Generally, students and practitioners are unable to travel to conferences, to other countries to look at social work in these countries, or to sustain a critical dialogue between colleagues continent-wide. The internet still has efficiency problems in much of Africa and servers can be down for weeks on end. Student exchange between African countries is not often possible because of the economic situation all over Africa. The professional social work community is then in danger of becoming an elitist group, leaving out those who are unable to afford contributing to this dialogue due to the fact that they can't afford to attend conferences.

So, what are the important issues that link social work practice to neo-liberal policies? It is important to teach the effect these policies are having on social welfare, education, and health (Ife, 2007). "The problems experienced by people with whom we work are, in large measure, linked to structural sources of oppression, exclusion and poverty at the global level, and if we are to seek adequate solutions, we need to engage with global structural forces" (Sewpaul, 2006, p. 430). Once social workers are aware of the impact of these policies, they can, individually and through their professional association, lobby their governments for fairer economic policies. "The challenge for African scholars is to interrogate the consequences of globalization on African politics, economies and societies in a post-colonial world" (p. 420). Paying off the IMF and World Bank debts and encouraging governments to place more value on the people of its country is important. In Ghana, radio talk shows are an important part of life. Social workers and their professional association could use these programs to provide a social work perspective to the issue at hand. They should also share that they are social workers, so people begin to understand that social workers are active in trying to deal with social issues. "Social workers need to think and act both locally and globally where we connect progressive social movements and communities and challenge inequities rooted in the International Monetary Fund, the World Bank and the World Trade Organization and the world's core imperialist nations" (Sewpaul, 2006, p. 422). Engelbrecht (2006) suggests that governments adopt retention strategies that would ensure "quality employees staying on the staff" (p. 132). He suggests sustainable and proactive retention strategies "which include a balance between the investment made in the recruitments of social workers and their retention, both receiving the same priority" (p. 143). He also suggests there be "efficient organisational communication between social service providers and professionals which is accessible and nation-wide" (p. 143). An example would be a social services professional publication. His hope is that the brain drain will be plugged of South African social workers migrating to the UK and that many will return to work in their own countries.

To promote fairer trade is to develop contracts with businesses that promote fair trade and develop community economic programs for the rural areas. An example can be seen in the work of one of the research group members who was a community worker in Northern Ghana. The village women had secured a contract with Body Shop to make shea butter. The women processed the shea nut and made the butter, and it was shipped to Body Shops around the world. Yunus (2007) suggests a social business approach to counterbalance the economic imbalance of the times. "Social business is designed and operated as a business enterprise, with products, services, customers, markets, expenses, and revenues – but with the profit-maximization principle replaced by the social-benefit principle. Rather than seeking to amass the highest possible level of financial profit to be enjoyed by the investors, the social business seeks to achieve a social objective" (p. 23). In other words, the business provides a product or service that generates income but it benefits the poor or society at large. Other examples of how countries and peoples are working around the neo-liberal ideologies of dependency are in the areas of fair trade and cooperatives. In Uganda, fair-trade brands have helped coffee cooperatives develop, empowering people and supporting sustainability. "Of the 200,000 smallholders, who grow coffee on Mount Elgon, only 6,000 are members of the cooperative – but that figure has doubled since early 2007. Protected from falling prices and the predatory tactics of private buyers, those farmers are empowered" (Purvis, 2008, p. 26–27). In the UK, ethical shoes, called Soul of Africa, are sold to raise money for "orphans in South Africa who have lost their parents to AIDS by training and employing local women to stitch shoes" (Butler, 2008).

E. Conclusion of chapter

This chapter has painted a somewhat bleak picture of the many challenges that confront the African continent and the negative impact that neo-liberal policies have had on the countries, communities, and the social work profession. Despite these challenges, the continent has survived historical oppression, and it is growing and making its way out of dependency on the western world and is showing signs that economic and social development are happening despite its financial predicaments (Kenny & Sumner, 2011). Maathai (2009) describes how the continent, in half a century, has seen the independence of all countries and has "moved forward in some critical areas of governance and economic development" (p. 10). More importantly, "civil society ... is becoming bolder in speaking out in support of human rights and good governance" (p. 11). The international financial institutions are slowly accepting the fact that some of their policies were not beneficial for Africa and reforms are being made. However, as Sewpaul (2006) asks:

> If democracy is indeed about human rights, social justice, people participation and respect for human dignity, where is its convergence with the marketplace that has no room for justice and compassion, that creates indifference to inequality, hunger, exploitation and suffering, that excludes the voice of the Other, with highly centralized power negotiated by the World

Bank, the International Monetary Fund and the World Trade Organization and by the world's superpowers? (p. 425)

This imbalance between national democracy and the international global economic order is what social workers and educators need to address in the classroom, at the local, national, and international levels – helping to create practical plans to work for change. We need to "confront and deconstruct capitalism's ideological persuasion, envisioning and giving substance to a world beyond neo-liberalism; walking along with people whom we work with in the struggle towards an alternative world based on redistributive justice; and drawing strength and inspiration from THEMBA[5] (**T**here **M**ust **B**e an **A**lternative)" (p. 431).

As I am writing this chapter, the United States is trillions of dollars in debt. Civil society and Congress are questioning this now as American people seem tired of these neo-liberal policies that favour the rich. In a tongue and cheek article in the Los Angeles Times, Brooks (2007) welcomes the United States to the Third World and offers IFI assistance to help bail them out. It is a provocative article that turns the tables on the superpower that has ruled the economic world for many years. Maathai (2009) challenges Africans to reach beyond all the barriers that have been put in the way of progress: "Despite the unfair trade practices and the heavy debt burden under which Africans have labored; the challenge is for Africans to escape the culture of dependency that leads to passivity, fatalism and failure … and to challenge the leadership to break free of the corruption and selfishness that exists, from high offices to the grassroots" (p. 5).

Alongside these economic policies that have not been kind to Africa, development theories have emerged that have supported the neo-liberal policies or have critiqued them. These main theories, modernization theory and dependency theory, reflect and critique the present economic policies in relation to development. These theories have assumptions that have affected social development in Africa. These will be discussed in the next chapter.

V. Development and Aid

The idea is that poverty is endemic, rooted. In my own community, they have a proverb that sustains that idea. "Poverty is king, money is like a stream, it passes so don't worry, it passes." ... So if you get money soon it will pass, it will go to the next one, it will pass, it will never stay. And that is the sad nature.

A. History of development theories

The above statement was shared with the research group by a guest speaker summarizing his observations of rural Ghana. It portrays a sense of helplessness concerning poverty and the belief that, once a person is born poor, they will always be poor. To rural people, poverty is a condition or situation that is natural. It is unfortunate that many development projects inadvertently feed into this mentality. As one group member stated:

People have resigned themselves to fate ... because you go to a community and for so many years there is an impending problem but it appears that they have exhausted all of their energy as to solving their thing but they have come to the realization that they can't do anything about it and have resigned to fate.

When I was carrying out my PhD research in Ghana, I heard two stories that I think summarize how recipients of development projects general feeling about many of the local development projects that have been administered by overseas organizations. The first story concerns a village in which a foreign donor had visited and assessed that the water situation in the village needed to be changed. In this village, every morning, the children would get up and do their chores, which included going to fetch water from a distant stream and bring it back to the house before going to school. The donor decided that a borehole should be built in the village which would save the children from having to go so far to fetch water. The borehole was built and the next year the donor came back to evaluate its use. What they found was that lots of grass and weeds had grown up around the well, showing that it had not been used. When asked why the borehole had not been used, the people of the village had a very simple response. They explained that when the children went to fetch the water, it was the only chance for the parents to be together intimately and thus provided an important alone time for couples. Construction of the closer borehole intruded on this intimate time and it was, therefore, not acceptable. Villagers were clear, however, that if the donor had asked them, they would have told them the situation and saved a lot of time and money. Unfortunately, they were never asked.

The second story tells of a volunteer whose organization deemed it necessary that each volunteer should do a project in their village within the two years of their volunteer appointment. One volunteer noticed that people were racing their cars through the village, thus putting women and children at risk of being hit. The volunteer's solution to this was to build mounds in the middle of the road through the village that would slow cars down and decrease the risk of people getting hit. This was a very noble gesture. Unfortunately, overtime, cars began to go around the mounds thus putting women and children at even greater risk, as going around the mounds meant driving further off of the road.

Both were initiated with the best intentions, but both failed to ask and listen to the local people. Ownership was in the hands of the donors and not the people. Volunteers, westerners, and development workers often come into a community with their own ideas of what should be done, spending little time or effort in understanding or learning about the local culture and values. Culture has deep and often unexpected influences on behaviour, but unfortunately cultural questions are not often asked before projects are implemented. If the village, in both scenarios, had been invited to discuss the issue, possibly a locally appropriate solution that met everyone's needs could have been agreed upon. Learning about culture and building relationships takes time. Over and over again development projects don't spend enough time listening and consulting with local people. Projects have to be approached with humility and with a teachable spirit by the donor agency. Pertinent questions to ask include: 1) whether the project is really needed; 2) what possible solutions are available; and 3) whether the local community been included in the planning and decision-making process. This is true in any development project.

1. Development through modernization

Walsh (2010), in critiquing development, concludes that "the very idea of development itself is a concept and word that does not exist in the cosmovisions, conceptual categories and languages of indigenous peoples" (p. 17). In fact, she, as well as many others, see the development industry as "signalling more than just material progress and economic growth; it has marked a western model of judgement and control over life itself" (p. 15). How did this happen?

The term 'under-developed' first appeared in U.S. President Harry Truman's Inaugural Address in 1949. Known as 'Point Four,' the address begins by stating that "we must embark on a bold new program for making the benefits of our scientific advances and industrial progress available for the improvement and growth of the underdeveloped areas" (Rist, 2008, p. 71). This set the stage for the development era whereby "'underdeveloped' and 'developed' were members of a single family: the one might be lagging a little behind the other, but they could always hope to catch up ... so long as he continues to play the same game" (p. 74). "The term became active ... thus 'development' took on a transitive meaning (an action performed by one agent upon another)" (p. 73). There are assumptions around these terms that promote an industrialized western model of social and economic development. Simpson (1994) explains:

> Terms such as undeveloped, under developed, least developed, less developed, have all appeared and been used by bodies such as the United Nations. Underlying all these labels is a perceived distinction of differences in poverty and wealth, and a belief that there is a process called development during which the condition of poverty is replaced by one of comparative affluence. (p. 4)

These categorizations and terms, fuelled by neo-liberal economic policies, shaped an evolving modernization theory in the 1950s and 1960s. Critics describe modernization theory as a reflection of the neo-liberal view of laissez-faire economics, competitive capitalism, and private property accumulation (Mullaly, 1993; Prigoff, 2000; So, 1990). This theory has the optimistic belief that through westernization, mainly economic development (Midgley, 1995), all countries would see economic growth, the benefits of which would trickle down and alleviate poverty (Roberts, 1984; So, 1990; Wilson & Whitmore, 2000). Wilson & Whitmore (2000) describe this modernization theory, based on W.W. Rostow's book "The Stages of Economic Growth," as having five sequential stages: "1) the traditional society; 2) the period when preconditions for take-off are developed; 3) the take-off stage; 4) the period of sustained growth and 5) the age of high mass consumption" (p. 17). The goal of modernization is to replace traditional societies with modern industrial societies (Midgley, 1995). The theory assumes a cultural value shift from traditional values to industrialized values, which could mean a shift from a community-based society to an individualistic society, and a shift from a sharing of resources to a competitive consumer society. It could also mean a shift from a work ethic that revolves around local culture and environment to one of hardworking individualists, often at the expense of the family and community. It assumes "the applicability to Third World countries not only of First World economic institutions, but of their political institutions as well"

(p. 18). Waters (2001) describes this development theory by using the metaphor of mountain climbers. The strongest are at the top of the mountain, while the weak are lagging behind due to smallness in stature, natural calamity, poor resources, or lack of training. The strong try to help by throwing ropes down but the ropes are not strong enough. However, most of the weak, still struggling up the mountain, long for the top of the mountain so that "when everyone gets to the summit they will join hands in mutual congratulation because they are all in the same place" (p. 34).

The perceived need to 'develop' the rest of the world was a way for western countries to rationalize maintaining economic and political influence in post-colonial countries. Through exploitation of 'developing' countries for their resources and supporting the overthrow of many governments to combat the spread of communism, development took on a political agenda (Meredith, 2006).

Over time, major criticism of this type of theory came from different areas, including neo-Marxism and feminist thinking. As Simpson (1994) states:

> The concept of development when viewed from inside the Developing World has often been neglected. The poor peasant of Peru or the slum-dweller of Calcutta would no doubt, if asked, conceive of development as the amelioration of his dire poverty. Others in the developing world often regard development as the intrusion into their societies of European and North American values imposed upon their own cultures, to them development is a mixed blessing. (p. 11)

Other countries and their people began to question this approach. "Not only were they not seeing prosperity, poverty was increasing, the gap between the rich and the poor was increasing, and there was no evidence of any 'trickle down' of economic benefits to the poor" (Wilson & Whitmore, 2000, p. 18). Another critique of development emerged known as the 'dependency theory.' Wilson & Whitmore (2000) historically identify this theory as coming from "the experience of Latin America, Andre Gunder, Theotoniao Dos Santos" (p. 20) and summarize this as follows:

To dependency scholars (*dependentistas*), underdevelopment is seen as a result from a growth process induced from the outside rather than from within. Underdevelopment is not seen as a *condition*, the obvious solution to which would be 'modernization'; rather, it is seen as a *process* coming out of historical experience shared by Asia, Latin America and Africa. This includes the experience of colonial rule, and of economic dependence on the sale of certain commodities (agricultural, mineral, some industrial goods processed by cheap labour) to the West ... the underdevelopment and impoverishment of Third World countries (the periphery) is produced by their dependent relationship with the exploitative rich countries (the core or centre). (pp. 20–21)

Simpson (1994) supports this by stating that "development must allow both peoples and nations the self-respect that comes from participation in the world economy as equals. Any 'web of interconnections' in a post-colonial world must develop not between exploiter and exploited but between partners with a reciprocal respect for the values of each other" (p. 11).

Along with western-style development the issue of the effectiveness of aid has been critiqued in recent times. Moyo (2009) challenges the notion that aid "can alleviate systemic poverty" (p. xix) and points out that the US$1 trillion in development-related aid has not made African people better off. "In fact, across the globe the recipients of this aid are worse off; much worse off. Aid has helped make the poor poorer, and growth slower. Yet aid remains a centrepiece of today's development policy and one of the biggest ideas of our time" (p. xix). Mammo (1999) agrees.

During the post-colonial period, poverty has been exacerbated from two fronts – external and internal. The external influences exhibited through development assistance or aid programs have made many African countries heavily dependent on external factors; financial institutions have accelerated African debt; imbalance in international trade has forced prices of primary goods to fall; and multinational corporations use African cut-price labor and natural resources to their advantage. In these processes Africa stands as a loser and is exposed to further poverty. (p. 6)

An example, concerning who benefits from aid, was given by one group member when he told of his work as a community worker in Northern Ghana. The agency he worked for was supported by USAID. In the food distribution program, local people were not given cash to buy locally but were given wheat from the subsidized farmers in the United States. Who is benefiting? The people who are now dependent on USAID wheat (who were not wheat eaters before this food distribution started) or the U.S. government who conveniently sent wheat left over from their production in the United States? His local agency was also instructed to drop programs if they no longer served the interest of the U.S. government. According to this group member, the local people would have wanted to have cash so they could buy from the local market, thus supporting the local economy. Who is this development project serving? Is it serving the well-being of the local community or the country from which the aid was sent?

Before the G8 meeting in Hokkaido in 2008, there was a warning concerning the anticipated rise of global food prices. According to Wintour & Elliott (2008), a British Cabinet Office report concluded that "world cereal production needed to increase by 50% and meat production by 80%, between 2000 and 2030 to meet demand, while noting that up to 40% of food harvested in the developing world is lost as a result of storage and distribution problems" (p. 2). If the developing world continues to be dependent on aid for food, sustainability of communities to provide for themselves will be lost and Africa will continue its dependency on the world for its food. As seen above, world food supplies are no longer a stable commodity and more sustainable development needs to be encouraged so Africans can feed themselves as they did before colonization.

2. The effects of modernization theory on poor countries

The results of a world in which neo-liberal economic policies and modernization theory have made their mark have not produced what was expected. Not everyone is on the mountain top experiencing economic and social prosperity. Is it really conceivable that the world can sustain prosperity for every country at the level of the industrialized societies? The world is already suffering with the amount of the western world's consumption of natural resources, the increase in population growth, and economic imbalance. The gap between the rich and the poor is growing every day (Worldwatch, 2003). Unfortunately, development agencies are slow to change their attitudes and ways of 'doing' development. This type of development continues to this day with experts continuing the trek to 'underdeveloped' countries to modernize them. Heron (2007) researched the need for western countries, particularly white western females, to continue to 'develop' these countries. The way in which development projects are carried out has "been normalized and operationalized in the work of development agencies, bilateral aid projects and so on. In this process, the unspoken subtext is that what really counts and must be preserved are our standards, our perspectives, our national fantasies, our imaginings of the Other, and, when we do development work, our experiences 'there'" (p. 4). Many development projects still aren't working for the people; they often continue to promote dependency and are often caught in bureaucracy with very little to show for the work these projects have started. One of the researcher group members commented: "NGO's have worked with the communities for a very long time and apart from fiscal infrastructure such as school buildings, health centres and boreholes you cannot see a significant or drastic change in the lives of the beneficiaries themselves." Although some attitudinal changes have taken place within development agencies, western 'experts' continue to design and prioritize many of the development projects delivered to the non-western world (Mouelhi & Ruckert, 2007).

We cannot assume that our ways of understanding are necessarily the same as those of others or are any nearer the truth. However, in the present development state of mind, "the message that Northern countries have a special role to play in alleviating the woes of the poor global "Others" (Heron, 2007, p. 5) seems true today. "In the case of Canada, this has become one of the most significant narratives of the *res publica*, a kind of national calling, that coalesces in both aid/development commitments and peacekeeping activities" (p. 5).

This modernization theory has influenced the phenomenon of globalization. There is a range of perspectives on globalization that elicits a whole body of discourse on its influence in the world today (Lechner & Boli, 2000; Waters, 2001). To some, globalization signifies interdependence, prosperity, modernity, and progress (Martin, 2000), while others see globalization as an advanced stage of modernization causing poverty, fragmentation, corruption, and marginalization (Lechner & Boli, 2000; Midgley, 2000). Scholte (2000) divides common conceived notions of globalization into five components: (a) internationalization (cross-border relations between countries), (b) liberalization (creating open borders between countries and international economic integration), (c) universalization (the spreading of world objects and experiences to all corners of the world), (d) westernization (modernization or Americanization that tend to destroy local and indigenous cultures), and (e) deterritorialization or globality (a reconfiguration of geography so that time and space are not seen in terms of territories/transplanetary and supraterritoriality). The accelerated process of globalization includes the compression of time and space and this is challenging life today (Waters, 2001).

Although globalization has made some positive contributions, it is presently dominated by neo-liberal policies of the most powerful nations of the world. Wilson & Whitmore (2000) call this ideological orientation 'globalism' (p. 14). Robertson (2003) describes challenges with this particular brand of globalization concerning equity and justice in the world. The first challenge is the "deepening of democratization and enhancing the centrality of civil society" (p. 12). In the present system of privatization, short-term profit-maximizing strategies are pursued "at the expense of human capital and infrastructure ... the result is increased inequalities brought on by war, debt and policies of exclusion" (p. 12). The second challenge is the environmental challenge. "Just as democracy cannot survive in a sea of poverty, it cannot survive in an environmentally damaged and disease-ridden world." The third challenge is the fact that nations are becoming more diverse in their populations. "Skewed development, within and across nation states and continents, reflects the fact that race, class, gender and other factors such as culture, ethnicity, sexual orientation and disability intersect in powerful ways to influence people's access to power, prestige, status and resources" (Sewpaul, 2006, p. 424). Robertson (2003) shares his thoughts of what an unequal globalization process is capable of doing and its consequences:

> People need to reclaim ownership of globalization and democratize the process. The alternative has confronted humans before. Actions that seek to marginalize human agency and creativity, and undermine democratic gains, will not only make societies more vulnerable to economic and political shocks, but will also deny humans the mass global dynamism they now need to address problems that exist in global proportions. Every child that starves is a child denied the ability to contribute to society to the best of his or her ability. Every child refused education represents a loss in social and human potential. In one way or another, all peoples and their societies pay the penalty for such neglect. (p. 6)

With the present-day modernization theory of development still functioning in most parts of the world, social workers are in a unique position, working with the more vulnerable in society to change attitudes and beliefs concerning development in order for people to experience a more equitable outcome. This begins by integrating experience with teaching about development models in the classroom. A shift in thinking plus understanding of the different development theories can help clients at the individual, group, and community levels to find more inclusive and equitable patterns of development. The understanding of structural systems that affect Africa's growth and development should be known by all social workers in Africa as well as how these systems affect their own national policies and their clients and communities.

B. Social work and development

Social work can play an important role in strengthening civil society and advocating for poverty reduction policies that support the local communities. Unfortunately, one of the results of modernization and skewed globalization is a concentration of power and money, both inside the country by elitists as well as some countries of the world while others, like Africa, continue living in a survival mode. This imbalance has also created a dependency cycle between western and non-western countries that perpetuates a colonial mentality. The historical and ongoing attitude of the west towards Africa has resulted in an attitude of distrust. Countries that are in the survival stage (just trying to get enough food, clothing, housing, etc.) that are now used to depending on the western world for food and clothing experience a kind of greed among their peoples that is understandable. For example, in Accra, Ghana, there is a cooperative art gallery that was set up so that artists could sell their paintings without the middle person and the proceeds would be distributed among the artists in an equal cooperative fashion. When it came time to distribute the money, the cooperative distribution didn't work because the artists only wanted their own money for themselves. Another example can be drawn from the time I spent in a Liberian refugee camp in Ghana. When second-hand clothing came in to the centre, the women designated to distribute the clothes among camp residents usually took most home for themselves and their families (Kreitzer, 1998). Trying to survive can bring out both the worst and the best in people. Unfortunately, the historic patterns of development and aid in Africa tend to perpetuate this mistrust and greed. The game of development is played by all, and the people 'being developed' have learned to fight for what they can get, not trust anyone other than their own, and not give any information that would put their culture and life into jeopardy. One research group member stated that

> True development is about contributing towards the communities own ideas, pursuits and dreams and supporting them, through skill training and financial backing, to fulfil those dreams and not just handing them something. Let people themselves also come up with their own talents ... helping people to use their own abilities to do things for themselves.

Social workers have the opportunity to change this attitude of dependency, empowering clients to think for themselves and create a better life for themselves. One group member states: "Sometimes it is just encouraging confidence and courage in people to find answers to their own problems because the solution lies within the problem." A social worker has to be very sensitive when entering a community because the people will suspect that he/she is there to disturb things and the social worker will not be accepted. There may be good intentions but communities can be frightened of change. This is where working with traditional authority or elders, spending time in the community, knowing the different coping mechanisms, building relationships, and including the community in any plans for the community are essential. Otherwise, people may be grateful for your help but may not use what you have initiated because they don't own it.

A good question to ask when creating a development project is "who benefits"? According to UNESCO (1982) "placing culture at the heart of development policy constitutes an essential investment in the world's future and a pre-condition to successful globalization processes that take into account the principles of cultural diversity" (p. 1). Development policy needs to include "the qualitative dimension, namely the satisfaction of man's spiritual and cultural aspirations. The aim of genuine development is the continuing well-being and fulfilment of each and every individual" (p. 2). One of the consequences of donor-controlled development is what I call "research or development fatigue syndrome." This is the negative reaction that people have to yet more researchers or development workers coming in to try and help a community. One of the group members described this well:

When I did my research for my long essay I went to the village and people started narrating stories for me.... I had to explain that I wasn't from the government or NGO but from university.... Everybody thought that when you come into a community and do research, basically you have come to give them some help. Unfortunately, people come and make all of these promises and so it affects the subsequent ones, when they are coming the villagers are not willing to give information because the other people came and made promises they couldn't fulfil.

Heron (2007) sees development as meeting the needs of the donors and their staff and volunteers. "Here again is a story where 'developing countries' appear to be in a state of unmanageable disarray, and where what seems to matter is not just the assistance that is given, but the helping imperative and the effect that 'helping' the passive Other will have on our [development worker] own life experiences" (p. 5).

At its best, development is about empowering local people to use their own resources so they don't depend on external assistance, take out loans, and end up in debt thus continuing the dependency cycle. Moyo (2009) suggests that African countries need to wean themselves off of foreign aid and this will improve Africa's poverty levels and their economies. However, this kind of 'rehabilitation' lacks political will from western countries involved in the aid industry and for African leaders who find it easier to accept aid. Mammo (1999) explains that "when post-colonial African countries made their decisions to adopt a certain path of development they simply followed Western footsteps – without thorough examination of the model(s) adopted to ensure that they could address the desires of African societies" (p. 11). It is now time to correct this error (Moyo, 2009). African leaders could take the step of decolonizing from aid and this takes a selfless leader. "Economic prospects in a non-aid environment require a long-term and selfless vision and not the myopia so many policymakers are afflicted with today" (p. 148). It is also about people thinking for themselves and using their own experience, knowledge, and talent to produce projects that are positive and innovative and which use and foster the inner strength of the people (Mammo, 1999). It is about sustainable development. An example of this type of development was given by the same research group member concerning his project in Northern Ghana. A training program was set up called Participatory Farm Management with the goal of cultivating an acre of land for maize. Using Participatory Rural Appraisal techniques, local farmers were asked to come up with what would be needed to achieve this goal. They came up with what they needed, thought through the task and came up with their own local workable solutions with the help of a local community worker. Yunus (2007), the founder of the Grameen Bank, speaks of a social business model that "recognizes the multi-dimensional nature of human beings" (p. 21). The social business principles aim for "full cost recovery, or more, even as it concentrates on creating products or services that provide a social benefit" (p. 22). These and other initiatives could change the way development is perceived and delivered in Africa. Social workers can implement positive change by using and teaching these various methods in their day-to-day work.

1. The role of social welfare institutions

Within each country it is important that social support systems exist to support the development of the community. A style of remedial social services was imposed upon anglophone African countries during the colonial times, with little consideration of traditional systems. According to Crown Colonist (1945), this was already frowned upon by a special correspondent for the Crown Colonist. Warning against transplanting social service institutions from western countries to Africa, the correspondent remarked that "by concentrating their attention on the application of borrowed and foreign solutions to their local problems, these colonies tended to overlook the possibility of finding other solutions, rooted in their own institutions, which may be more appropriate to their own particular needs" (as cited in ASWEA, 1976a, Doc. 11, p. 28). Exceptions were countries like Ghana and Tanzania where the indigenous Community Development Movement was encouraged to promote literacy and self-sustainability (Abloh & Ameyaw, 1997). Both the Department of Social Welfare and the Department of Community Development have felt the cutbacks to their programs through the various IFI programs. As well, little critique of these institutions has occurred in Africa as to their effectiveness in today's society (Laird, 2003). "Indeed over three decades, African scholars have consistently argued that the national Departments of Social Welfare set up by the former colonial powers of Britain and France should be reoriented to undertake interventions which support the objectives of social development not rehabilitative modes of casework" (p. 259). Important questions to ask concerning these institutions are: 1) who do these institutions serve; and 2) what is their purpose? These critical questions should be asked with students in the classroom, academics researching these institutions, and practitioners. Reformation of some type is possible or ultimately getting rid of them if they are not meeting the needs of society. South Africa is a good example of a country trying to change a social welfare system that was mainly remedial to better serve poor white South Africans (Earle, 2008). After apartheid, the whole social work ethos had to change and this challenged and continues to challenge the social work profession concerning the different roles and social services institutions that are needed in the new system (Gray & Mazibuko, 2002; Patel, 2005).

In Ghana, the traditional system of social care was that people in the whole community looked after each other. However, the present system depends on the Department of Social Welfare, NGOs, the Department of Community Development, and external organizations to provide social welfare services. As a result, the government has reduced its funding for social welfare, people have not been trained for self-survival, and many simply wait for handouts that are not forthcoming. Communities seem less self-motivated and more dependent on someone else, an outsider or the government, to motivate them to effect change. This apathy may be partially a result of not being involved in the planning of the past projects and having projects put upon them that they did not want.

2. National development and social policy

For many countries in Africa, since independence, national planning was a priority. This can be seen in the ASWEA documents in regards to social work education. In order to have a relevant social work curriculum, there needed to be social policy as part of national planning. "Governments need to have a balanced, integrated and coordinated national development plan; a commitment to social development and to formulate social policy and to involve social workers at different levels of planning and implementing the national development programmes.... Governments should have a policy of balanced and decentralized services and social work educators and practitioners should start to be active and involve themselves in rural development where most of the needs are found and the majority of the people live" (ASWEA, 1974c, Doc. 6, pp. 11–12). In 1976, at another ASWEA conference, it was noted that development was not reaching the poor rural people but only the privileged few.

"A growing number of observers are beginning to perceive – sometimes with a felling of disgust – that so many of the efforts put in a large number of countries in the process of development have not assisted, up until now except to enrich further an already privileged minority, this without benefit for the underprivileged minority" (p. 81). The speaker goes on to say: "The aim of development is the improvement of man before the improvement of the economy. In other words, the economic resources must be of service to man and not vice versa" (p. 82). Four important aspects of development are as follows: "1) Social services support including nutrition and education; 2) popular participation; 3) respect of traditional cultures and 4) integrated character of rural development" (ASWEA, 1976a, Doc. 11, p. 82),

In 1982, the same themes emerged again. "There is a growing realization in Africa today that the neglect of the social dimension of development has substantially contributed to the lack of progress in development effort both in the colonial and post colonial eras" (ASWEA, 1981, Doc. 17, p. 24). One speaker relates this to present remedial social work education.

> With the type of social welfare systems and national planning approaches that have been around in Africa for some time now, it is easy to see why social work training programmes and approaches could not be different. This is because the type of services produced their own appropriate workers. Training programmes were geared to producing workers that would fit in the service models of the time. Since service models were dominated by non-African influences, Jan de Jongh was justified in remarking: "I don't know of any developing country in which social work education was an original product of national development: the origins can always be traced back to strong foreign influences." (ASWEA, 1981, Doc. 17, p. 87)

In 1986, ASWEA conferences were geared towards trying to alleviate the many crises' affecting Africa at that time.

> The deterioration of African family's levels of living has been underway for many decades. Contributing factors have

been the distortion of rural economics plus high under and unemployment, large population increases, constantly decreasing availability of land and even that land available being steadily degraded in an ecologically disastrous trend. Add to this inappropriate food policies, the impact of world recession and heavy debt payments, political instability and mal-development through policies that have given little attention to the needs of the majority rural dwellers, particularly women and children and the dimensions of the problem emerge. (ASWEA, 1985, Doc. 20, pp. 23–24)

There needed to be a social development approach to social services and appropriately trained social development workers to help alleviate suffering caused by the above factors. South Africa began this process through a positive social policy initiative called the White Paper for Developmental Social Welfare in South Africa. This policy advocates for the social development approach to development. Social development is "essentially a people-centred approach to development that promotes citizen participation and strengthens the voice of poor people in decision-making and in building democratic and accountable institutions ... social welfare policies and programmes from a social development perspective set goals that are likely to lead to tangible improvements in people's lives" (Patel, 2005, p. 30). The White Paper for Developmental Social Welfare "sets out the government's strategy for transformation which includes five key policy objectives: the provision of basic needs, developing human resources, building the economy, the democratization of the state and society and the implementation of the Reconstruction and Development Programme (RDP)" (p. 92).

It is imperative that social workers are involved at the national planning level and at the social policy level in particular and together influence government social policy for the future. This may mean actively protesting the present economic strategy and to also question the growing number of NGOs who are taking on the role of providing for poor people instead of what was once the government social welfare plan. Critiquing the role, responsibilty and influence of the non-government organization sector is crucial to social work education.

3. NGOs and development

As governments are decreasing their funding for health, education, and welfare, pressure is put on the private sector to provide these services. In Africa, where funding health, education, and welfare is not a profitable business, NGOs are taking up the task of filling in the gaps that neo-liberal economic planning is leaving behind. "The combination of a weak African state and the New Policy Agenda of the IFI's and donor countries (emphasizing neo-liberal economics and liberal democracy) has created not only a vacuum in the development space (by de-emphasizing the state), but also a fertile ground for the mushrooming and operations of NGO's in all their shades, largely seen as the favoured child of the financial institutions as beginning from the late twentieth century" (Matanga, 2010, p. 117). These can be national or international organizations. NGOs have grown considerably in African countries, often serve the governments in the countries where they are based, and can play into the neo-liberal agenda (Manji & O'Coill, 2005; Onyanyo, 2005; Sankore, 2005; Wallace, 2004). Cohen, Kupcu & Khanna (2008) call these NGOs the 'New colonialists.' They recognize that many NGOs are holding weak states together, for example, Afghanistan, but question whether they have gone too far "in attempting to manage responsibilities that should be those of governments alone" (p. 75). Beyond that, "they often tackle challenges that donors and developing country governments either ignore or have failed to address properly" (p. 76).

On the other hand, NGOs are also a voice for human rights abuses and can play a significant role in putting pressure on governments to serve their people in a better way (Roff, 2004). A growing number of critics are questioning what positive effect there has been after decades of development projects through NGOs. As Wallace (2004) states: "NGO's are now becoming increasingly tied to global agendas and uniform ways of working. This reality threatens their role as institutions providing an alternative, as champions of the poor, as organizations working in solidarity with those marginalized by the world economy.... It is hard to see how NGO's can really be watchdogs and monitors of those they have to go to for funding" (pp. 216–17). In a report concerning partnerships between Africa and the Northern countries, Heron (2007) points out that "from the perspective of Southern development agency personnel,

Northern organizations privilege the views of Northerners over those of African 'partners'; this was considered an especially egregious issue in partnership relations" (p. 13). There are questions being raised as to why there has been a huge increase in NGOs (around 25,000 groups are now qualified as international NGOs) and whether this is a healthy scenario for an equitable world (Onyanyo, 2005).

Increasingly, social workers are being hired to work in a variety of international, national, and local NGOs. This is good news for social workers as NGOs often have better pay and working conditions than government jobs. As one group member pointed out, in more and more NGO job advertisements, the qualification of a social worker is increasing. What is this saying about the influence of NGOs in society? Cohen et al. (2008) admit that these NGOs, although ideally they should be working their way out of a job, will stay in these countries doing what government should normally be doing for their people. They recommend that at least there should be a system of accountability. Recently a code of conduct was signed by international NGOs "pledging to pursue practices that bolster the public sector in the countries in which they operate" (Bristol, 2008, p. 2162). There is concern that "the number of NGO's operating in Africa has grown nine-fold and that governments are struggling with the myriad of different operating styles and approaches. He hopes that the code helps to standardise operations and encourage use of the public system as the platform for the delivery of services" (p. 2162). Social workers need to critically look at the role of NGOs in their countries. Are these NGOs filling in gaps that should be filled by the government? If so, should social workers lobby their governments to push for accountability for the lack of funding to human services? Do they need to be involved at the social policy level advocating for change? By working for NGOs, are social workers buying into the top-down modernization approach to development? If so, are social workers trained to influence these organizations to work in a more collaborative way with their clients? These and other question should be part of social work education curriculum in this world of NGOs.

Kreitzer & Wilson (2010) see the social work role as being part of a global solidarity movement, advocating for a fairer and just world for the millions who are not benefiting from neo-liberal policies. This begins with educating oneself to these issues. It also means setting an example for positive partnerships, particularly between North and South partners. They highlight three important areas to consider in partnerships: 1) preconditions for effective alliances; 2) planning and implementation; and 3) personal qualities and skills. Preconditions for effective alliances involves a common understanding of the key issues; forming appropriate alliances; awareness of the issues of power and dependency; and availability of sufficient resources. Planning and implementing partnerships involves addressing the following: 1) creation of a safe place to work; 2) addressing power issues and the role of the outsider; 3) ongoing reflection and evaluation; 4) flexibility and responsiveness to emerging unexpected situations; 5) respectful use of host-country resources; 6) sustainability; and 7) dissemination to all people of project outcomes. Personal qualities and skills needed in the individuals involved in the project are: 1) self-awareness; 2) conceptual skills; 3) openness to and respect for different ideas and worldviews; 4) transparency/honesty/trust; 5) mutual respect; 6) sensitivity; 7) humility; 8) sense of humour and fun; 9) flexibility/adaptability; 10) willingness to share the challenges of daily life; 11) resourcefulness and commitment; and 12) relationship building skills (pp. 711–14). All of these areas reflect social work values and ethics and can be taught as part of social work curriculum. In the context of Africa, other areas can be added as well.

C. Conclusion of chapter

'Development' is a term that is loaded with assumptions about how a country should be. It is defined by a Eurocentric understanding of the world with little recognition of other ways of knowing and living. Development, so far, has had mixed success. What is missing is that people in the western world do not listen to the people. Listening, *really listening*, building relationships and advocating for full participation of the community or group is essential. Promoting self-awareness, encouraging people to come up with their own solutions and working towards a dynamic approach to development is a way forward. A group member sums it up very well:

It is important for us as social workers, and I think that is some-times the problem or misconceptions that we have that in help-ing people we let them become sometimes dependent on us to the point where they cannot be on their own. I think that is the confrontational aspect of our work that we need to tackle very much ... we need to develop a system where people will not be dependent but will be independent of themselves, to be able to contribute to society irrespective of their handicap. But we also need to recognize that for them to do that they need to start from a point ... so as social workers we come and assist people and try to build up their own lives in terms of development ... to do this we need to put into place structures or systems that will make those people not just survive but help them to develop themselves to the extent that with or without us whatever process we have started with them could continue.

Vanbalkom & Goddard (2007) speak about development as not only being sustainable but also dynamic. "Sustainability is about leaving something behind that will last" (p. 257). A dynamic approach is the ability to "be willing and capable of responding in creative ways to shifting circum-stances and priorities" (p. 255). Sometimes these two are in tension with each other but flexibility to the needs of the community is critically im-portant. The most important aspect of any development project is listen-ing. This has been the major criticism of development projects. Social workers have been trained to listen and it is up to them, whether they work in NGOs or government organizations, to keep listening as a prior-ity to any work they do.

A true measure of mature development is the ability of local individuals and organizations to change the course of reform in response to emerging needs and changing circumstances. Thus, the goal of development is not merely to have local part-ners carry on with programs started by or with international collaborators, but rather to develop in them the capacity and deeper understanding of development that creates the confi-dence to improve existing approaches, create new programs and indeed drop initiatives that no longer serve the country's needs well. (p. 256)

Cultural identity, hegemony of western knowledge, and neo-liberal policies and development agendas have all contributed to the success and challenges to the social work profession in Africa. Each of these factors, and not exclusively these, should be critiqued in all social work programs. The result will be a critical body of knowledge that will create a new curriculum in Africa that is culturally appropriate and more suitable to the needs of the continent. So, what is the future of social work in Africa? Should the profession stay or should it go? If it stays can it change to be more culturally appropriate? The next chapter brings practical suggestions to these questions and is based on the reflections of the research group in Ghana.

VI. Creating Culturally Relevant Education and Practice

In my opinion the time has come for serious and critical re-examination of social work training in Africa.... Twentieth-century Africa expects social work to be creative and revolutionary ... unless the profession of social work is prepared to take a new path, social workers will for a long time to come remain ineffective in developing countries. (Mumenka cited in ASWEA, 1974c, Doc. 6, p. 32)

A social work theory must therefore respond to the contemporary social construction of reality both by clients and workers and their social environments; if it fails to do so, it will be unsuccessful. (Payne, 2005, p. 20)

A. Introduction

The success and effectiveness of the profession of social work in Africa remains uncertain. Considering my personal teaching and research in Ghana, the issues arising from African and international conferences concerning African social work, and the diversity of recent scholarly articles and books on the topic of culturally relevant social work education, there is reason for both optimism and discouragement of the progress of the profession in Africa. It is discouraging that internal and external barriers identified in this book have impeded social work from becoming African-centred and these barriers continue to exist today. It is discouraging that in parts of Africa, western social work education is still considered superior, not because it has been critically evaluated, but because being educated in a western curriculum and teaching style allows social workers to move to the western world, escaping from the challenges of living and working in their own countries. It is discouraging that resources are so scarce, that, in many African countries, social workers still do not have a textbook to call their own and rely on second-hand books from the west to teach social work. Constantly adapting practices from a western textbook that don't relate to African history, tradition, and culture is something that students shouldn't have to do. It is particularly troubling that many articles about African social work still are not available to African social work students to read and study due to technological difficulties and copyright issues. It is discouraging that social work associations have not critically looked at their codes of ethics and rewritten them in a way that reflects their history and culture. Finally, it is discouraging that many of the issues brought up in the ASWEA documents of the 1970s and 1980s are still issues today.

Despite these continuing challenges, I remain optimistic and am encouraged by what I have read and by the creativity produced through my own research and through the writings of African colleagues and discussions with them concerning the issue of culturally relevant social work education. African nations are definitely gaining their identity in the world. The pioneers in social work in West Africa were great thinkers and were eager to blend western social work education and practice with traditional African values and practices. This can be seen in the GASOW and ASWEA conference documents described in chapter I. South Africa is also going through an important and critical process of redefining its social work education in the post-apartheid era. Recently, the International Association of Schools of Social Work held its conference in Durban, showing the international social work community that Africa has an important voice in the profession worldwide. I am encouraged by the openness and honesty exhibited by my group of PAR researchers in Ghana who were willing to look critically at the social work curriculum at the University of Ghana and come up with ideas about how their curriculum could be more effective. Even more impressive is their passion for the profession, their concern that it is still on the periphery, and their commitment to the professional association in Ghana.

The primary focus of the book to this point has been to identify the current and historical issues challenging social work in Africa. Simply identifying problems, however, is of modest value unless it leads to the creation and implementation of effective solutions. The unique makeup and personal commitment of the Ghana PAR group provided an opportunity to do just that. This chapter focuses on the PAR process and ideas identified by the group and our suggestions concerning how to implement practical solutions to the challenges identified.

B. Recognizing the need for change

Mumenka, who is quoted at the beginning of this chapter, challenges the profession to take a new path in order to be relevant to modern society. What would a creative and revolutionary social work education in Africa look like? "Education should be the means by which people reclaim their African identity and affirm their independence from colonial ideologies and practices" (Ndura, 2006, p. 94). If Africans had to begin again, where would they start and who would be included in creating a curriculum that met the needs of Africans? "Social work education agenda cannot be dictated by foreign or domestic experts, but must be grounded in the realities of the practitioners and educators coming from diverse geographical and social locations'" (Tsang, Tan, & Shera, 2000, p. 156). Mwansa (2010) and other African social workers mentioned earlier all agree that something needs to change. "Social work in Africa has unlimited opportunities to deal with human needs … the focus is on the rediscovery of indigenous knowledge for both teaching and practice purposes" (p. 132). In starting from the traditions and culture of each African nation, what will emerge is a culturally relevant curriculum that may or may not keep western education and practices. The issue of culturally relevant social work curricula is being debated in Africa and this is where changing curriculum begins. It begins by Africans in the profession accepting that there needs to be a revisiting of the past in order to move forward in the future and a critical look at what is being taught and practised presently. "Social work has to be redefined as being able to unleash its potential and create innovative responses to current social problems rather than constituting a maintenance profession" (p. 133). The process of decolonization begins with a rediscovery of the history and culture of Africa and the profession.

1. Rediscovery of history and culture

Maathai (2009) speaks of the need for all Africans to rediscover their history and culture. This is true with the profession of social work. How society took care of its people before colonization, the influence of colonialism concerning social work practice, the evolution of social work in Africa, and its present state in Africa need to be examined by social work educators and practitioners. The challenge is building the confidence in educators, many of whom are presently holding on to the western education, and empowering them to move on to create new programs. As far back as the 1970s, there was concern that it was just easier to go with the western curriculum than to spend the time and energy to create new programs (ASWEA, 1974c, Doc. 6, p. 11). However, the 'civilized'/'uncivilized' mindset, still ingrained in the human psyche of many educators, is difficult to let go.

> One way of reclaiming the African spirit of empowerment is to research, discover and appreciate their own cultural background. Such programs could be in the form of discussion groups organized and run by local communities.... Most importantly, such programs should be a major part of the academic curriculum at all levels of instruction.... It needs to be transformed in order to engage students and teachers in a

process of knowledge construction that reflects and validates the differing perspectives that characterize multi-ethnic and culturally diverse nations. (Ndura, 2006, p. 98)

In the 1970s a new school of social work was set up in Mali to replace the old existing ones that were out of touch with society. Emphasis was on encouraging Malians to "return to their own origins and evaluate their potential with a view to developing [an appropriate education] wisely" (ASWEA, Doc. 6, 1973, p. 60). Planners went to the villages "in order to get a better understanding of local institutions and conducted a house-to-house survey in the suburbs of our urban centres" (p. 61). As a result, a new program was created that was "in perfect harmony with the targets set by the country's economic and social development plan" (p. 63). In Tonga, Mafile'O (2004) critically researched some of the differences between western social work theories and knowledge and those of the Pacific Islands. As a result, changes have been made to the curricula to incorporate Pacific Island values into social work practice. Recognizing the need to rediscover and appreciate cultural traditions and historical influences in social work can lead the way to critically looking at the present curricula in order to go forward with curricula changes.

The PAR research group started the research using the above process of rediscovering the past, looking at traditional practices in order to think about changes in the curricula. This took the form of a variety of skits that the group did to remind the group of how things had changed in Ghanaian life from pre- to post-colonial times (see Appendix 1). As the research progressed, the group was challenged to look at the past and how many historical influences had shaped social work in Ghana. The following is a list of acknowledgments that the group wrote that reflects this 'rediscovery of the past' and shows the conscientization process that took place during the research process:

- We acknowledge the negative and positive influences of colonialism and its effect on the Ghanaian society. On the negative side, loss of identity, labelling everything of African origin as primitive and fetish, abuse of non-human and human resources, and creating dependency has affected African development and creativity.

On the positive side, colonialism brought formal education, the social work profession, and a new understanding of the rights of individuals including the handicapped in this society. One group member states: "Now we have to sit down, see what colonialism has left us with and see how we can Africanize the system that they have left and see what ways we can make it more applicable in our situation."

- We acknowledge the continual influence of western society on Ghanaian culture and practice. As a nation we live in many different worlds at the same time. As a group we feel that both the western and traditional approaches to solving social issues have been embraced by the country and this should be reflected in social work training.

- We acknowledge that culture is dynamic, constantly changing, and sometimes intangible. It encompasses the past, present, and future. This is reflected in continual changes in social issues and these changes need to be addressed in social work training. Regular evaluations of the courses should be part of the Department of Social Work's continuing assessment of its program.

- We acknowledge that Ghanaian culture has its differences from and similarities to other cultures. The importance of consensus in decision-making, expressing emotions externally, community, saving face, and hospitality are principles identified as important in Ghanaian culture.

- We acknowledge the importance of understanding traditions and cultural practices in society and how they evolved in light of social issues. Social workers need to know the cultural aspects of the people and communities they work for.

- We acknowledge the work of the social work pioneers in Ghana in introducing and strengthening the profession of social work and its training.

- We acknowledge that the introduction of social work in Ghana was developmental in nature but over the years has become remedial with the individualization of services. The dwindling political interest and funding in social welfare services has been a factor in the decrease of service delivery, and new ways of providing social welfare services need to be created. This, however, is not to negate the fact that social work has been active in Ghana for many years. The citizens and government have not always recognized this contribution.

- We acknowledge that the past twenty years in Ghana have been difficult economically, socially, and politically due to changes in governments and debts incurred through structural adjustment programs, and this has affected the public perception of social work generally. Social work as a profession has not been accepted in Africa up to now. It lacks social acceptability. It has been on the periphery of Ghanaian society and this has affected the progress of social work training and job placement. There needs to be a concerted effort to change people's perceptions of social work in Ghana. This could entail a strengths-based approach to practice that empowers clients, builds upon their strengths, and encourages growth of their inner abilities and creative spirit.

- We acknowledge the importance of learning from other African countries concerning their social work education and practice. A lot can be learned from communication and dialogue between countries on the continent. We also acknowledge that our own social work training and practice could be more user-friendly to students and clients and society at large.

- We acknowledge the continual lack of resources that have plagued the Department of Social Work since the 1980s and appreciate what has been accomplished with minimal finances and minimal staffing, which often affects one's motivation to work creatively. This includes teaching that is done outside the Department of Social Work, for example, administration of social services. This is taught by business people in the School of Administration, who know little if anything about the social work profession. This stifles creativity in the classroom when the lecturer is not clear on what social workers do.

- We acknowledge that there was a strong traditional society in which to develop a social welfare system traditional to Ghanaian culture before colonialism, and the positive aspects of this tradition should be taught in all courses in social work. Work should be completed at the academic and practitioner level, developing social work interventions that are based on traditional cultural practices that may be pre-colonial but are still relevant in today's society. Work with the Institute of African Studies would help with this endeavour.

- We acknowledge an imbalance of western social work knowledge and practice in social work training in Ghana and encourage training to be more traditional to Ghanaian society. We acknowledge that African knowledge is not primitive and uncivilized and is just as important as western knowledge.

- We acknowledge the difficulties within the University of Ghana with regards to salaries and conditions of lecturers, specifically, the very poor pay and conditions of lecturers and the strict requirements for being employed as a lecturer. The profession of social work is a very practical profession and years of practice need to be acknowledged and rewarded by the university when hiring lecturers.

- We acknowledge that for a society to develop there must be dreamers. We acknowledge that social workers are like artists in that they create ways for positive change to occur in society. Therefore the importance of creating a class environment through participatory teaching methods that encourage dreamers and visionaries within the profession is necessary. This includes using art, group work, group projects, community-based projects, and role-playing to critically look at an issue. In practice situations, Participatory Rural Appraisal techniques can be used to initiate change in the whole community. Several people use this in their work with children, youth, and adults, and more training could be provided for this type of hands-on assessing and implementation of change.

- We acknowledge the importance that research can play in developing social policy, and research needs to be encouraged in agencies and at the university level. However, financial constraints and time often prevent research from happening for university lecturers and agency staff. Research can be used to verify what kinds of interventions are useful and which are not. It can also define social problems in Ghana and identify interventions for these problems. We acknowledge the appropriateness of Participatory Action Research as a research methodology in Ghana. We all come from different backgrounds and experiences and the group process is an effective way to bring these differences together for creating change. It promotes a democratic and creative way to facilitate research that allows people to be involved, thus counterbalancing the research fatigue syndrome found in many communities today.

- We acknowledge the importance of the revised bachelor's curriculum and the new master's program and the significant impact these will have on the future of social work training and practice in Ghana.

These acknowledgments reflect the outcomes of the conscientization process that emerged from the group concerning their own understanding of Ghanaian society and social work in Ghana. After rediscovering the history and culture and the past influences concerning social work in Ghana, a critical look at the curriculum is the next step in the process of curriculum change.

2. Critically evaluating present curricula

Payne (2005) views social work as a social construction that needs to change with society and the world:

> So theory is constructed in an interaction between ideas and realities, mediated through the human beings involved. How clients experience their reality affects how workers think about their practice theories; agencies constrain and react to both and together they make some social work. The social work they make influences what social work is and how it is seen elsewhere. A social work theory must therefore respond to the contemporary social construction of reality both by clients and workers and their social environments; if it fails to do so, it will be unsuccessful. (p. 20)

If social work is to be effective in a particular society, it needs to respond to social and cultural contexts. In other words, social work curricula need to be sustainable (stability, continuity, and sustainability) and need to be dynamic (responsive, dynamic, and creative) (van Balkam & Goddard, 2007). The beauty of social work is that it can adapt, change, and develop with the environment in which it is working. However, if social work curricula need to change according to the needs of society, a regular evaluation of their effectiveness in that society is important.

For Fook (2002), a critical reflective approach to change "holds the potential for emancipatory practices ... in that it first questions and disrupts dominant structures and relations and lays the ground for change" (p. 43). Smith (2008) agrees: "To achieve social change, social work education thus needs to critically engage with post-colonial and post-apartheid socio-political realities of inequality, oppression, racism and cultural hegemony, and facilitate critical conscientization" (p. 371). The PAR research group asked these kinds of questions throughout the process and answers were sought but were not always found. For example: 1) what cultural practices, institutions, and beliefs in the pre-colonial, colonial, and post-colonial eras are reflected in social work today; 2) how much of the colonial structures and practices can we see in social work education, welfare, institutions, and government and non-government organizations;

3) in pre-colonial Ghana, did we have the knowledge available to create a social welfare system that met the needs of Ghanaians; 4) what institutions, organizations or society does the Department of Social Welfare serve; 5) if we were given the task of starting a culturally relevant social welfare system, how would we do this? Finding the answers to these questions is crucial to the future of social work education and practice. Ndura (2006) suggests more questions that help focus the issues:

> Another way of reclaiming the African spirit of empowerment is questioning Western motives.... Why is Western literature elevated to the center stage of the educational experience while African languages and literatures remain under-explored? Why is Western financial assistance used to hire Western expatriates instead of preparing local educators for local schools? Why are most school textbooks imported from Western nations? Why do Western governments provide financial and military assistance to warring African ethnic factions? Why do Western nations grant asylum to persecuted Africans and yet make it almost impossible for those in exile to reunite with their families? Why do Western institutions deny so many African academic credentials when they were educated under Western philosophies and standards? Reclaiming the African spirit of empowerment will become a possibility only when the Africans begin to raise such questions and lift the veil of blindness that has obstructed their true independence from the colonial master's stronghold. (pp. 98–99)

Answering and critically reflecting on these questions and continual dialogue among academics, bureaucrats, community leaders, and practitioners will create new theories and interventions that are culturally relevant and that will respond to the needs of people in African society. This dialogue has happened over a period of time with the ASWEA and GASOW conferences, among African social work writers, and more recently in western social work publications. Gray et al. (2008) understand the importance of this dialogue, giving examples from different parts of the globe of how social work educators and practitioners are dealing with the issue of culturally relevant social work education and practice. Osei-Hwedie & Jacques (2007) edited a book concerning the indigenization of social work in Africa with lively debates from Osei-Hwedie and Arnon Bar-On on the issue of whether it is indeed possible to have African-centred curricula. Once the past has been revisited for cultural and historical rediscovery and a critical look has been taken at the curricula from historical influences, then a new kind of curriculum can emerge.

One of the pioneers of social work in Ghana, Dr. Blavo, stated that "Social work has not yet been born in Africa." This is a surprising statement in a country where formal social work education has been offered since 1945. What is that statement really saying? Is it saying that the profession is still trying to be born, has it been born and still trying to walk, or are we walking around banging our heads against the wall trying to fit a western concept into a culture where it may not fit? When I ask myself these questions, I think of two metaphors: 1) a square peg trying to be pushed into a round hole, and 2) a new-born baby still attached to the umbilical cord of its mother. African social work academics, students, and social workers need to come to terms with the possibility that the many western social work approaches don't fit. They need to quit trying to teach inappropriate practices, cut the umbilical cord with western social work, and begin growing on their own. Once this new form of social work develops, it may be appropriate to take what is useful from the western social work knowledge and practice but create a new and vibrant child (profession) that will grow up to meet the needs of its own people. Mwansa (2010) suggests that as the "continent enters a postmodern phase some of the knowledge will be useful if it is reworked to fit local needs. Most educators are dependent on material to which they are accustomed and this spiral of dependence on foreign information for education and training continues unabated" (p. 133). With a rediscovery of the history and culture of Africa and a critical reflection on the present curriculum, how can African-centred curricula emerge in a diverse and complex continent like Africa?

C. Using the Ghanaian context for a case study on curriculum change

The opportunity arose, through my PhD research, to go back to Ghana and work with students, practitioners, educators, and community leaders in the area of culturally relevant social work curriculum. After years of teaching, studying, and learning in Ghana, the need to critically examine and revise social work education and practice became clear to me. It was also clear to me that Ghanaians needed to take the lead in critically looking at their own curricula, recommend changes, and take action accordingly. The purpose of the research was to give space for Ghanaians to critically reflect on the need for curriculum change through their own rediscovery of history and culture, evaluate the present curricula, and suggest concrete changes in how to adapt or start again in regards to culturally relevant African social work education and practice.

D. The process of identifying culturally relevant curricula

Participatory Action Research provided the framework within which Ghanaian practitioners, academics, and government workers could critically look at social work in Ghana, assess current social work education and practice, evaluate its effectiveness, and instigate appropriate change. Although most of the group had not experienced this type of research, it proved to be meaningful and educational. A few group members commented on the process:

> When we started the project, like others have said, this is a unique way of data collection, which is not the same as what we are used to. One interesting thing about it to me is the way we dialogue in the group.... We always discuss things in some detail and sometimes very hot and by the end of it we have consensus.... The research project has given us the opportunity to contribute our ideas as to what should be done to the curriculum to make it suitable to changing needs.

This group has enabled me to critically examine some of the things that we have been thinking through as social workers.... This research has been a process where we all dialogue together, agree on and we have to reach a consensus in making decisions and for me it has been very interesting to know the other side of research where you have to involve people in dialogue.

We started with a weekend in the mountains to get to know each other and to challenge our perceptions of the world. One of the most important exercises we did was the map exercise.

Understanding who we are in the world, how we perceive the world, and how we are perceived by others was a consistent source of discussion in the research group. As part of the preparation for the project, a perception exercise was introduced. Four maps of the world were put up on the wall; the Mercator Map (traditional map), the Peters Projection Map (a map showing the Mercator Map as a product of colonization), the Upside Down South Map (the north is in the south and the south is in the north); and a traditional African map (using western terminology). The research group members were asked to visit each map (in groups of three) and answer the following questions: 1) Does this map seem correct to you; 2) Does this map seem different from the map you are used to and why; 3) Whose worldview is being portrayed in this map, and 4) What does this exercise say about our perception of the world? (See Appendix 2 for more details.) The learning that took place in the exercise was extraordinary. In challenging the group to "look outside their own frame of reference," subtleties of their perceived identity in the world came through which are important to highlight. For many, the initial response to the Upside down map was that it was wrong.

But as people reflected on the different maps, they realized that the world is a sphere and, whichever way you turn it, it doesn't change the position of any country or place. Here are two key insights expressed by group members after the exercise was completed:

No matter where we come from in the world, no matter the continent that we are in, we think differently depending on where we stand. You interpret from how you view things. So the world over we should not kind of look down upon certain people and their values and what they think how society ought to be run.

If we take that map for the fact that it was presented differently and you look at it and say it was wrong, who decides what is wrong and what is right? Does it mean because a certain white man somewhere does it and it is right? Or do we have to look at it critically and then criticize it and just say "no" because it is coming from this end therefore it is right?

What the group began to do was to recognize and question their own socialization and belief system and learn to critically examine what they actually believe and where that belief system comes from. Who decides what is true and where this knowledge originates? All of us have been socialized to believe that the Northern Hemisphere is developed and more civilized and the Southern Hemisphere is developing and is still primitive. Psychologically, this is very important and affects how we look at ourselves, our profession, our country, and our continent. When the map is turned upside down, it goes against our familiar way of thinking. Why is this so? What events took shape that condemned the African continent to a self-destructive cultural identity from which it is still trying to recover today? Who decides how Africa is perceived as a continent? We can look at the world from any point of view. Africa can be at the top and the others can be down, but the dominant viewpoint has continually put Africa as down, underdeveloped, primitive. We interpret from how we view things. The world doesn't change. It's our view of the world that changes. Why was this exercise important? Conscientization[1] occurs when people are challenged to think differently. People tend not to like to think differently because to think differently and to challenge one's beliefs is uncomfortable. What the group understood, in the end, was that there are different viewpoints to reality, and no one way of looking at the world is more correct than another.

After the weekend, the group met twice a month. At the first meeting of the month, the group talked about the evolution of social work in

Africa, and later in the month, they talked about African and Ghanaian culture. The meetings usually had a guest speaker who talked about the particular subject. These speakers were pioneers of social work in Ghana and professors from the Institute of African Studies at the University of Ghana. Each session was opened with a time for reflection on what the group members had learned from the last session. The group also critiqued the different course outlines obtained from professors who taught in the social work department. Throughout the process, the group had time to reflect and critically think about what had been discussed in previous meetings. Each meeting was recorded and transcribed. Group members were encouraged to read the transcripts and come up with themes from the transcripts. Data analysis occurred as part of the group process as well as individual analysis throughout the research.

What follows are the important findings of this case study from Ghana concerning culturally relevant social work for Ghana.

E. Ghanaian Research findings

The research findings will be addressed in two different sections. The first are recommended changes to the present curriculum as well as recommended new courses that could be offered to address the needs of Ghanaian society. This includes a discussion on field practica. The second section addresses other issues that arose from the research process. They are not necessarily related directly to curricula but have an important effect on how social work is taught and practised in Ghana. These include: 1) social work's relationship to Ghanaian society; 2) the professional association; 3) institutional structures; and 4) intercontinental relationships.

1. Changes to the present curriculum

Each group's first task was to identify different jobs that social workers do in Ghana and to identify a range of issues that social workers in Ghana respond to in their jobs. This was important so that the group could then focus on the curriculum to see if there were any gaps between what was taught and what social workers are responding to in their work. Social workers worked in government and non-government organizations, the prison service, orphanages, education service, industry, community development, social welfare, and hospitals, to name a few. Their work included: 1) Employment issues – unemployment, child labour, poverty alleviation, prostitution, micro-financing, armed robbery/crime, lack of employable skills, and labour unrest; 2) Family issues – domestic violence, childlessness, irresponsible parents, the *trokosi* system, marital disputes, family welfare, care of the elderly, and disabilities; 3) Child issues – child labour, street children, child defilement, the *trokosi* system, and child trafficking; 4) Teenage issues – school dropouts, teenage pregnancy, gender issues (both male and female), and prostitution; 5) Education issues – school dropouts, girl-child education, and illiteracy; 6) Health issues – HIV/AIDS, female genital mutilation, guinea worm, maternal mortality, and provision of potable water; 7) Environmental issues – pollution; 8) Mental health issues – drug abuse; 9) Community issues – conflict resolution and mediation, community empowerment, and conscientization; 10) Migration issues – refugees and urbanization; and 11) Housing issues.

The research group analyzed the curriculum outlines to see if any of the above issues were being addressed in the classroom.[2] Once analysis was completed, a document outlining changes to the diploma, bachelor's, and master's degrees was published for the Department of Social Work and for the public to review and consider. The critique of each course will not be detailed here, but similar themes emerged from all three levels of degrees and will be summarized here. What is important to understand about these changes is that they emphasize a shift from the western-style social work practice to ideas of how the curriculum could be more African in content and in which African-centred social work practice would be encouraged. As Smith (2008) states: "Educators of social workers have the responsibility of stimulating this process of developing critical reflection and consciousness" (p. 374). There were no social work books giving the Ghanaian or, for that matter, an African perspective on social work. The following categories show the many areas we felt could change concerning the curriculum.

Language and course titles. Language is an important tool for cultural understanding and teaching. Some of the most important things that we experience are described through language. Using culturally appropriate language that speaks clearly to the student is extremely important.

One guest speaker stated: "We look for the essential elements in our language and we think these elements are the defining features of this particular language." To name something is to express ownership of it. In the colonizing world, "naming was to think about the world, one might say, on one's own terms" (Willinsky, 1998, p. 35). Some of the course titles needed to be updated to reflect African language and culture. I gave an example earlier of being asked to teach "Framework for Social Diagnosis" and "Framework for Planned Changed," titles from earlier American and British social work books. African-specific terms should be used to reflect the course names. This could be done in a creative manner by asking students to come up with new titles for courses that reflect their society.

History and philosophy of social work. Although this is a course in itself, the group felt that any history and philosophy taught in any class needed to be African-specific. Too much emphasis is placed on teaching western social work history and western philosophy. A more balanced approach should include how social work has developed in Ghana and other parts of Africa including North, South, East, and West Africa. The evolution of social work in Central and South America, as well as Asia, would be helpful for African students as these continents have been through colonization and have suffered the effects of the present economic order. The countries of the Americas have also looked critically at the past in relation to social work education, an example being Nicaragua (Wilson, 1992), and Asian countries are also engaging in this process (Gray, Coates, & Yellow Bird, 2008).

Gathering bodies of knowledge that are African-specific may feel like a daunting task, and many articles on African social work are in western journals and are hard to access in Africa. A good starting point is looking at the United Nations Surveys and Monologues mentioned in chapter I and in the ASWEA and GASOW documents. These documents, as well as the United Nations Surveys and other United Nations documents on social work, should be taught as part of the history of social work in Africa. There are also books written about the history of social work in South Africa (Earle, 2008; Gray, 1998; Patel, 2005), and I am sure each African country has some sort of document relating to their local history of social work education and practice. Apt & Blavo (1997) explain the history of Ghanaian social work in their article on social work in Ghana.

Documentation concerning activities of social welfare institutions in African countries is important and ASWEA has two documents outlining these institutions and their purposes (see chapter I of this book). Recently, a small project, funded by the International Association of Schools of Social Work, the African Association of Schools of Social Work, and the University of Calgary, have collected ASWEA documents, copied and bound them, and sent them to African social work libraries in order to make them available to professors, research students, and students for their own learning. In addition to making these documents available, there is concern that pioneers of African social work are very elderly and their stories and experiences will be lost once they have died. Research, video interviews, and historical documenting need to be completed to record these stories of how social work developed in the different African countries and the experiences of these pioneers before it is too late.

Another concern that the research group identified was the fact that many African universities teach philosophy from a European perspective. African philosophy has an important part to play in social work training. "African philosophy should be able to respond to the problems and human conditions in modern Africa. It should also clarify the concepts, beliefs and values that we hold, use and live by, through sustained discussion and dialogue" (van Wyk & Higgs, 2007, p. 62). van Wyk and Higgs go on to say that "through philosophy we can study pronouncements of persons, create texts of indigenous philosophical discourse which can then be further interpreted and discussed; this provides insight as to how individuals shape culture and society, and leads to a better understanding through a clearer idea of any society's internal intellectual dynamics" (p. 63). They also caution that there is not one universal African philosophy but these can be different depending on culture. A need to connect African philosophy with social work values and practice is crucial in strengthening African identity in social work. If theory is influenced by the social, political, and economic realities of people, African philosophy should be part of social work curricula.

Local case studies. Early on in the evolution of social work in Africa, there was collaboration between Zimbabwe and Ghana concerning sharing case examples of social work practice. However, for the most part, one of the consistent themes throughout the ASWEA documents, subsequent articles on African social work, and this PAR research group was the lack of local case examples for students. Efforts have been made to collect case studies (ASWEA, 1973) from the local context, but in places like Ghana this has not been successful. One research group member stated that she was tired of reading about social work in urban Chicago and having to adapt it to the rural Ghanaian situation. She questioned whether it was fair to put social work students through this adaptation process when the amount of mental energy this takes could be better channelled to creative thinking and studying. Another group member gave an example of a social policy course he took. It wasn't until he was a research assistant after graduating that he realized the Ghana Poverty Reduction Strategy was a key national social policy. No one gave him an example of social policy in Ghana to study or critique. There is a complacency concerning the acceptance of western case examples and this has to change. This is a result of the other challenges described in previous chapters concerning the lack of funding for higher education and lack of resources and faculty time to address these concerns, including updating case examples. Publishing textbooks is very difficult with limited finances available. The lack of local case examples is partly due to the use of western textbooks as well as the need to constantly update case studies for use in the classroom.

Rediscovering historical traditions. For many African countries, oral history and cultural language is very important. In Ghana the use of proverbs is important in many professions and in the community. They bring people in close contact with the local natural environment. For example "An elephant dies because of many spears" (Ibekwe, 1998, p. 27) speaks to co-operation. "The usefulness of a well is known when it dries" (p. 9) refers to appreciation or "Do not tie up a dog with a chain of sausages" (p. 75) refers to futility. A teaching style that brings out these proverbs and stories to communicate principles would enhance social work training. This also reminds students of their own heritage and it may promote seeking more knowledge about life before colonization. These proverbs could effectively be used to support more traditional social work interventions and other forms of social work training.

In discussing how to move on from oppression, systemic racism, and power dynamics, Smith (2008), in her study on South African education, revealed that the "lethal multiple oppressions that they had experienced, and sometimes continued to experience, had created a devaluation of self, identity and culture" (p. 380). One of her student interviewees remarks: "When the master of the slave is gone, within that domain it keeps on going, it's an ugly cycle but it keeps on going you know, and I think that's what happens when you are not free, mentally, although oppression is not physical, it's in our minds" (p. 378). Themes identified from her research were: 1) internalized oppression; 2) identity development and psychological defence; 3) responses of denial, anger, and helplessness; 4) critical conscientization and feeling more powerful; and 5) an understanding of oppression and the need for critical, anti-oppressive practice. She found that the interviewees, social work students, upon reflecting and discussing their experiences, were helped to be liberated from these feelings. This sharing of experiences left them feeling more powerful and able to act. Finally, she found that a "respect for and embracing of traditional culture (such as the use of the talking stick) symbolized a decolonisation that was found to be liberating, dignifying and empowering" (Smith, 2008, p. 380). Social work training should allow for this reflection and discussion to take place in a safe environment and should respect and use the tools available in traditional culture.

There is a rich history of community development in Africa, and this should be strengthened in the classroom (Abloh & Ameyaw, 1997). Community development needs to take into account the changing nature of culture. Historical traditions may or may not be appropriate to keep in a changing world. On the other hand, cultural identity is tied to traditional ways and useful components of these traditions should be preserved and taught. With the consistent poverty experienced in Africa, innovative techniques for community economic development must be part of the curriculum concerning appropriate community development. Like the women in the Northern Village who sold shea butter to the Body Shop, these are the types of case studies that should be taught and encouraged in order to alleviate poverty. Businesses that give back to the community while paying people a good salary (Yunus, 2007) should be promoted.

A good understanding of the international financial institutions (IFIs) and the historical effects of their policies should be part of social work training (Ife, 2007).

Social workers need to understand the role of the U.N. and its agencies, the role of NGO's, the role of the World Bank and the IMF, the neo-liberal and neo-conservative agendas, globalisation and the power of the global corporations, the complexities rather than the simplicities of the Middle East, of Africa, of Latin America, of Asia, of Eastern Europe, the legacy of the cold war, and the origins of cultural and religious tensions, on all continents, that go back centuries if not millennia. (Ife, 2007, pp. 19–20)

I believe that Africans have a much greater understanding of these policies than social workers in the western world, as they touch their everyday lives. The many programs of the IFIs, including the poverty reduction programs, and SAPs are programs within a neo-liberal agenda that does not favour poverty reduction. The new poverty reduction strategy program from the IMF "seems to merely add new social and governance elements to former reforms, which have been unsuccessful over the past two decades in achieving progress toward these goals.... it is unclear how policies emphasizing the primacy of the market mechanism in such areas as trade, finance and agriculture can be reconciled with the improved access of the poor to productive assets, and to actually mitigating the negative outcomes of structural adjustment" (Mouelhi & Ruckert, 2007, p. 289).

Using different research methods. Traditionally, research has been quantitative in nature in many African universities. This is understandable, given the history of university education in Africa, which was heavily influenced by western university models in both structure and content (Ajayi et al., 1996; Ashby, 1964; Boateng, 1982). However, it is also puzzling, given the historical tendency for oral history and consensus tradition. Laird (2003) challenges the notion that quantitative research is the most appropriate for African social work:

The particular socio-economic circumstances of developing regions, the disparity of cultural context vis-à-vis western nations and the wider parameters of social development activity in the context of meagre direct welfare services provision, are prima facie grounds for a critical consideration of the applicability of the research methodologies advanced by western social work scholars. (p. 252)

She identifies various problems such as using western instruments, designed by British and American professionals for the industrialized world, and Eurocentric language and assumptions made in the outcome. "In short, quantitative methodologies are compromised because their instruments of inquiry are over determined by a particular socio-economic and cultural milieu" (p. 256). She goes on to encourage a more participatory approach to research and in particular using Participatory Rural Appraisal, first used by Chambers (1997). This tool addresses power relations within the research itself and uses many tools for knowledge-gathering, as well as empowering local people to look at the issues in their community. "The concentration on group settings for the gathering of information rather than through individuated processes such as the questionnaire or interview is an interpersonal encounter more consonant with African social structures" (Laird, 2003, p. 267).

Research methodologies should be more consistent with the society in which researchers are collecting their data, and this is why this particular methodology was used in Ghana. It is time for qualitative research to have a more prominent role in research education in African universities.

Addressing mental health issues. Considering the predominance of the HIV/AIDS pandemic and its affect on the mental and emotional state of families and the traumatic experiences of child soldiers and refugees in many parts of Africa, mental health issues and interventions need to be addressed in all social work courses. Post-traumatic stress disorder is increasingly becoming an important issue with these vulnerable groups of people. Kabeera & Sewpaul (2008) found in their study concerning the after-effects of the Rwandan genocide that "returnees developed mental problems, but on account of lack of psychiatric facilities they were unable to access proper treatment. The experience of life-threatening and shocking events, like rape and murder, robs one of a sense of integrity and wholeness. Some survivors reported experiencing nightmares and recurring images of frightful events; they had difficulty sleeping, felt tense and extremely sad" (p. 326). Straub, Pearlman, & Miller (2003) recognize healing from trauma as the first important step in healing and reconciliation. While working in Rwanda, they made information available to the public that explained in detail the symptoms of post-traumatic stress disorder and how to get help for this disorder. This was an important part of their reconciliation process in Rwanda. Participants were provided with trauma information through the radio and written forms on how to heal through "engagement with painful experiences, empathic support from others and the reconnection to and renewed trust in people" (p. 289). In the Liberian refugee camp in Ghana, there was little attention paid by different NGOs and the UNHCR concerning funding trauma programs. In a camp with over 20,000 refugees, there was only one group addressing this issue. I believe this is true in many refugee camps, where the priority is to provide food, shelter, and clothing. However, trauma counselling in refugee camps is a vital and important service that can be provided by appropriately trained social workers. Pearn (2003) graphically presents the traumas that children experience through war, conflicts, and soldiering:

> Post-traumatic stress disorder ... has been very much a featured disease of the late 20th and 21st centuries. Children are less likely than adults to talk about such episodes or to understand their genesis. Nevertheless, recurring obsessive thoughts of horror, flashbacks and recurring dreams either of stark reality or of symbolic illusion are some of the chronic symptoms of this childhood disorder. (p. 170)

In particular, the effects on the child soldier's psyche are particularly damaging: 1) desocialization and dehumanization; 2) loss of childhood including schooling; and 3) a society-induced psychopathy, which causes post-traumatic stress disorder and is very difficult to rehabilitate. "Exposure to violence, to cruelty and to the systems of war where the resolution of problems is perforce solved by force during childhood years is inimical to the development of conscience ... war-imposed terror and cruelty, directed against others but observed by the child determine the norm in the evolving conscience of a growing child" (pp. 169–70). Social workers have an important role to play in rehabilitating these children of war to stop the normalization of violence of a generation of children who are prone to suicide as a result of this exposure to violence. Training to support this role is important, but it is often excluded from the social work curriculum.

Changing the face of field practica. Field practicum is considered crucial to effective social work training. As one lecturer in social work states: "It wakes you up. It makes you see how poor people are, how people are suffering … when you see these things, and then you start learning how to deal with real issues." As far back as 1972, field work and supervision was highlighted as an important part of social work training (ASWEA, 1972). There was emphasis on fieldwork in rural areas as in the 1970s this was where most of the people lived. Group and community work were emphasized as important to social work education (ASWEA, 1974c, Doc. 6). In many African schools, field practicum programs seem to have some problems, including length of time in the field, lack of supervisors, lack of choice of placement, and integrating theory and practice. The field practicum component of social work training should be extended with more emphasis placed on community fieldwork.

Gray and Simpson (1998) give a good example of a social-development-based practicum. It is called a 'community-based student's unit,' where a group of four students go into a community, for months at a time, and work alongside the community in identifying developmental needs, prioritizing those needs and identifying local resources in order to find solutions with full community participation. The value of this type of practicum is that it gets students out of the somewhat elitist classroom and into the rural areas. "The community recognizes the contribution of the university via its students and the students themselves attest to the value of the experience gained even though, at times, they felt they were attempting a 'mission impossible'" (p. 236). Early social work training in Ghana did the same type of practicum. Students were taken to rural communities, on the weekends, to work with people, particularly with women and children.

Other innovative ways for field work practica need to be created and tested with the goal of providing the best possible experience for students and also enhancing the individual and community in which the students are placed. A good practicum example was explained by a research group member concerning children in fishing villages not attending school but going fishing instead. They explained: "if a social worker is attached to the community, study how the children come into the fishing rather than the school, find out their interest and try to see what the person can do either to the small group of boys trying to encourage them.... We can really see whether they could go back to school or if their interest is elsewhere." Through organizing community leaders to discuss this issue, an appropriate plan could be created that meets the needs of the children and the expectations of their school. For example, fishing could be considered part of the school curriculum and used as an incentive for children to go to school once they are finished fishing. Another example of an effective field practicum is letting students go into the villages and conduct community meetings as part of their educational experience. Finally, concerted effort should be made and programs established for student exchanges between other parts of Africa instead of Europe and America. This can only help to increase the awareness of social work issues on the continent and will help to bring together social workers in Africa in order to share knowledge, skills, and experiences amongst each other.

When I was a volunteer at the University of Ghana, 2004–2006, there was little support for students in the field. I, along with another volunteer, devised training for supervisors, revised the grading system and made a commitment to visit each student once in their three-month practicum. This was easier said than done. Visiting students meant a few days travel on mediocre roads, spending the night in rural areas, and meeting with the student and supervisor. The idea of a full-time fieldwork coordinator may seem like a luxury, but the research group felt very strongly that this is missing in social work education. Supervisors and students need that support from the Department of Social Work.

2. Developing new courses

The group identified new courses that they felt should be introduced to the social work curriculum at the University of Ghana. These courses reflect issues that are of concern to Ghana presently and integrate some of the ideas from the research project. The new courses include: 1) traditional mechanisms for social change; 2) social work and power issues; 3) social work and social action; 4) social work values and ethics in African society; 5) social work and refugees; 6) persons in need of protection in institutions; 7) development theory and practice; and 8) mediation and conflict resolution. These were mainly thought to be appropriate for the BSW level. Laird (2003) suggests appropriate questions to ask when evaluating and creating new curricula:

> 1) Does the present social work curriculum include and fit into the psychological, spiritual, economic, social, political and environmental issues in society; 2) Is the curriculum holistic in nature; 3) Does it emphasize African traditional knowledge; 4) Does it explore the continent's different social welfare experiences and international policies; 5) Does it address gender issues; 6) Does it include international perspectives; 7) Is it up-to-date with current African issues; and 8) Are the courses using local case examples for teaching? Concerning the results of this curriculum in local practice does it encourage and produce social work activities that 1) work in the local setting; 2) achieve appropriate results; 3) worthwhile interventions and 4) resource efficient? (p. 252)

Although we did not have these specific questions at the time, I believe that, through the process of reviewing the present courses and identifying new courses, the group critically asked these questions.

Traditional mechanism for social change. This course would explore the idea of linking social work interventions that build upon the core traditional practices in the country. It would begin with a study of traditional social mechanisms before colonialism and identify which traditions are still effective in society today. All societies have developed systems over the years to solve their own social problems. The course would be jointly taught by a social work professor and a professor from the Institute for African Studies or an equivalent. Traditional mechanisms for coping with social issues would be identified and work would be completed around creating new social work interventions that incorporate those mechanisms. During the research process, a professor from the Institute of African Studies shared three examples of traditional mechanisms to deal with social issues: 1) women pounding fufu (ground cassava),

2) disregarding protocol and 3) a mock battlefield. All were used as tension-releasing activities and the group talked about how these could be incorporated into social work interventions.

Women pounding fufu. There are times in which women need to speak their minds without the pressure of the elders or men around. One such tension-releasing activity that allows women a place to speak their minds is around pounding fufu. As women are pounding and grinding the cassava, they are also singing about life, about birth, their husbands and lovers and all kinds of things about family life, marriage, negatives and positives of life. This balance between physical labour and oral communication allows for life's stresses, joys, and worries to be vented to each other. Social work group interventions could create space like these traditional practices for women who are vulnerable.

Experiencing Asafo. The second example is a period of time in the year in which common people can say what they want to say to the elders and chiefs without repercussions. In Fante, this is called *Asafo.* Because of the respect inherent in the life of the elders and chiefs, it is not possible to complain too much about their leadership. There is certain protocol that is used in addressing these leaders. However, a certain time is set aside for the men of the village to be able to speak any way they like to or about the elders and chiefs, often using very profane language. They can dress any way they want and say anything they want in this context and the elders and chiefs can't respond. This is a way to relax a somewhat heavy protocol system in order to relieve tension in the group. This type of community-building process could be used in other areas where the community has an important issue to discuss and where space is created for people to talk about their concerns in a non-hierarchical way.

Mock battle. There was a Nigerian festival that consists of a mock
battle between two groups who have been feuding. A
mock battle is played out and they conquer each other and
then eat at a banquet together. It uses art, theatre, songs,
and poetry and is done every year to try to resolve a particular conflict. Again this is a good community-building
exercise that can be completed with the whole community or parts of the community, depending on the issue.

The above mechanisms and others can be seen in festivals and rituals, and
the principles behind them can be useful to social workers looking at new
interventions for practice. The use of oral tradition, belief systems, drama,
song, and language could be explored. Other ways in which social workers could work within traditional systems, including traditional health
clinics, chieftaincy system, traditional healer, women's movements, etc.,
should be explored. Potential conflicts between traditional and modern
interventions should be examined using practical examples.

Educational programs should develop awareness of and appreciation for people from different ethnic groups and their experiences. As they acquire empathic ability, individuals would
also learn to respect and value the humanity that unites their
diverse ethnic groups and understand that such unity is a major prerequisite for local, national, and regional lasting peace
as well as individual prosperity. Most of all, these programs
would enhance participants' awareness of and appreciation for
the increasing and unavoidable inter-ethnic interdependence
that is engrained in the very fabric of African history, traditions
and customs. (Ndura, 2006, p. 98)

Finally, the course should include a critical reflection on the social worker's role in intervening with cultural behaviours that are unhealthy and
inappropriate. This assumes that all students will have some training in
the local culture. If the intervention is appropriate, can it be completed in
a culturally sensitive and successful way? One group member states: "if

we are social workers and we are supposed to practice things that we are taught, which don't actually fit in our society we have to try to indigenize it so that if social workers are not having the results then we could use traces in our culture to try and make it more applicable to our setting."

When the group considered the topic of traditional mechanisms for social intervention, it was pointed out that, in the Sociology department alone, every year students do long essays on social issues in Ghana. These essays are put on shelves and few people look at them. Also, in the Institute of African Studies, students and scholars have researched many ceremonies or festivals, and as the works of social workers and researchers these essays are great resources in gathering information about societal traditions. This idea of incorporating traditional social mechanisms for social work interventions is a shift in thinking and members of the group began to believe this was possible. One group member states: "I feel [current interventions] are not too acceptable and we understand those things in principle and we accept them and we want to make it more practical, we could create ceremonies, we could change some of the things to make it more acceptable." The idea had been planted that we can be creative with social work interventions and that we can use our knowledge and skills to produce interventions more appropriate to the African setting. Once these mechanisms are identified, questions need to asked: 1) How can we implement these mechanisms and take it from a state level to the home; 2) Can a rural mechanism fit into the urban setting; and 3) Can you shift them, and, if so, do they still make sense in a new setting or should they be modified and/or abandoned altogether? There are many traditional mechanisms in society that are there to relieve tension, conflict, and present problems, and they just have to be identified and looked at in relation to social work. This class would help students to enhance their knowledge of these traditional mechanisms and to develop the skills to use these mechanisms to design and implement effective social work interventions.

Finally, an introduction to traditional authority structure would be helpful in this course. Kreitzer (2004b) shows similarities between the role of the queen mother in villages and the role of the social worker. Closer collaboration between queen mothers and social workers when working in the village is important. The queen mother in the research group confirmed this by saying: "What I will advise all social workers, whenever you are sent to a village or somewhere to the people, the first people you are to meet to make your work easier is the chief and the queen mothers and the elders in the village. When you meet them and you tell them why you are there, they will welcome you and help you to make your work there with them easier." If possible, a queen mother should be included in this course as a guest speaker or a guest lecturer as she is the expert on culture.

Social work and power issues. The objective of this component of the curriculum would be to have students examine in depth the different ethnic groups in the society. Because of the intricate details of power issues within ethnic groups, outside resource people could come to speak about their particular ethnic group. Issues of power, authority, class, ethnicity, racism, and oppression could be discussed as well as traditional approaches to empowerment and positive change in society. Rural and urban issues should be explored in light of power issues as well as tensions between religious and cultural systems. The importance of language in culture could also be explored in light of power issues.

Social work and social action. A practical course teaching the history of social action and successful techniques for social action at the local, national, and international levels is becoming increasingly important in a world where there is a large gap between the 'haves' and the 'have nots.' Social workers in the west have tended to favour individual therapeutic intervention (Midgley, 2001) while social workers in the South, particularly in Latin America, advocate for social activism for social change. Mmatli (2008) advocates for social workers "to adopt political activism as an intervention strategy aimed at creating a conducive environment in which other social work methods can be practiced" (p. 297). Gray & Mazibuko (2002) also advocate that social workers, previously tending to stay out of politics and economics, should play "an active role in the political and social arena at all levels" (p. 198). Mmatli (2008) suggests that social workers should be involved in lobbying to exert pressure on politicians and other decision-makers to address important issues.

Firstly, where possible "social workers should work closely with their clients to develop an alternative vision or agenda that addresses their concerns, initiate a debate on such an agenda, and lobby for bipartisan support" (p. 303). This will show social work's interest and presence at the government level and will also benefit the clients. Secondly, social workers should stand for electoral positions on tickets of political parties that are consistent with social work values. Social workers need to occupy positions of power. Thirdly, political education can raise the consciousness of the poor in order that people can make informed choices about whom to vote for. Finally, voting is an important social work activity. Practical skills on how to lobby Parliament, write letters, and organize demonstrations could be taught. How to promote the profession of social work publicly should also be explored. Important to this course would be a practical application of social action as a required assignment. This could be to speak on current affairs programs on the radio and TV and to publicly acknowledge that one is a social worker. In the end, promoting social justice is about "actively working towards more egalitarian societies" (Kabeera & Sewpaul, 2008, p. 333). "Political activism in Africa should seek to achieve a common goal, that is, to influence policy decisions in order to maximize the benefits for social work clients" (Mmatli, 2008, p. 302). In Rwanda social workers have an important role to play concerning the Gacaca courts for healing and reconciliation by "ensuring that the hearings are fair and impartial … securing legal assistance for alleged perpetrators and victims where necessary; and doing on-site debriefing and support for victims as the hearings engender a great deal of emotional trauma" (Kabeera & Sewpaul, 2008, p. 329). Social workers can advocate for change, and there are techniques and skills that can be taught for effective activism, South African anti-apartheid social workers being a group that has the experience in this type of social work.

Social work values and ethics in African society. This course would look specifically at national and international social work values in relation to African societies. The universality of social work values would be explored and, in particular, a detailed examination of African societal values and culture in light of African philosophy and traditional beliefs systems (Gray, 2005; Kreitzer, 2006; Taylor, 2000). This would begin with a deconstruction of the concept of culture in order to identify culture in a particular society and in Africa generally. In order to have culturally specific interventions, knowing the different cultures in society is paramount (Mafile'O, 2004). One group member states: "I came to learn that we need to know the relevance of the cultural aspect of the people we are dealing with. Because it will enable us to be creative in developing relevant programs and projects that will be based on their specific cultural values which people will accept as their own and will believe in that."

Once a critique of values and beliefs in relation to African philosophy have been explored, a further step is to critically look at how these values and beliefs may or may not contradict the values put forth by IFSW and IASSW Ethics in Social Work, Standard of Principles (2008). Each professional association should rewrite its code of ethics to reflect in content and language its own society. An earlier example was given in Chapter 3 of this book of the Indian code of ethics that was revised, through the help of Dr. Richard Ramsay at the University of Calgary, and this code of ethics now reflects more of the Indian society (TISS, 1997).

Ross (2008) gives four examples where traditional practices and values and beliefs can cause difficult ethical decisions for social workers in their practice. She advocates the development of an "indigenous Afro-centric model of social work to promote healing, and as a way of teaching social work students about the dilemmas inherent in respecting cultural practices which impinge on the rights of others" (p. 385). An example she gives concerns traditional medicine. Seen as combining mental and spiritual guidance, herbal medicine, nutritional therapy, and physical therapy, she asks: "why then should there be a conflict between African and traditional healing, western medicine and human rights?" (p. 386). If the traditional belief is that a person with a disability has this disability due to the ancestor's wishes or a punishment for wrong-doing, the ethical dilemma for social workers is that they "are expected to respect the cultural beliefs of different groups; or on the other hand, they are expected to consider the rights of the affected individuals" (pp. 386–87). These are difficult decisions that will be faced by social workers, and students need to be aware of and skilful in dealing with different values. A second example is ritual animal slaughter. This has been denounced by the Society for the Prevention of Cruelty to Animals, and yet it is an important ritual for cleansing. For the social worker, the ethical dilemma is whether they honour animal rights or "respect the rights of the cultural groups" (p. 389) because it is an important part of many ceremonial rites of passage. A third example is organ donation. "Cultural taboos often stand in the way of organ donation ... many black South Africans believe that they cannot be buried without their organs as their ancestors will not accept them" (389). And yet many people die daily due to the lack of organs being donated to save their lives. A fourth example is virginity testing. Condemned by the South African Human Rights Commission for young girls under the age of sixteen, it is an extremely important practice amongst the Zulu.

> The basic antagonism between modern-day human rights and African cultural rights emanates from the fact that while the former hold that the full realization of the human potential lies in the absolute freedom and independence of the individual, the later espouses the notion of Ubuntu and the common good, that is, that no man is an island. The concept of Ubuntu involves putting people first and reflects the communal values of collective humanity, compassion, solidarity, respect, humility, caring and sharing. In other words, a person is a person through other people. (p. 391)

This course will not only provide the opportunity for students to critique their own value base and how this evolved but should raise awareness of (and develop skills to deal with) ethically difficult social work situations.

Social work and refugee issues. The number of refugees in the world, as of the end of 2009, was 10.4 million with 22 per cent in Africa (UNHCR, 2010). With civil wars breaking out, this figure will surely rise in the future. Not only does war determine movement between countries, but economic, ecological, and political reasons often send people to seek refuge in another country. This course would look at refugee policies and refugee issues, including externally and internally displaced peoples, hosting refugees, repatriation, social work practice in refugee camps (practice issues and intervention strategies, child soldiers, unaccompanied minors, counselling services for post-traumatic stress disorder, etc.), and the role of international organizations in refugee issues. The pros and cons of integrating refugees into society versus a refugee camp should be critically discussed, and visits to a number of camps in the country should be undertaken. Many African countries have been host to thousands of refugees, and this course is extremely important to address, especially as working in refugee camps is often seen as being sentenced to the dreaded 'outpost' where no social worker wants to work. The profile of effective social work in refugee camps would help eliminate this attitude and fear so that it is seen as an important option in social work practice. Community-based counselling services like ones that have been developed in Rwanda (Kabeera & Sewpaul, 2008) should be part of the discussion in this course.

Persons in need of protection in institutions. This course would explore major issues surrounding institutional care versus community care in light of developmental approaches to social work. Resettling people back into the community (for example, people living in witch communities, long-term institutions, and orphanages) and appropriate strategies for doing this in an African context would be discussed.

Development theories in the context of Africa. A course should be taught that specifically looks at the social development approach to social work that has already been advocated for by twenty years of ASWEA conferences and other authors, including Midgley (1995), Gray (1998), Sewpaul (2006) and Patel (2005). A look at the South African White Paper for Developmental Welfare, as well as other countries working on this approach, would be part of the course. Criticism over the usefulness of the medical model and casework model for communal countries in Africa has been debated. New models that go beyond the casework and community work practice are needed from a social development approach (Laird, 2003; Lombard, 1999; Sewpaul & Lombard, 2004).

Mediation and conflict resolution. For many African countries, consensus has been a part of the traditional way of solving issues in the community (Gyekye, 1996). And yet social work curriculum often does not include conflict resolution as a skill needed in social work. Patel (2005) emphasizes the importance of this skill in social work. "The emphasis of mediation on finding a 'win-win' solution resonates well with social work's core values of the dignity and the recognition of the worth of each person" (Patel, 2005, p. 288). This course would develop skills for successful mediation and conflict resolution with individuals, families, groups, and communities. Patel (2005) identifies three stages of conflict resolution as being peacemaking, peacekeeping, and peacebuilding. Kabeera & Sewpaul (2008) suggest a "shift from a worldview that supports violence as a means of conflict resolution to embracing dialogue, mediation and non-violent means" (pp. 332–33). This should be integrated into all curricula from primary school to university level, including social work curricula.

New courses had been introduced, a few years before this research, to the University of Ghana social work program and in particular members of the group were enthusiastic about two courses: Development and Social Issues I and II, which covered the whole year in the new MSW program. These courses critically looked at those aspects of globalization in the international system which impacts directly on the development of Ghana. They covered the main concepts of development theory and considered the controversies surrounding definitions of development, underdevelopment, and sustainability. They also cover North/South relations and the dynamic relationships between education, infrastructure, access to information, and poverty. The second half looks at effective and ineffective strategies for development and the role of NGOs and government agencies and then explores their relationship to each other. The topics addressed in these courses are crucial for social work training in Africa.

Other important courses introduced were: 1) people living with HIV/AIDS; 2) social work and law; and 3) school social work. These courses are not guaranteed to take place due to the lack of lecturers and the ability to pay them. Funding is the overriding determinate of whether courses can be taught. This is directly linked to the government's priority with secondary education and infrastructure within the university itself. The more recent interest from the World Bank (2009a) may help in providing more professors to teach these courses. Our research group felt that courses for work with children and youth and a course on aging and life cycle should be offered at the bachelor's level and not just at the master's level. Also, each course should include an international element and a gender relations element and, in particular, knowledge, theory, and interventions from other African countries. Finally, there needs to be a concerted effort to educate and teach all students IT techniques that they can use in their practice.

These changes to the present curriculum and the suggestion of new courses in social work are the practical outcomes from the work of the research group. The whole knowledge base of social work history in Africa needs to be developed and critically analyzed in an African context. Social workers need to be politically involved because "when social workers have been involved in social and/or political activism, they have been able to influence social policy" (Mmatli, 2008, p. 301). Case examples should come from Africa so that students can get the most out of their learning without spending the mental energy of adapting theories and interventions from a western textbook. Articles from Africa should be used in the reading list and have preference over western articles. Classrooms should minimize the lecture-style teaching and use adult learning approaches that create an environment for creative thinkers and visionaries. The use of drama, art, oral tradition, group projects, role-playing, practical activities, videos, and practitioners from the community coming in as speakers and instructors are appropriate to include in the classroom. This would require the creation of a safe and collaborative teaching environment where social work academics could develop new teaching skills and methods and develop a reciprocal arrangement by which community people could come and talk to the class and in turn academics give something in return to the community. In practice this could mean a community social worker could teach and in return the professor could volunteer time with the social worker's agency.

Ideally, an African social work textbook is important in the development of social work in Africa and indigenous writers should be encouraged to contribute to this production. There needs to be an opening up of libraries around the world so African students, academics, and practitioners can access articles for teaching and learning. Finally, there should be programs set up so that students can do field practica in other countries in Africa instead of in Europe and America. This will increase African knowledge concerning social work that will contribute to the overall development of social work in Africa.

3. Other issues arising from the research process

Often, in a PAR process, other important issues arise that may not have been part of the original research proposal. These issues can often be as much or more important than the goals of the research itself. The group had other issues that they wanted to address and the following are other issues that emerged from the research process.

Social work on the periphery. One common theme that emerged from this research in Ghana and is expressed consistently at African conferences is that social work is not a recognized profession in many countries in Africa and people want this to change. No doubt the work of both the IFSW and IASSW has helped in promoting social work worldwide, but it has a long way to go in Africa. On the continent, a body that brought social work together was the ASWEA conferences. However, in the early 1990s it was disbanded and became the Eastern and Southern African Association of Social Workers. More recently, the Association of Schools of Social Work in Africa (ASSWA) was formed to bring the continent together in social work education and practice. Their role includes developing relevant curricula and regional standards, undertaking joint research and representing the interests of African schools of social work at national, regional, and international levels. Each country's national association needs to be strengthened so that they are the voice for social work to their governments and people. At the moment many are struggling to survive. Public awareness campaigns and educational videos can also help give a higher national profile to social work. Trained social workers in high positions can educate and encourage the profession to have a voice in national social policy. At the local level, social workers can be involved in radio call-in programs stating that they are social workers and this is their point of view. Sometimes other professionals do not even know what social workers do and each social worker can be a voice for the profession. There would also be value in collecting records and documenting what social workers are already doing. One group member states: "we need to avoid creating the impression that Ghana social work has no basis at all in the Ghanaian culture. There is a need to have the impression corrected." Kabeera & Sewpaul (2008) suggest that social workers in Rwanda could play a huge role in coordinating and organizing community-based interventions such as the monthly community service activities initiated by the government, micro-credit schemes and soft loans to improve household incomes and innovative services for returnees. The more visible social workers are in the community, the more people will see, understand, and value their contributions.

Professional Associations in Africa. Mazibuko & Gray (2004) provide a good history of social work associations in South Africa. At one point there were five different associations depending on race and social divisions. "Professional associations ... have had a chequered history in South Africa ... due to the deep social and racial divisions engendered by apartheid and attempts by the government to control every aspect of social life" (p. 140). They give a list of major functions of a professional association as follows.

> 1) advance the interests of social workers by attending to matters relating to salaries, service conditions and benefits, and line of promotion, 2) promote the professional development of social workers through theory and research, and the introduction of professional journals to facilitate this development, 3) encourage ethical professional conduct by providing codes of ethics to guide social workers, including practitioners, managers, policy-makers and educators, towards ethically and politically sensitive practice, 4) ensure the promotion of relevant and appropriate social work education and practice aimed at the alleviation of poverty and the reconstruction and development of communities and 5) monitor service provision so as to ensure a just and equitable distribution of social work services. (p. 132)

This is a tall order for professional associations that are struggling to stay alive. One of the issues confronting the Ghanaian professional association (GASOW) was that it had not successfully brought social workers together from parts of Ghana and if this didn't happen, then collective national action would be difficult to achieve. In Ghana, many people have passed through the social work program at the university and the school of social work, and yet there are few professionals involved at the association level and some practitioners don't even know that the association exists. There were several other issues pertaining to the running of a vibrant and successful association: 1) there needs to be new and younger people interested in the association; and 2) it must be established who can be called a social worker in the country and continuing education must be provided for trained social workers. It is the association's responsibility, working with the government, to determine who can call themselves a social worker and who can't, doing this in a culturally appropriate way.

Another concern is that the Ghanaian government is not using the association as a source for professional advice in social policy issues. If an association is not working well, if it doesn't have its own professional people behind it, then it is less likely that the government will use it as a resource. In Ghana, other NGOs have taken on this role of advising government on social policy and filling in the gap. One in particular, the International Social and Development Centre (ISODEC), has built an image for itself, and people respect their views. They are a watchdog for the government, and they continually analyze and respond to the government's social policy issues. The professional association should strengthen its voice to advocate on behalf of the health and social welfare of its people.

Intra-continental work. Another important element for the growth of social work in Africa is intra-continental cooperation among the different countries in Africa. The new continental organization, the Association of Schools of Social Work in Africa (ASSWA) was developed in order to, amongst other things, create and maintain a regional network of critical debate and exchange of innovative ideas in social work education and practice. As Mwansa (2010) states:

> The process of transformation must be steered by an organization that has legitimacy and the will to offer leadership, direction and focus. This should provide a forum for academics to debate the challenges of training a cadre of professionals who will respond to the specific needs of the people. It will also enhance information flow, the development of networks, faculty and student exchange, regular reviews, research and standards of excellence.... An organization for schools of social work is therefore essential for the transformation of the social work profession in Africa. (p. 131)

One of the main barriers to the growth of this organization is the culture of inertia (Mwansa, 2010). "The inability of social work to effectively respond to problems on this continent has opened it to criticism, scepticism and, at times, outright ridicule" (p. 134). Another issue is attempting to create culturally relevant social work curriculum. "Failure to deal with these issues will spell doom for social work in Africa. ASSWA has to take the lead in this endeavour" (135).

Other issues around intra-continental collaboration concerns finances. Unfortunately, many African social workers are not paid enough to be able to attend conferences regionally, let alone nationally or within the continent. The other barrier to the pan-African meetings is the perennial tight security around visas. So many conferences I have attended have had gaps in presentations because someone couldn't get a visa to travel to another country in Africa let alone another country in the world. It is a continual struggle just to get together as a continent. But it is crucial for the growth of social work. Collaborative research between countries, student exchanges, and conferences within the continent help with the critical challenge of making social work more relevant to the African situation. This dialogue has to continue and, as schools of social work begin to exchange their programs and ideas, others can benefit from these different programs and together a new and better curriculum and practice can emerge.

Institutional changes. One area of concern for the research group was the effectiveness of the colonial institutions that have remained since independence.

Government organizations. The group spoke about the effectiveness or ineffectiveness of the colonial institutions like the Department of Social Welfare. This topic also emerged in the ASWEA conferences. They were pleased that something, an institutionalized organized structure, had emerged that helped in the transition from traditional life to colonial/modern life. What the group was challenged by was the question of whether this type of institutional structure is still effective, or if major changes needed to be made. It is possible that, in order to implement the necessary positive changes in social welfare delivery, the entire institution should be replaced. Built on a remedial approach from the colonial era, its appropriateness has to be critically looked at. According to Laird (2003), debates have been going on over the past decades concerning the appropriateness of these institutions. "African scholars have consistently argued that the national Departments of Social Welfare set up by the former colonial powers of Britain and France should be reoriented to undertake interventions which support the objectives of social development not rehabilitative modes of casework" (p. 259).

This critical reflection and institutional change in service has still not happened. Social work needs to advocate for effective social welfare services at the government level. To change a large institution like social welfare takes much time, planning, and resources. It will affect both the beneficiaries of this institution and the way social work is taught at the diploma and bachelor's level. However, if people begin to think about a new approach to social welfare, this is a start. As one group member stated: "How do we look at the whole content of social work and make it useful to our needs and not necessarily to the needs of those people that brought it or people that said we should learn it? How do we make it friendly to our own needs?" This critical thinking concerning social welfare institutions needs to begin at the university level of social work education and students should be given the opportunity to be creative and revolutionary in their ideas around relevant institutions. The professional association should also be involved in this discussion. One group member thought that a solution was to create "a Ministry of Social Welfare because that seems to be the only way something gets attention." It seems that if something becomes a ministry in Ghana then issues are addressed more rapidly. There are examples of other countries who have implemented changes to their colonial institutions. For example, in Zimbabwe they also took a developmental approach at looking at the effectiveness of social welfare institutions. Instead of these institutions using only government money that is constantly dwindling, these institutions began generating money and becoming self-sustaining.

4. Outcomes of the research project

One of the main concerns among the members of the research group was whether or not anything that we did would be implemented, or were we just doing research for research's sake. Having a history of good ideas that were never implemented due to financial constraints, hierarchical issues, and oppressive environments, the group members were reluctant to put their time and effort into something that might never make any difference. It was difficult to know how the research would make a difference and trusting the process was hard for everyone. All we could do was to do the best analysis we could and then disseminate the information and encourage the University of Ghana's Department of Social Work to implement the curricula changes. A group member explained: "What impact can we also as a group bring to bear on this situation so that at the end of the day the work that we do we will see our fruits being utilized … what can we do to push the agenda forward as far as the adaptations or the changes that we want to see in the social work curriculum?" Another group member stated: "If we are not careful it is going to be a talk shop and it will appear that we will not be able to do anything about it. And then we also one day will sit here with the next generation and tell them how social work was in our time and here too we were not able to do anything about it."

A key component of Participatory Action Research is the actions generated from a project. Political action sets PAR apart from other forms of action research. Political action can take place at many different levels of society from individual to societal changes. Each action was meant to challenge social work education and practice in Ghana with the hope that it would move forward in a positive way. Our action plans came out of creating new knowledge and the conviction that this new knowledge needed to be made available to everyone interested in the study. Always in our minds was the importance of returning our knowledge to the community (Department of Social Work, social workers, students, and the community). The action plans were all political in that each confronted power relations from the individual to the societal level. Disseminating this knowledge to the public was also important. Fals Borda (1988) describes four levels of communication concerning the "production and diffusion of new knowledge": "It incorporates various styles and procedures for systematizing new data and knowledge according to the level of political conscience and ability for understanding written, oral or visual messages by the group" (pp. 95, 96).

A consensus process was used to decide on the types of actions we would be involved in and how we would implement them. Of the five plans we proposed, each had its own trajectory. The need to reinvigorate the professional association issue in Ghana was nearest and dearest to the group's hearts, and there was a sense of urgency in getting this sorted out and establishing a working and vibrant association. Concerning the issue of social work being on the periphery, we considered different avenues to make our profession known to the public, including appearing on TV, being involved in current affairs programs on radio and TV, and doing a public education video. The latter was agreed upon. The following describes the way in which each action plan emerged, unfolded, and was implemented. The action plans were presented to the Department of Social Work at a Presentation Day held at the university. The two final plans evolved from my own work in Calgary, Canada.

Recommendations for changes to the curriculum. Throughout the research process, we talked about the curriculum and our experiences with it. Three workshops were specifically designed to allow group members to share their experiences with the program and to comment on the course outlines. Towards the end of the project, we put our thoughts together and produced a document concerning recommended changes to the curriculum that is discussed above.

At the end of the project, a copy was presented to each of the part-time and full-time lecturers who taught in the Department of Social Work, as well as lecturers from other departments who taught social work students. A copy was also given to the library so that all students and the general public could see our recommendations. It was important that the research outcomes were transparent and open to the public.

Public Education Video: Social work in Ghana: Education and Practice. One of the main themes that emerged from the research project was the concern that social work was on the periphery in Ghana and the group had several ideas on how to educate the public about social work. Radio, Ttelevision, talk shows, and a video were discussed. However, the idea had been floating around about filming a video. The group agreed that the best idea was for one of the TV stations to film it. Dialogue centred on how to do the video, what should be in it, who should be in it, and how long the video should be. Once we had decided on producing a video, each person was to write a three-minute script on what they did as a social worker. Once these scripts were collated, I narrated the larger script, bringing the different scripts together. The group then looked at it and made corrections. Ghana TV (GTV) was approached with an agreed-upon price. A producer from GTV was invited to come and a schedule was organized. This schedule included travelling to the north of Ghana for a weekend of filming in the rural areas. The video was a way for the group members to participate in a practical educational activity and to show their own work and skills as social workers. Copies were given to heads of the Department of Social Welfare, the Department of Community Development, and the University of Ghana, Department of Social Work. Unfortunately, we were never able to show the film on TV due to the fact that Ghana TV wanted money to show it and the agreement beforehand was that it was a public education film that should have been shown free of charge.

Re-energizng the Ghana Association of Social Workers (GASOW). By far the most pressing issue was the state of GASOW. Some group members were fed up with the association and others didn't even know if it still existed. The group used the workshops with different speakers to identify problems and to discuss the idea of starting a new association. In the end, three options came forward. The first was to start a new association based at the university. The second was to revive the old association. The third was to scrap the old one altogether and create a new national association. It was finally agreed that we would try to revive the old association by instigating a 'friendly coup' which would identify the issue of the lack of respect for the present association and send a message to the executive association that social workers were not happy with the professional association. Another important point was that members of the present association was frustrated with the apathy among social workers concerning the profession and the association. It was important to find the best way to attempt a 'friendly coup' so that a positive action could result that would include social workers from all over Ghana. The group decided to hold a general meeting for all social workers in Ghana to discuss the issue and decide on how best to go forward with re-energizing the association. Project money was used to advertise in two national newspapers and over 250 letters were sent to government and non-government organizations.

On November 1, 2003, a general meeting was held, and over seventy people came from across Ghana. It was the largest general social work meeting that had occurred in recent times. People from the prison service, education service, community development, social welfare, industry, and non-government organizations came to give their thoughts and opinions concerning the future of the association. Group members and faculty at the university took a risk in supporting this meeting, as it was extremely political. After three hours of tense discussion, the meeting adjourned with the challenge for social workers to go home and think about what they wanted to do in regards to the association. The result of this meeting produced changes to the make-up of the association. A follow-up meeting was held and the executive of GASOW was relieved of its duties and an interim executive was established. Approximately a year later, fair elections were held and a broader representation of social workers was elected. The president of the association subsequently was elected as the African regional representative for the International Federation of Social Workers at their Nairobi meeting in April 2005. This is an excellent example of PAR methodology. A stakeholder group was created, opinions and information were shared, and knowledge and recommendations were produced. Most importantly, the final step involved implementation of these recommendations, and positive changes were implemented.

Presentation of a TV and video recorder. One of our recommendations was that the department should invest in audio-visual equipment to be used as a teaching tool in the classroom. The group bought the above items and we presented this at the Presentation Day. It was acknowledged that the money came out of the project funds, something many foreign researchers do not think to do in appreciation of an institution's support for their research.

Articles for publication. The group agreed to write a joint article concerning the research process. In January 2004, I wrote to all group members asking them to give me their thoughts and feelings about the research, the strengths and challenges, and anything else they wanted to include in an article about the research. I also asked them to give their comments on the role of the queen mother in the group process for an article concerning the topic of social work and traditional authority (Kreitzer, 2004b). The article has now been published (Kreitzer et al., 2009).

African articles for courses. The group suggested during the course of the workshops that we collect all the indigenous articles we had or knew about and put them in a reader for the library. On my return from Ghana, I collected many articles concerning social work in Ghana. I have copied the proceedings of the GASOW seminars held in the 1970s, the ASWEA proceedings from the 1970s, and the four United Nations international surveys on social work conducted in the 1950s and 1960s. These documents were transported to the Department of Social Work in May 2004 for use by students there. Technology is geared towards the rich of society, and information via the internet and global libraries, although improved for many countries, is still not accessible for the average person living in an economically poorer country.

ASWEA project. Between 2008 and 2011, a joint project by the Association of Schools of Social Work in Africa, the International Association of Schools of Social Work, and the University of Calgary, Faculty of Social Work, was facilitated by which the ASWEA conference proceedings were collected, copied, tidied up for printing, and printed for distribution in Africa. As a result, hard copies and DVDs of the documents were produced and the material was also placed on line for access through the Wits University historical archives (http://www.historical-papers.wits.ac.za/).

5. Dissemination of information

The group suggested that we have a Presentation Day in order to show what we had completed through the project. The day was planned and over a hundred people attended the day.

Presentation Day. The group agreed to hold a Presentation Day at the Department of Social Work to present our different actions to the staff, students, and community people. On October 17, 2003, we met with all interested people to explain the research project and to present the action plans we had produced as a result of our research. The recommendations for changes were presented to the Department of Social Work. The full video was shown as part of the program and copies were presented to the

Department of Social Work and the School of Social Work, Osu. The television and the video recorder were presented to the department, and the presentation produced huge applause from everyone. Finally, it was announced that a meeting concerning the association would be held on November 1, 2003.

Publication of the research. After the research the group wanted to write about the research. We agreed that any member of the group who wanted to participate in writing an article about the research could do so. In 2009, an article was submitted and accepted for publication with multiple authors from the group Kreitzer et al., 2009).

The personal experiences of the group were collected at the end of the project. Each person was asked to express two positives and two challenges regarding the project and these were put onto video. Excerpts from this video affirm the conscientization of a group of people willing to critically look at their own lives, society, and profession.

> Any time I attended a meeting I would just sit down quietly and listen to them. Now I know the work of the social worker. I am part of the system and I appreciate the work that they do. I am going to sing their song about them wherever I go and wherever I meet the community.... I have learned that we don't say problems, but rather they use the word issues.

> Another challenge is with my own thoughts and feelings about social work in Ghana and about colonialism and about these different factors that have affected the evolution of social work in Ghana.... I feel I have made friends with nine people that I hope I will always be in contact with.

> Being in this group has enabled me to read lots of articles concerning social work in other parts of the world, especially developing countries like ours, country's like Zimbabwe and South Africa and what they are doing. And this has really gingered (shakened) in me how to do developmental social work.

When we started the project, like others have said, this is a unique way of data collection, which is not the same as what we are used to. One interesting thing about it to me is the way we dialogue in the group.... We always discuss things in some detail and sometimes very hot and by the end of it we have a consensus.... When we are sitting as individuals in our homes or villages, either as former students or current students, we wouldn't have had the opportunity to do that. But the research project has given us the opportunity to contribute our ideas as to what should be done to the curriculum to make it suitable to changing needs.

When I came into the group, naturally I am a little bit loud and sometimes I forget that this is a participatory group that every-body's thoughts and views are to be expressed ... but with time I have learned to control myself and then allow anything to go and then after that I will make my comments.... It is a sort of a revolutionized type of research and I am looking forward to using it.... Another benefit that I have gained from this research is the friends I have made.

I have been proud to be part of this participatory action re-search. And what fascinates me is this aspect of, the positive aspect of, democracy; the democratic way in which we con-ducted this research.... I was faced with the challenge of per-sonal biases. I felt that if western influence was not also proper then it was equally right for me to say that some of our cultural aspects were not also proper.... I saw that a big challenge for us Africans to start thinking about is that we need to give women and children their rightful positions so far as human rights is concerned.

The group has enabled me to critically exam some of the things that we have been thinking through as social workers.... This research has been a process where we all dialogue together, agree on and we have to reach a consensus in making decisions and for me it has been very interesting to know the other side of research where you have to involve people in dialogue.... What role are we going to play after this group work has gingered (shakened) us more or less to re-examine the role social workers can play or should play in our society? What is the way forward? What are the next steps as group members?

This research has caused me to think, it is a very positive aspect that it has had on me. Before we started the whole research program, we were taken through some exercises [the map exercise] to think outside box. And that has stayed with me ever since. I mean for the first time I have seen that it is very necessary to sometimes not only respect the common, what people are used to, but to also consider other methods of knowledge which are equally important.... It is a vision of the research to establish a professional association. I know it is not going to come very easily because we have been doing some running around and it appears that people are not too enthusiastic about it so that is a big challenge.

This research will benefit me in my master's preparation because most of the articles given to us contained information about things that I have been looking for quite a long time which I had not been able to find.... I hate to say that when I was in my final year or so well as for social work, I only did it as a discipline and I will move to finance or law. But I think through this particular research method I have learned to love social work. The discussion with Dr. Blavo was actually asking me to stick to social work in the future.

F. Conclusion of chapter

Much has been written concerning the need to create a culturally relevant African social work curriculum; however, few writers give examples of practical ways to go about doing this task. The information in this chapter contains practical ideas that the group came up with in order to begin this process. The chapter also highlights other important social work issues that needed to be addressed in the Ghanaian setting and no doubt other social work professionals in other countries will have similar issues. Sharing how the research group tried to tackle these issues will be of value to others academics, students, and practitioners in other countries of Africa. In detailing the research process, it is hoped that other PAR projects will emerge and that the academia of the universities in Africa will see the value of this type of research and open the door to qualitative research methodologies. Finally, the action plans for this research were life-changing for the group members and for social work in Ghana. Like a pebble thrown into a still pond, the ripple effects are still being felt in Ghana. Discussion and debate about social work curricula continues, research group members have gone on to obtain higher degrees of education and others have continued in their practice. The history of social work in Africa, through the ASWEA documents, is being distributed all over Africa for use in teaching, research, and writing. The goal of a more culturally relevant social work curriculum continues to move slowly in African debates and discussions and in practice.

VII. The Future of Social Work in Africa

In any examination of the challenges of Africa, one natural resource often goes underappreciated: Africans themselves. As I have said, the disempowerment of ordinary people, especially at the grassroots, underlies Africa's gravest problems. In all their incredible diversity, Africans share common bonds that tie them together and that they must cherish in their communities, nations, regions, and across the continent. It is fundamental that Africa's leaders create the conditions under which their peoples gain confidence, dignity, and a sense of self-worth – with the citizens themselves actively participating in their effort. (Maathai, 2009)[1]

Recently, I read *The Challenge for Africa* (Maathai, 2009) and was heartened by the themes she discussed. The themes from that book are similar to the themes I discuss in this book. She speaks of an Africa that has a unique and strong history which came from many micro-nations. These culturally sophisticated nations had their own systems of governing and community living and working. When Europeans came to the continent, the African way of living was deemed savage and the Europeans felt the strong need to civilize this continent and took full advantage of doing so. Not only were the people exploited but the resources were taken and used to create the industrialized world we now call the west. This exploitation has continued beyond the independence of the countries on the continent through devastating world economic rules, the denial of historical facts about the continent, the continual negativity concerning its place in the world, and the negative consequences of development. According to Williams (1987), African civilization has suffered much oppression from which it is still trying to recover. It continues to struggle to find its place and purpose in today's world. "Advances in information technology, combined with that of neo-liberal capitalism has profound influences on people's identities, cultures and on their material conditions" (Sewpaul, 2006, p. 421). Both external forces and internal forces seem to keep Africa from finding its path. These forces have affected the identity of Africans as individuals and the identity of the continent in relation to other countries of the world. However, Africa has a resiliency that has kept it going. Despite everything, it is a continent that continues to exist and grow despite what the rest of the world throws its way. "The peoples of the region continue to show resiliency, determination and initiative in strategizing to meet the challenges that face them, as is reflected in growing numbers of indigenous NGO's, many with a commitment to supporting a human rights agenda" (Heron, 2005, 787).

African universities could contribute to creating a new shift in thinking concerning what is important in education for the continent. What is needed is a blending together of modern and traditional knowledge that honours its own traditions as well as accepting other worldviews when appropriate. The simplistic primitive/civilized dichotomy instigated during the colonial rule must be replaced by a proud recognition of African knowledge and culture. The failure to do this so far has been due to poor "faculty planning, the obstruction of interested individuals, the miseducation of the university teachers, and the confusion of political leaders" (van Wyk & Higgs, 2007, p. 69). "The African university has to provide a service to the continent and its people. The African continent is immense, not only in terms of its size, but more important, with respect to the cultural, linguistic and ethnic diversity that characterizes the people who live in its various parts. The challenge that awaits the African university is to improve the quality of the lives of all those who inhabit this continent" (p. 70). The educational system needs to nurture visionaries who are prepared to ask questions and think differently in order to come up with creative solutions to issues and not revert to back to the old solutions that are no longer relevant. One research guest speaker comments: "The foundation for all education must be creative education. Creative foundation for people or for young people to look at solutions other than the existing solutions.... It should be nurturing and bringing out of a person a creative attitude to life." African universities need to provide opportunities for students and faculty to push beyond what is acceptable and allow visionaries a chance to offer long-term solutions to the many issues facing the continent. It should be a university that is

> ... grounded in African communities and concerns itself with knowledge production that takes the African condition and identity as its central issue – knowledge production that recognizes the African condition as historical, not biological and defines its key task as coming to grips with this condition critically.... [I]t actively is involved in the reclamation and promotion of indigenous knowledge systems and the deconstruction of colonial discourses. It considers the African experience as a source of ideas that leads to exceptional and original scholarship as well as informed public policy. (van Wyk & Higgs, 2007, p. 69)

African social work, too, has to find its own unique style of training and practice in order for it to be an influential force for change in Africa. It needs to cut the umbilical cord of western social work education, stop using interventions that don't work, and find a new pair of sandals that fit the African situation. It needs to emerge as a revolutionary and creative alternative to western social work theories and knowledge. "Given the history of colonization and oppression, class and race stratification and the hegemony of western world views, the struggle for social justice by social workers must be linked to ideals of emancipatory, anti-oppressive and anti-hegemonic practice" (Smith, 2008, p. 374). The challenge is to find a balance in the African and western approaches to social work, so as to reflect the diversity of society that many African countries are working towards in this modern age. "There is much of value in Western thinking about social work, but this must not stifle the wisdom and experience of local cultures" (Gray, 2005, p. 236). Gray (2005) suggests a "grounded approach where we celebrate and recognise commonalities while at the same time valuing and including differences; an expansive approach to professional definition rather than a self-protective stance" (p. 233). The problem has been that western social work has been dominant and the balance needs to shift. It can shift in two ways: 1) move the pendulum all the way over to a total African approach to social work, or 2) adopt a slower convergence of the two with an emphasis on critical evaluation and replacement of western social work theories and knowledge that are not relevant to the African situation. Some countries have done the former and others the latter (Gray, 2005).

One research guest speaker states: "How do we create creativity … creativity is nurtured by exposing individuals to challenges that have no answers necessarily.… Any situation that is a challenge without a ne-cessarily prescribed answer to it becomes a creative situation. Instead of exams that are passed by a prescribed answer, people's minds need to be challenged to think. African social work needs to define itself regard-less of how others want to define it and needs to move forward to be an important and influential profession in Africa and in the social work profession worldwide." A good example is South Africa. Presently, South African social work has been challenged with changing their social work curricula in a post-apartheid era. They have been challenged to recreating a curriculum and practice that focuses on social development. As a result, the changes have forced social workers to revisit their values relating to social justice, to redirect their services to the poor, to find more effect-ive ways of addressing poverty, and to practice community development on a broader scale. It called upon them to make a greater impact on the problems of mass poverty, unemployment and social deprivation through greater use of diverse social work methods, such as advocacy, community development, empowerment, consultation, networking, action research, and policy analysis (Gray & Mazibuko, 2002, p. 199).

Social work is an art and a science. Like a painter who looks at society, observes both transient and static activities, and then paints what she sees, so a social worker looks at a client, group, family, or community and builds a picture of their life. That picture can emphasize the positive or negative of that life. Often society is portrayed through the media as violent and negative. But the true artist creates something truly beautiful, unique and lasting. Similarly, social workers can achieve a goal that brings out the best in the client, be they individuals or communities. They can work with and bring hope and positive living to their clients in an African way.

The role of the social work profession needs to be addressed at three levels: the micro (individual), mezzo (organizational), and macro (national). At the micro level, social workers need to embrace their profession and be proud of it in public forums, in workshops, and in their everyday lives. They need to break away from the destruction and disempowering concept of 'western knowledge as civilized and traditional knowledge is primitive.' Their confidence in critical thinking, taking risks, and boldly going where no one has gone before in curriculum development needs to be nurtured in a safe environment. "International social work is not just about the spread of professional social work across the globe, it is also about the development of practices that are relevant in local contexts. As such, different forms of social work emerge and take hold, moulded and shaped by the social, political, economic circumstances, the history and culture of particular contexts, as well as prevailing social work knowledge and values" (Gray, 2005, p. 236). At a mezzo level, there needs to be a strengthening of the professional association as well as ongoing evaluation of the curriculum so that the organizational body can work together for positive change in the profession. At the macro level, a concerted effort by both the individual social workers and their association to make the social work profession known and respected in the country is crucial. This includes supporting the Association of Schools of Social Work in Africa. This involves developing a relationship with NGOs, IGOs, and government officials in showing them the uniqueness of the profession and how it understands and influences important social issues in both rural and urban settings. Individual social workers, organizations, and the government need to work together, critically evaluating existing social services agencies to see if they are still relevant to the country. If the institutions are strengthened, they need to be made workable and more effective in modern society and, if they are not, then get rid of them.

Social work education should be a process of "critical conscientization; engagement with oppression and issues of power; a commitment to radical transformation; changes in epistemologies; and efforts to change material conditions" (Smith, 2008, p. 381). Social workers can help to educate their clients and communities concerning their own human rights so that clients can more effectively advocate for themselves when confronting human rights abuses. They can also challenge the government to enact effective legislation, regulation, and policy protections for human rights. How the social worker addresses these challenges will determine their effectiveness as agents for positive social change. One group member stated: "We need to create creative people in all areas. If there are creative people performing then they bring about change, positive change in society and that is progress; that is development." Finally, with questions around curricula and what is valid and what is no longer relevant came a sense from some of the group members that maybe their training didn't equip them to deal with modern social issues in Ghana. This sense of inadequacy highlights the need for continual evaluation of social work education, something that has not been developed in Ghana. The research group knew the importance of ongoing and advanced training but also acknowledged the difficulty of delivery. Not all social welfare agencies in Ghana provide further education. However, secondments are offered, particularly for diploma graduates to obtain their BSW at the university.

Recently, I was at an African conference in which I asked people to get into groups and think about how they would recreate social work curricula that was more relevant to their culture. Afterwards, there was feedback about the exercise and I was struck by one African social worker's frustration. The comment was made that the western world is again telling Africans what to do. They gave Africa their curricula, telling them it would work for them, and now they are telling them that it isn't correct and that we need to do our own thing. This book is not about telling the African social work profession what to do. In fact, much of it comes from Africans themselves through the participation of local professionals, academics, practitioners, and community leaders in the PAR research group process. Not everyone will like or agree with the book and that is fine. What I hope for is that African social workers and academics be challenged to critically look at the ideas in the book through discussion groups, classrooms, academic workshops, writing, research, etc., and decide for themselves what curricula are relevant for their culture. This critical evaluation should in fact be completed on a regular basis, in all societies, as cultures continue to change. I strongly believe that African academics and social workers could revolutionize the profession and take it in a different direction that will challenge western social work in a way that it has not been challenged before. I strongly believe that a more African-centred social work curriculum is needed and that it can be achieved through critical thinking, collaboration, and hard work.

> All Africans must change the mind-set that affects many colonized peoples everywhere. They must believe in themselves again; that they are capable of clearing their own path and forging their own identity; that they have a right to be governed with justice, accountability, and transparency; that they can honor and practice their cultures and make them relevant to today's needs; and that they no longer need to be indebted – financially, intellectually and spiritually – to those who once governed them. They must rise up and walk. (Maathai, 2009, p. 20)

This is the challenge for social work educators and practitioners in Africa.

The newly formed ASSWA has a critical role to play in addressing social work issues in Africa. Not only does it have a web-based forum to critically discuss African social work issue but in future the website can be used to fill the gap of the lack of case studies (by having a case study database) and the lack of access to African social work articles (by having a database for articles). A database of curriculum and course outlines from each country would also be available.

In North Luangwa National Park in Zambia, there is a tree called the 'winterthorn.' It is a tree that seems to be at odds with the rest of the trees and plants that spring forth new leaves during the rainy season. "In the midst of this celebration of new life and color, the winterthorn stands barren and leafless. A stranger to Africa will say, 'Look at that huge tree; too bad it's dead ... when the plains and rivers dry up, the green trees wither and fade.' At that moment, when it has the stage all to itself and life seems too hard to bear, the winterthorn begins to sing. At first only a whisper of green touches the tips of the thorny branches, but soon a rich deep color spreads across the towering limbs. And then the stranger will ask, 'What is that magnificent tree'? Like Africa itself, the winterthorn dances in its own season" (Owens & Owens, 1984, p. 34).

"There is evidence that indigenous cultures are enriching and adding to new discourses in social work beyond the conventional, radical and postmodern; they are opening up new ways of thinking about social work in tune with indigenous ways" (Gray, 2005, p. 234). So too, a revolution needs to take place in African social work. Now is the time for social work in Africa to explode forth and lead the way in creative and revolutionary social work. And colleagues in other parts of the world need to sit up and listen and learn from this explosion. There are signs that African social work education and practice have changed and the discussions about this curriculum continues. Governments are beginning to recognize the critical value of the profession in regards to national development and social planning. Maathai (2009), an international African, describes the complexities of living in many different worlds and challenges Africans to define themselves and to embrace the continents diversity:

> My dual identities – both 'western' and 'African,' local and international, a member of the elite and someone from a rural background-capture the essence of what might be perhaps the deepest and most complex issue of all facing Africa; what it means to be an African today. Part of this identity is one not determined by Africans themselves. Too often, it seems, Africa has been seen as ungovernable, incomprehensible, and immune to the efforts of more enlightened nations' attempts to civilize it – in short, as unable to help itself. Africans too often have allowed themselves to be defined by these retrogressive stereotypes and have not seen themselves as they are: a spectacularly varied and dynamic cluster of what I call 'micro-nations' – communities bound together by their environment,

experiences, culture, and history that interact with other communities within the larger nation-state and region. Africans must reclaim and embrace their diversity if they are to flourish. (p. 22)

African social workers need to reclaim their profession, make it African-centred, embrace the diversity of the continent, and work together to revolutionize the profession in order for it to be an integral part of African life. To this effect, I believe this research has added to the growing number of African social workers who are challenging academics, researchers, and practitioners to critically think through their social work education and practice and to turn the critical dialogue into action concerning social work in Africa.

Appendix 1

Role-playing exercise examining pre-colonial, colonial, and post-colonial Ghana

Was there a systematic body of knowledge that could be drawn upon in order to create a social welfare system and were there people to do this job?

Set 1 – Pre-colonial Ghana – How were social needs met?

Characters: mother, father, two children (one is handicapped), aunt, uncle, ancestor, witch doctor, chief, elders, queen mother, pawns, slaves, refugees, priest, etc.

What was the role of the father in this society?
What was the role of the mother?
How did the children receive their education?
Who controlled children's behaviour?
What happened to people who were physically or mentally challenged?
Who took care of the health of the family?
How did the family provide for itself economically?
How were the spiritual needs met in the family?
What language did people speak?
How did people entertain themselves?
How were justice and law carried out?
Are there any other social institutions that I have forgotten?

Set 2 – Colonial Ghana – "Of all the factors of change, colonialism was undoubtedly the one with the greatest impact on our social institutions as its effects were felt with almost equal force throughout the length and breadth of the country" (Nukunya, 1992)

Characters: mother, father, two children (one is handicapped), missionary teacher, regional commissioner, university student, western doctor, cash crop farmer, traditional authority, etc.

What was the role of the father and mother in colonial Ghana?

How did the children receive their education? Was it encouraging of traditional knowledge?

Who set up the higher education system?

Who controlled children's behaviour?

What happened to people who were physically or mentally challenged?

Who took care of the health of the family? What happened to the witch doctor?

How did the family provide for itself economically?

How were the spiritual needs met in the family?

What language did people speak?

How did people entertain themselves?

How were justice and law carried out?

Who provided for the welfare of people who had no one to look after them?

What Government and non-government organizations were present at this time?

Set 3 – Post-colonial Ghana

Characters: mother, father, children, traditional authority, western experts, World Bank expert, preacher, university student, etc.

What was the role of the father and mother in post-colonial Ghana? How did the family change from traditional style family?

How did children receive their education? Whose educational curriculum were they taught?

Who determined what was taught at the university level?
Who controlled children's behaviour?
What happened to people who were physically and mentally challenged?
Who took care of the health of the family?
How did the family provide for itself economically?
What factors have influenced the economics of Ghana?
How were spiritual needs met in the family?
What language do people speak?
How do people entertain themselves?
How are justice and law carried out?
Who provides for the welfare of people who have no one to look after them?

What cultural practices, institutions, and beliefs of these three eras are reflected in social work knowledge nowadays?

This is a very brief outline of Ghanaian society and how it has changed over the years. The question I pose to you is: Was there a systemic body of knowledge that could be drawn upon in order to set up an indigenous social welfare system?

What institution, organization or society does the Department of Social Welfare serve?
What institution, organization, or society does the Department of Community Development serve?
What institution, organization, or society do non-government organizations serve?

If you were given the task of starting a social welfare system, how would go about this, and who would implement this system? Think outside your box!

Appendix 2

A. Cultural awareness

Exercise 1

Map exercise – The purpose of this exercise is to get people to think 'outside their own perspectives' and to see that the world can be viewed in different ways. The maps I used were the traditional Mercator world map (1569 from Germany), the Peters Projection World Map (map that represents countries accurately according to their surface areas. It points out the inaccuracies of the Mercator map that favours European colonial empires), and What's up? South! World map (this questions the development concept of North/South and who says that the North is up and the South is Down? The world is in fact a ball and has no top. The world is presented with the North in the South and the South in the North), New Zealand No long down under map (This puts New Zealand in the middle of the world and in the North), old maps of the world (You can use any old maps of the world), Fuller's Dymaxion Map (it challenges spatial and directional relationships with the earth and is designed to help us view the world from above), etc., and I put them up on the walls around the room. In groups of 3 or 4, they go around and answer the following questions: 1) Does this map seem correct to you; 2) Does this map seem different to the map you are used to; 3) Who do you think designed this map? What language is used in the map? What countries are prominent? What countries are not obvious? Whose worldview is being used in these maps; and 4) What are the differences between this map and the first one you saw?

Give the groups at least thirty minutes for the exercise and then get back together and have each group present its answers. A discussion can then be around different perceptions and how we bring our own perceptions to what we read and experience. The exercise should bring out the importance of critically looking at our assumptions and perceptions and that any issue can have many different viewpoints.

Exercise 2

Tree of Life – This is a good exercise for the beginning of a project or course so people can get to know each other better and acknowledge one's own cultural and identity and place in the world. Each person is to draw a tree with its roots under the ground, the trunk, the leaves, the buds, and the fruit. The roots represent: 1) the family from which we come, and 2) strong influences that have shaped us into the person we are now. The trunk represents: 1) our job, 2) family, and 3) organizations, communities, movements to which we belong. The leaves represent our sources of information like the newspaper, radio, television, books, reports, traditional knowledge, experience, friends, and contacts. The fruit represents our achievements: 1) projects we have organized, 2) programs, 3) groups we have started or helped to develop, and 4) materials we have produced. Finally, the buds represent our hopes for the future. Each person is filling in the tree of life with examples of the above under the appropriate part of the tree. After each person has finished, each one shares his or her tree with the group and they are put on the wall to display. Construction paper, marking pens, and sticky designs are used. The exercise is flexible enough to adapt to any culture. The purpose of the exercise is to reflect on one's own class origins, recognizing where one's values, beliefs, and assumptions come from. It is also a nice way to get the group to know each other and understand where people are coming from.

Exercise 3

Knowing ones culture – The purpose of this exercise is to get people to explain and express their culture in a non-verbal way. With construction paper, pens, sticky symbols, and magazines, each person is to describe their culture through drawings and art. No words can be used. After twenty minutes, have each person share his or her drawing with the others.

Exercise 4

This exercise can be used to remind people of their history and to reflect on how different historical factors have affected their cultures, values, and beliefs. There are three role-plays: 1) pre-colonial, 2) colonial, and 3) post-colonial. Five or six people can volunteer to play a typical family in pre-colonial Ghana. This could consist of a mother, a father, a disabled baby, a daughter, etc., and it is good if they can dress up for the part that they are playing. So this group gets up and sets the pre-colonial scene. Then, the audience asks the following questions for each time period. (For details, see Appendix 1.) This is then repeated (with new actors) for the colonial period and the post-colonial period. The exercise gave people a practical example of their own assumptions and ideas of how the past was for Ghanaians, and sometimes members of the group disagreed with each other and brought out the differences that colonialism made to the economic, social, political, and cultural aspects of life.

Exercise 5

This exercise brings together different ethnic groups to discuss the whole concept of culture. Each person comes up with a word or phrase in their ethnic culture that defines or identifies the concept of culture. The purpose of the exercise is to show that people perceive culture differently and language has a role to play in how culture is defined. Culture involves the past, present, and future. After everyone has come up with a word, the discussion can centre on what culture is, who defines culture, and how these different words to define culture are used in their particular ethnic group. It is an exercise that is quite difficult but provides stimulating dialogue. In talking about culture, it brought out a sense of pride and a way to open the door to cultural attitudes and values important to the project.

B. Neo-liberal agenda exercise

Exercise 6

Global debt – The story of the debt crisis

This exercise helps to inform students in a practical way how the IFIs affect their countries. Divide the class into groups of 5 to 7 people, leaving two students out. Give them a big piece of paper or four flip-charts taped together to make a large sheet and ask them to go off and build an ideal society. They can use words, drawings, magazine pictures, etc., to make their own country. They are to be as specific as possible, thinking about the environment, jobs, food, security, industry, etc. This takes about thirty minutes. The students who are left out will be the facilitator's assistants. The facilitator is usually the teacher. Once the societies have been created, the facilitator and his or her assistants visit the society. They introduce themselves as visitors. They ask questions about the important things in the society and generally chat with the society members. They then announce that they are from the IMF and that the society borrowed money from the IMF and hasn't been able to pay back the debts. Therefore, the IMF team is here to dictate a certain set of conditions (structural adjustment programs) in order that the society can pay back their debt. The IMF team explains the conditions, i.e., cutting back on education, health care, and social welfare. The IMF team continues to explain the program further while they rip away these programs from the society. (The facilitator literally rips away the 'education'-related pieces of the society. This is done with great force.) Any pictures of schools, etc., are ripped out of the mural. The second is health care. (The facilitator rips away anything to do with health, like hospitals and health centres). Welfare services are then ripped out of the mural. In the end, the society looks like Swiss cheese with holes in it.

Some of the reactions from students will be that they want to protect their country so they may stand on it or take it away or take the IMF people hostage or become violent.

A discussion at the end could have reflection questions like:

1. What was your reaction to how the IMF treated your society?

2. How did you feel about its attack on your way of life and your values?

3. How are these issues related to North/South relations?

4. Why did you not protect your country or why did you do the things you did to protect your country?

For further information and details of this exercise go to www.united-church.ca/websight.

Look for Global Debt – The Story of the Debt Crisis. There are other games on the website for your use as well.

References

Abbott, A. (1999). Measuring social work values: A cross-cultural challenge for global practice. *International Social Work, 42, 4,* 455–70.

Abloh, F., & Ameyaw, S. (1997). Ghana. In H. Campfens (Ed.), *Community development around the world: Practice, theory, research and training* (275–91). Toronto: University of Toronto Press.

Adeofe, L. (2004). Personal identity in African metaphysics. In L.M. Brown (Ed.), *African philosophy: New and traditional perspectives,* pp. 69–84. Oxford Scholars Online Monographs.

Agbo, A.A. (1999). *Values of Adinkra symbols.* Kumasi: Ebony Designs and Publications.

Ajayi, J.F.A., Goma, L.K.H., & Johnson, G.A. (1996). *The African experience with higher education.* Athens: Ohio University Press.

Allen, M., & Leipziger, D. (2005). *2005 review of the poverty reduction strategy approach: Balancing accountabilities and sealing up results.* New York: IMF and the World Bank.

Amonoo-Neizer, E.H.,(1998). Universities in Africa – the need for adaptation, transformation, reformation and revitalization. *Higher Education Policy, 11,* 301–9.

Amponsah, P. (2003). The earthquake of 22nd June 1939 and its effect in Ghana. (Abstract) *Geophysical Research Abstracts,* vol. 5, 14097, 2003.

Ani, M. (1994). *Yurugu: An African-centered critique of European cultural thought and behaviour.* Trenton, NJ: Africa World Press.

Annan, K. (2007). Interview with Kofi Annan. *Globe and Mail,* Feb. 17, 2007, p. 18.

ANZASW. (2004). *Aotearoa New Zealand Association of Social Workers Code of Ethics.* http://anzasw.org.nz.

Apt, A.A., & Blavo, E.Q. (1997). Ghana. In N.S. Mayadas, T.D. Watts, & D. Elliott (Eds.), *International handbook on social work theory* (320–43). Westport, CT: Greenwood Press.

Aryeetey, E., & Peretz, D. (2005). *Monitoring donor and IFI support behind country-owned poverty reduction strategies in Ghana.* London: Commonwealth Secretariat.

Asadourian, K. (2000). *Beginning where the Soviet ends: A study of social work in Armenia.* West Hartford, CT: Seeroon Productions: University of Connecticut.

Asamoah, Y.W. (1995). Africa. In T.D. Watts, D. Elliott, & N.S. Mayadas (Eds.), *International handbook on social work education* (223–40). Westport, CT: Greenwood Press.

Asamoah, Y.W., & Nortey, D.N.A. (1987). Ghana. In J. Dixon (Ed.), *Social Welfare in Africa* (22-68). Beckenham: Croom Helm.

Asamoah, Y.W., & Beverly, C.C.. (1988). Collaboration between Western and African schools of social work: Problems and possibilities. *International Social Work, 31,* 177–93.

Ashby, E. (1964). *African universities and western tradition.* Cambridge, MA: Harvard University Press.

ASWEA. (1972). *The important role of supervision in social welfare organization,* Doc. 3. Addis Ababa: ASWEA.

ASWEA. (1973). *Case studies of social development in Africa,* vol. 1. Addis Ababa: ASWEA.

ASWEA. (1974a). *Case studies of social development in Africa,* vol. 2. Addis Ababa: ASWEA.

ASWEA. (1974b). *Curricula of schools of social work and community development training centres in Africa,* Doc. 7. Addis Ababa: ASWEA.

ASWEA. (1974c). *Relationship between social work education and national social development planning,* Doc. 6. Addis Ababa: ASWEA.

ASWEA. (1975a). *The directory of social welfare activities in Africa,* Doc. 8. Addis Ababa: ASWEA.

ASWEA. (1975b). *Techniques of teaching and methods of field work evaluation,* Doc. 9. Addis Ababa: ASWEA.

ASWEA. (1976a). *Realities and aspirations of social work education in Africa,* Doc. 11. Addis Ababa: ASWEA.

ASWEA. (1976b). *Techniques d'enseignement et methods d'évaluation de travaux pratiques,* Doc. 10. Addis Ababa: ASWEA.

ASWEA. (1977). *The role of social development education in Africa's struggle for political and economic independence,* Doc. 12. Addis Ababa: ASWEA.

ASWEA. (1978a). *AESA réunion du groupe d'expert sur l'élaboration d'un programme de formation en bien-être familial,* Doc. 14. Addis Ababa: ASWEA.

ASWEA. (1978b). *Guidelines for the development of a training curriculum in family welfare*, Doc. 13. Addis Ababa: ASWEA.

ASWEA. (1978c). *Guidelines for the development of a training curriculum in family welfare*, Doc. 15. Addis Ababa: ASWEA.

ASWEA. (1979). *Principes Directeurs pour l'établissement d'un programme d'étude destine à la formation aux disciplines de la protection de la famille*, Doc. 16. Addis Ababa: ASWEA.

ASWEA. (1981). *Social development training in Africa: Experiences of the 1970's and emerging trends of the 1980's*, Doc. 17. Addis Ababa: ASWEA.

ASWEA. (1982a). *Seminar on the organization and delivery of social services to rural areas in Africa*, Doc. 19. Addis Ababa: ASWEA.

ASWEA. (1982b). *Survey of curricula of social development training institutions in Africa*, 2nd ed., Doc. 18. Addis Ababa: ASWEA.

ASWEA. (1985). *Training for social development: Methods of intervention to improve people's participation in rural transformation in Africa with special emphasis on women*, Doc. 20. Addis Ababa: ASWEA.

ASWEA. (1986). *Association for Social Work Education in Africa*. Addis Ababa: ASWEA.

ASWEA. (1989). *Social development agents in rural transformation in Africa*, Doc. 21. Addis Ababa: ASWEA.

Austin, D. (1975). Et in Arcadia Ego: Politics and learning in Ghana. *Minerva, 13*, 2, 236–69.

Bamgbose, A. (1983). Education in indigenous languages: The West African model of language education. *Journal of Negro Education, 52*, 1, 57–64.

Bar-On, A. (2001). When assumptions on fieldwork education fail to hold: The experience of Botswana, *Social Work Education, 20*, 1, 123–36.

Baylis, F. (2003). Black as me: Narrative identity. *Developing World Bioethics, 3*, 2, 142–50.

Bernstein, A., & Gray, M. (1991). Introducing the South African student to the social work profession. *International Social Work, 34*, 3, July, 251–64.

Black, S. (2001). *Life and debt*. DVD documentary. New York: New Yorkers Films artwork.

Boahen, A. (1975). *Ghana: Evolution and change in the nineteenth and twentieth centuries*. London: Longman Group.

Boateng, N.A. (1982). *Western education and political leadership in Africa: The Ghana experience*. Paper presented at the 5th National conference on the third world, Omaha, Nebraska, October 27–30, 1982.

Bodor, R., Zuk, G., Feehan, R., Badry, D., Kreitzer, L., & Zapf, K. (2008). Stories about social work education in rural, northern, and First Nations communities in Alberta, Canada. The 33rd National Institute on Social Work and Human Services in Rural Areas, Boise, Idaho, U.S.A.

Bogo, M., & Herington, W. (1986). The universality of western social work's knowledge base in the international context: Myth or reality? *Social Development Issues, 10, 2*, 56–65.

Bradshaw, C., & Graham, J.R. (2007). Localisation of social work practice, education and research: A content analysis. *Social Development Issues, 29, 2*, 92–112.

Bridges, W. (1991). *Managing transitions: Making the most of change*. Toronto: Addison-Wesley.

Briskman, L. & Noble, C. (1999). Social work ethics: Embracing diversity? In B. Pease & J. Fook (Eds.), *Transforming social work practice: Postmodern critical perspectives* (57–69). New York: Routledge.

Bristol, N. (2008). NGO code of conduct hopes to stem internal brain drain. *Lancet, 371, 9631*, 28 June – July 4, 2008, p. 2162.

Brooks, R. (2008). Hey U.S. Welcome to the Third World. *Los Angeles Times*, September 2008, opinion.

Brown, P.T. (1971). Social work education in Zambia: An integrated approach. *International Social Work, 14, 1*, 42–47.

Burke, J. & Ngonyani,,B. (2004). A social work vision or Tanzania. *International Social Work, 47, 1*, 39–52.

Busia, K.A. (1951). *The position of the chief in the modern political system of Ashanti*. London: Oxford University Press.

Butler, S. (2008). Trade rather than aid. *Guardian Weekly*, June 27 – July 3, *179, 2*, p. 43.

Caffentzis, G. (2000). The World Bank and education in Africa. In S. Federici, G. Caffentzis, & O. Alidou (Eds.), *A thousand flowers: Social struggles against structural adjustments in African universities* (3–18). Trenton, NJ: Africa World Press.

Cham, S.B. (2008). The problem of African orphans and street children affected by HIV/AIDS. *International Social Work, 51, 3*, 410–15.

Chambers, R. (1997). *Whose reality counts? Putting the first last.* London: Intermediate Technology.

Chossudovsky, M. (1997). *The globalisation of poverty.* London: Zed Books.

Cohen, M.A., Kupcu, M.F., & Khanna, P. (2008). The new colonialist. *Foreign Policy, 167,* July/August, 74–79.

Congress of Berlin. (2006). *Congress of Berlin.* http://courses.wcupa.edu/jones/his312/lectures/ber-cong.htm.

Conrad, J. (1995). *Heart of darkness and other stories.* Hertfordshire: Wordsworth Classics.

Court, D. (1999). *Financing higher education in Africa: Makerere, the quiet revolution.* Washington, D.C.: World Bank.

Cox, D. (1995). Asia and the Pacific. In T.D. Watts, D. Elliott, & N.S. Mayadas (Eds.), *International handbook on social work education* (321–38). Westport, CT: Greenwood Press.

Dakubo, C. (2001). *Collective learning: Lessons from Ghana.* http://www.itto.or.jp/newsletter/v11n3/7.html.

Demmer, C., & Burghart, G. (2008). Experiences of AIDS-related bereavement in the USA and South Africa. *International Social Work, 51, 3*, 360–70.

Drake, S.C., & Omari, T.P. (1962). *Social work in Africa.* Accra: Department of Social Welfare and Community Development.

Driedger, O. (2004). *Collaboration across boundaries: A Ukraine/Canadian experience in social development.* Paper presented at the Canadian Association of Social Work Conference, Saskatoon, June, 2000.

Drower, S.J. (2000). Globalisation: An opportunity for dialogue between South African and Asian social work educators. *Indian Journal of Social Work, 60, 1*, 12–31.

Duodu, C. (2008). The last mercenary? *New African,* Aug./Sept., 10–15.

Durst, D. (1992). The road to poverty is paved with good intentions: Social interventions and indigenous peoples. *International Social Work, 35*, 191–202.

Dzobo, N.K. (1981). The indigenous African theory of knowledge and truth: Example of the Ewe and Akan of Ghana. *Phenomenology in Modern African Studies, 13, 1&2*, 85–102.

Earle, N. (2008). *Social work in social change: The profession and education of social workers in South Africa.* Cape Town: HSRC Press.

Ecumenical Coalition of Economic Justice (ECEJ). (1990). *Recolonization or liberation: The bonds of structural adjustment and struggles for emancipation.* Toronto: Ecumenical Coalition of Economic Justice.

Elliott, L. (2008a). Children and pensioners getting poorer. *Guardian Weekly,* June 20–26, *179, 1,* 17.

Elliott, L. (2008b). What a difference a year makes. *Guardian Weekly,* July 11–17, *179, 4,* p. 18.

Engelbrecht, L.K. (2006). Plumbing the brain drain of South African social workers migrating to the UK: Challenges for social service providers. *Social Work/Maatskaplike Werk, 42, 2,* 127–46.

Faiola, A. (2008). The seeds of change. *Guardian Weekly,* 20.06.08, 44.

Fals Borda, O. (1988). *Knowledge and people's power: Lessons with peasants in Nicaragua, Mexico and Colombia.* New Delhi: Indian Social Institute.

Fals Borda, O. (2001). Participatory (Action) Research in social theory: Origins and challenges. In P. Reason & H. Bradbury (Eds.), *Handbook of action research* (27–37). Thousand Oaks, CA: Sage.

FAO. (2001). Farmers implementing IPM in Ghana. Retrieved August 1, 2004. http://www.fao.org/ag/agp/agpp/IPM/Farmers.htm.

Federici, S. (2000). The recolonization of African education. In S. Federici, G. Caffentzis, & O. Alidou (Eds.), *A thousand flowers: Social struggles against structural adjustments in African universities* (19–24). Trenton, NJ: Africa World Press.

Fook, J. (2002). *Social work: Critical theory and practice.* London: Sage.

Foucault, M. (1980). Two lectures. In C. Gordon (Ed.), *Power/Knowledge: Selected interviews and other writings 1972–1977* (78–108). Brighton: Harvester Press.

Freire, P. (1997). *Pedagogy of the oppressed,* 20th ed. New York: Continuum.

Fuller's Dymaxion map. (n.d.) *Fuller's Dymaxion World Map.* http://www.bfi.org.

GASOW. (1972). *Social welfare, education and practice in developing countries.* Accra: Ghana Association of Social Workers.

GASOW. (1973). *Social planning in national development.* Accra: Ghana Association of Social Workers.

GASOW. (1974). *The role of agriculture and rural technology in national development.* Accra: Ghana Association of Social Workers.

GASOW. (1975). *Popular participation and the new local government system.* Accra: Ghana Association of Social Workers.

Gaventa, J., & Cornwall, A. (2001). Power and knowledge. In P. Reason & H. Bradbury (Eds.), *Handbook of action research: Participative inquiry and practice* (70–80). Thousand Oaks, CA: Sage.

Government of Ghana. (1992). Ghanaian constitution. http://www.parliament.gh/constitution_republic_ghana.html.

Graham, M.J. (1999). The African-centred worldview: Developing a paradigm for social work. *British Journal of Social Work 29,* 151–267.

Gray, M. (1995). The ethical implications of current theoretical developments in social work. *British Journal of Social Work, 25,* 1, 55–70.

Gray, M. (1998). Approaches to social work in South Africa: An overview. In M. Gray (Ed.), *Developmental social work in South Africa* (7–24). Cape Town: David Philip.

Gray, M. (2005). Dilemmas of international social work: Paradoxical processes in indigenisation, universalism and imperialism, *International Journal of Social Welfare, 14,* 3, 231–38.

Gray, M., & Coates, J. (2008). From 'Indigenization' to cultural relevance. In M. Gray, J. Coates, & M. Yellowbird (Eds.), *Indigenous social work around the world* (13–30). Burlington: Ashgate.

Gray, M., Coates, J., & Yellow Bird, M. (2008). *Indigenous social work around the world.* Burlington: Ashgate.

Gray, M., & Mazibuko, F. (2002). Social work in South Africa at the dawn of the new millennium. *International Journal of Social Welfare, 11,* 191–200.

Gray, M., & Simpson, B. (1998). Developmental social work education: A field example. *International Social Work, 41,* 2, 227–37.

Gulati, P. (1974). Social work roles in traditional societies. *International Social Work, 17,* 3, 50–54.

Gyekye, K. (1996). *African cultural values: An introduction.* Accra: Sankofa.

Hancock, G. (1997). *Lords of poverty.* London: Arrow Books.

Haug, E. (2005). Critical reflections on the emerging discourse of international social work. *International Social Work, 48,* 2, 126–35.

Healy, K. (2001). Participatory action research and social work: A critical appraisal. *International Social Work, 44, 1,* 93–105.

Healy, L.M. (2001). *International social work: Professional action in an interdependent world.* Oxford: Oxford University Press.

Hegel, G.W.F. (1956). *The philosophy of history* (J. Sibree, Trans.). New York: Dover.

Herbst, J. (1993). *The politics of reform in Ghana, 1982–1991.* Berkeley: University of California Press.

Heron, B. (2005). Changes and challenges: Preparing social work students for practicums in today's Sub-Saharan African context, *International Social Work, 48, 6,* 782–93.

Heron, B. (2007). *Desire for development.* Waterloo: Wilfrid Laurier University Press.

Hill House Newsletter. (2004). *Tribute by Christian Council of Ghana.* Accra: Hill House Quaker Meeting, No. 1.

Hochschild, A. (1998). *King Leopold's ghost.* Boston: Houghton Mifflin.

Hodge, D.R. (2006). Spiritually modified cognitive therapy: A review of the literature. *Social work, 51, 2,* 157–66.

Holscher, D., & Berhane, S.Y. (2008). Reflections on human rights and professional solidarity. *International Social Work, 51, 3,* 311–23.

Hutchful, E. (1997). *The institutional and political framework of macro-economic management in Ghana.* Geneva: United Nations Research Institute for Social Development.

Ibekwe, P. (1998). *Wit and wisdom of Africa: Proverbs from Africa and the Caribbean.* Oxford: New International Publications.

Ife, J. (2007). *The new international agendas: What role for social work?* Inaugural Hokenstad international social work lecture, San Francisco, October.

IFSW/IASSW. (2008). Ethics in social work: Statement of principles. *International Social Work, Supplement,* 7–11.

IMF. (2010). Debt relief under the heavily indebted poor countries (HIPC) initiative fact sheet. http://www.imf.org.

Jacques, G. (1993). Social work practice in Botswana: Principles and relevance. *Journal of Social Development in Africa, 8, 1,* 31–49.

Jeong, J.W. (1996). Ghana: Lurching toward economic rationality. *World Affairs, 159, 2,* fall, 64–71.

Kabeera, B., & Sewpaul, V. (2008). Genocide and its aftermath. *International Social Work, 51, 3*, 324–36.

Kaseke, E. (2001). Social work education in Zimbabwe: Strengths and weaknesses, issues and challenges, *Social Work Education, 20, 1*, 101–9.

Keeley, G., & Hooper, J. (2008). Flood of African migrants risking perilous journey at new heights. *Guardian Weekly*, July 18–24, *179, 5*, 3.

Kendall, K.A. (1995). Foreword. In Watts T.D., Elliott, D., & Mayadas, N.S. *International handbook on social work education*. Westport, CT: Greenwood Press.

Kenny, C., & Sumner, A. (2011). Escaping the poverty trap. *Guardian Weekly, 185, 8*, 44.

King, R., & Oppong A. (2001). *Ghana: Influencing policy: Urban market women and the Kumasi central market*. Kumasi: Centre for the Development of the People.

Konadu-Agyemang, K. (2001). Structural adjustment programs and housing affordability in Ghana. *The Canadian Geographer*, winter, *45, 14*, 528–45.

Kreitzer, L. (1998). *The experiences of refugee women in the planning and implementation of programmes at Buduburam Refugee Camp, Ghana*. Master's thesis, University of Calgary.

Kreitzer, L. (2004a). *Indigenization of social work education and practice: A participatory action research project in Ghana*. PhD thesis, University of Calgary.

Kreitzer, L. (2004b). Queen Mother and social workers: A potential collaboration between traditional authority and social work in Ghana. *Chieftain, 1.* http://dspace.ucalgary.ca/handle/1880/42980.

Kreitzer, L. (2006). Social work values and ethics issues of Universality. *Currents Journal, 5*, 1–14.

Kreitzer, L., & Wilson, M. (2010). Shifting perspective on international alliances in social work: Lessons from Ghana and Nicaragua, *International social work, 53, 5*, 701–19.

Kreitzer, L, Abukari, Z., Antonio, P., Mensah, J., & Kwaku, A. (2009). Social work in Ghana: A participatory action research project looking at culturally appropriate training and practice. *Social Work Education, 28, 2*, 145–64.

Kuykendall, R. (1993). Hegel and Africa: An evaluation of the treatment of Africa in the Philosophy of History. *Journal of Black Studies, 23, 4*, June, 571–81.

Laenui, P. (2000). Processes of decolonization. In M. Battiste (Ed.), *Reclaiming indigenous voice and vision* (150–60). Vancouver: UBC Press.

Laird, S. (2003). Evaluating social work outcomes in Sub-Saharan Africa. *Qualitative Social Work*, *2*, *3*, 251–70.

Lauer, H. (2004). *The contribution of women's traditional leadership to enlightened governance and national development in Ghana.* Paper presented at the International Conference on Chieftaincy in Africa: Culture, Governance and Development, Accra, Ghana, January, 2004.

Lebakeng, T.J. (1997). *Africanisation and higher education.* Sapem, July 15–Aug. 15, pp. 4–7.

Lechner, F.J., & Boli, J. (2000). Introduction. In F.J. Lechner & J. Boli (Eds.), *The globalization reader* (1–4). Oxford: Blackwell.

Levinsohn, J. (2003). *The world bank's poverty reduction strategy paper approach: Good marketing or good policy? G-24 discussion paper series.* New York: United Nations.

Lewis, S. (2005). *Race against time.* Toronto: Anansi.

Little Bear, L. (2000). Jagged worldviews collided. In M. Battiste (Ed.), *Reclaiming indigenous voice and vision* (77–85). Vancouver: UBC Press.

Lombard, A. (1999). Transforming social work education in South Africa: A contextual and empowerment issue. *Social Work/Maatskaplike Werk*, *36*, *1*, 97–112.

Maathai, W. (2009). *The challenge for Africa.* New York: Pantheon.

Mafile'O. (2004). Exploring Tongan Social Work: Fekau'aki (Connecting) and Fakatokilalo (Humility). *Qualitative Social Work*, *3*, *3*, 239–57.

Mamdani, M. (2001). *When victims become killers.* Princeton, NJ: Princeton University Press.

Mammo, T. (1999). *The paradox of Africa's poverty.* Lawrenceville, NJ: Red Sea Press.

Manji, F., & O'Coill, C. (2005). NGO's: A tainted history. *New African*, Aug./Sept., *443*, 16–20.

Maravanyika, O.E. (1990). *Implementing educational policies in Zimbabwe.* Washington, D.C.: The international Bank for Reconstruction and Development/World Bank.

Marley, B. (n.d.). *Redemption Song.* http://www.metrolyrics.com.

Martin, P. (2000). The moral case for globalization. In F.J. Lechner & J. Boli (Eds.), *The globalization reader* (12–13). Oxford: Blackwell.

Matanga, F.K. (2010). NGO's and the politics of development in Africa. *Development, 53, 1,* 114–19.

Mayo, P. (1999). *Gramsci, Freire & adult education: Possibilities for transformative action.* London: Zed Books.

Mazibuko, F. & Gray, M. (2004). Social work professional associations in South Africa. *International Social work, 47, 1,* 129–42.

McKenzie, B., & Morrissette, V. (2003). Social work practice with Canadians of Aboriginal background: Guidelines for respectful social work. In A. Al-Krenawi & J.R. Graham (Eds.), *Multicultural social work in Canada: Working with diverse ethno-racial communities.* Oxford: Oxford University Press.

Memmi, A. (1965). *The colonizer and the colonized.* Boston: Beacon Press.

Mercator Map. (2001). *Mercator Map.* http://en.wikipedia.org/wiki/Mercator_projection.

Meredith, M. (2006). *The state of Africa: A history of fifty years of independence.* Toronto: Free Press.

Midgley, J. (1981). *Professional imperialism: Social work in the Third World.* London: Heinemann.

Midgley, J. (1995). *Social development: The development perspective in social welfare.* London: Sage.

Midgley, J. (2000). Globalization, capitalism and social welfare. In B. Rowe (Ed.), *Social work and globalization* (13–28). Ottawa: Canadian Association of Social Workers.

Midgley, J. (2001). Issues in international social work: Resolving critical debates in the profession. *Journal of Social Work, 1,* 21–35.

Midgley, J. (2008). Promoting reciprocal international social work exchanges: Professional imperialism revisited. In M. Gray, J. Coates, & M. Yellow Bird (Eds.), *Indigenous social work around the world: Towards culturally relevant education and practice* (31–45). Burlington, VT: Ashgate.

Milne, S. (2008). Kiwis are in the tune with the times. *Guardian Weekly,* July 11–17, *179, 4,* 21.

Ministry of Education, Ghana. (2000). *Girl's education.* Retrieved May 19, 2004. http://www.ghana.edu.gh/present/girlsEducation.html.

Mmatli, T. (2008). Political activism as a social work strategy in Africa. *International Social Work, 51, 3,* 297–310.

Morrow, R.A., & Torres, C.A. (2001). *Reading Freire and Habermas: Critical pedagogy and transformative social change.* New York and London: Teachers College Press.

Mosha, R.S. (2000). *The heartbeat of indigenous Africa: A study of the Chagga educational system.* New York: Garland.

Mouelhi M., & Ruckert, A. (2007). Ownership and participation: The limitations of the poverty reduction strategy paper approach. *Canadian Journal of Development Studies, 28, 2,* 277–92.

Moyo, D. (2009). *Dead Aid: Why aid is not working and how there is a better way for Africa.* New York: Ferrar, Straus & Giroux.

Mullaly, R.P. (1993). *Structural social work.* Toronto: McClelland & Stewart.

Mupedziswa, R. (1996). The challenge of economic development in an African developing country: Social work in Zimbabwe. *International Social Work, 39,* 41–54.

Mwansa, L.K.J. (2010). Challenges facing social work education in Africa. *International Social Work, 53, 1,* 129–36.

Nagpaul, H. (1993). Analysis of social work teaching material in India: The need for indigenous foundations. *International Social Work, 36,* 207–20.

Ndura, E. (2006). Western education and African cultural identity in the Great Lakes Region of Africa: A case of failed globalization. *Peace & Change, 31, 1,* January, 90–101.

New Zealand map. (n.d.). *New Zealand no longer down under world map.* Christchurch: Hallifax Tourist Products.

Nimmagadda, J., & Cowger, C.D. (1999). Cross-cultural practice: Social worker ingenuity in the indigenization of practice knowledge. *International Social Work, 43, 3,* 261–76.

Ninsin, K.A. (1991). The PNDC and the problem of legitimacy. In D. Rothchild (Ed.), *Ghana: The political economy of recovery* (49–68). Boulder, CO: Lynne Rienner.

Noyoo, N. (2000). Preparing South African social workers for social development praxis. *Social Development Issues, 22,1,* 35–41.

Nukunya, G.K. (1992). *Tradition and change in Ghana: An introduction to sociology.* Accra: Ghana Universities Press.

Obeng, E.E. (1988). *Ancient Ashanti chieftaincy*. Tema: Ghana Publishing Corporation.

Onyanyo, M. (2005). NGOs pseudo governments or surrogates of western powers? *New African, 443*, 20–21.

Osei-Hwedie, K. (1990). Social work and the question of social development in Africa. *Journal of Social Development in Africa, 5, 2*, 87–99.

Osei-Hwedie, K. (1993). The challenge of social work in Africa: Starting the indigenization process. *Journal of Social Development in Africa, 8, 1*, 19–30.

Osei-Hwedie, K., & Jacques, G. (2007). *Indigenising social work in Africa*. Accra: Ghana Universities Press.

Osei-Hwedie, K., & Rankopo, M.J. (2008). Developing culturally relevant social work education in Africa: The case of Botswana. In M. Gray, J. Coates, & M. Yellow Bird (Eds.), *Indigenous social work around the world: Towards culturally relevant education and practice* (203–18) Burlington: Ashgate.

Owens, M., & Owens, D. (1984). *Cry of the Kalahari*. London: Fontana.

Pakenham, T. (1991). *The scramble for Africa*. New York: Perennial.

Palitza, K. (2011). Tobacco industry's smoking gun. *Guardian Weekly*, October 21–27, 185, 19, p. 45.

Palmer, K. (2010). *Spellbound: Inside West Africa's witch camps*. Toronto: Free Press.

Parton, N, & O'Byrne, P. (2000). *Constructive social work: Towards a new practice*. Basingstoke, UK: Macmillan.

Patel, L. (2005). *Social welfare and social development*. Cape Town: Oxford University Press.

Payne, M. (2005). *Modern social work theory*, 3rd ed. Chicago: Lyceum.

Pearn, J. (2003). Children and war. *Journal of Paediatrics and Child Health, 39, 3*, 166–72.

Peters World Map. (n.d.). *Map of the World: Peters Projection*. New York: Friendship Press. http://www.petersmap.com.

Prigoff, A. (2000). *Economic for social workers: Social outcomes of economic globalization with strategies for community action*. Belmont: Brooks/ColeThomson Learning.

Purvis, A. (2008). Uganda's black gold. *Guardian Weekly*, July 18–24, *179, 5*, 25–27.

Ramsay, R.F. (1999). Toward a common paradigmatic home: Social work in the twenty-first century. *Indian Journal of Social Work, 60, 1*, 69–86.

Rattray, Capt. R.S. (1929). *Ashanti law and constitution*. Oxford: Clarendon Press.

Ray, C. (2008). The dangers of 'brand aid.' *New African*, February, 18–19.

Ray, D.I. (1986). *Ghana: Politics, economics and society*. Boulder, CO: Lynne Rienner.

Reason, P. (1994). Three approaches to participative inquiry. In N.K. Denzin & Y.S. Lincoln (Eds.), *Handbook of qualitative research* (324–39). Thousand Oaks, CA: Sage.

Reason, P., & Bradbury, H. (2001). Introduction: Inquiry and participation in search of a world worthy of human aspiration. In P. Reason & H. Bradbury (Eds.), *Handbook of action research* (1–14). Thousands Oaks, CA: Sage.

Richmond, M. (1965). *Social Diagnosis*. Toronto: Collier-Macmillan.

Rimmer, D. (1992). *Staying poor: Ghana's political economy, 1950–1990*. Oxford: Pergamon Press.

Rist, G. (2008). *The history of development*, 3rd ed. London: Zed Books.

Roberts, G. (1984). *Questioning development*, 2nd ed. London: Alver Press.

Robertson, R. (2003). *The three waves of globalization: A history of a developing global consciousness*. Winnipeg: Fernwood.

Rodenborg, N. (1986). A Western-style counseling office in Somalia: A case study of cultural conflicts in social work. *International Social Work, 29*, 43–55.

Roff, S. (2004). Nongovernmental organizations: The strengths perspective at work. *International Social Work, 47*, 2, 202–12.

Ross, E. (2008). The intersection of cultural practices and ethics in a rights-based society. *International Social Work, 51*, 3, 384–95.

Sackey, V. (2001). *Democracy in Ghana*. Speech given by the former policy advisor for President J.J. Rawlings. University of Calgary, September 19, 2001.

Sachs, J. (2005). *The end of poverty: How we can make it happen in our lifetime*. London: Penguin.

Said, E. (1991). Identity, authority and freedom: The potentate and the traveler. *Transitions, 54*, 4–18.

Sainsbury, E. (1970). *Social diagnosis in casework*. London: Routledge & K. Paul.

Sankore, R. (2005). What are NGO's doing? *New African*, Aug./Sept., *443*, 12–15.

Sarpong, P. (1971). *The sacred stools of the Akan*. Accra: Ghana Publishing.

Sartre, J.P. (2001). *Colonialism and neo-colonialism* (1964). London: Routledge.

Sautoy, P. (1958). *Community development in Ghana.* London: Oxford University Press.

Schneider-Barthold, W. (1997). *Promotion of the informal sector for development in Africa: Analysis of the participatory and process-oriented approach applied by ECA.* Addis Ababa: UN Economic Commission for Africa.

Scholte, J.A. (2000). *Globalization: A critical introduction.* New York: St. Martin's Press.

Sefa Dei, G.J. (2005). Social difference and the politics of schooling in Africa: A Ghanaian case study. *Compare, 35, 3,* 227–45.

Semali, L., & Kincheloe, J. (2000). Series editors' Foreword. In R. S. Mosha, *The heartbeat of indigenous Africa* (ix–xvi). New York: Garland.

Sewpaul, V. (2006). The global-local dialectic: Challenges for African Scholarship and social work in a post-colonial world. *British Journal of Social Work, 36,* 419–34.

Sewpaul, V., & Lombard, A. (2004). Social work education, training and standards in Africa. *Social Work Education, 23, 5,* 537–54.

Shawky, A. (1972). Social work education in Africa. *International Social Work, 15, 3,* 3–16.

Simpson, E.S. (1994). *The developing world: An introduction* (2nd ed.). Harlow, UK: Longman Scientific and Technical.

Smith, L. (2008). South African social work education: Critical imperatives for social change in the post-apartheid and post-colonial context. *International Social Work, 51, 3,* 371–83.

Smith, L.T. (1999). *Decolonizing methodologies: Research and indigenous peoples.* London: Zed Books.

So, A.Y. (1990). *Social change and development: Modernization, dependency and world-system theories.* London: Sage.

Straub, E., Pearlman, L.A., & Miller, V. (2003). Healing the roots of genocide in Rwanda. *Peace Review, 15, 3,* 287–94.

Stewart, H. (2008). World trade talks collapse. *Guardian Weekly,* August 8–14, *179, 8,* p. 46.

Sultany, T., Lavie, Y., & Haimov, I. (2008). Correlation between ethnicity and filial responsibility among three ethnic groups in Israel. *International Social Work, 51, 3,* 396–409.

Sutherland-Addy, E. (2003). (Interview from transcript dated June 14, 2004, Accra Ghana). Unpublished raw data.

Tandon, R. (1981). Participatory research in the empowerment of people. *Convergence, 14, 3*, 20–28.

Tandon, Y. (1996). Reclaiming Africa's agenda: Good governance and the role of the NGOs in the African context. *Australian Journal of International Affairs, 50, 3*, 293–303.

Taylor, Z. (2000). Values, theories and methods of social work education: A culturally transferable core? *International Social Work, 42, 3*, 309–18.

Tete, R. (2007). Africans are too afraid to be free. *New African*, April, *461*, 44–46.

Tettey, W.J., & Puplampu, K.P. (2000). Social science research and the Africanist: The need for intellectual and attitudinal reconfiguration. *African Studies Review, 43, 3*, December, 81–102.

TISS Social Work Educator's Forum. (1997). Declaration of ethics for professional social workers. *Indian Journal of Social Work, 58, 2*, 335–42.

Torczyner, M.R. (2000). Globalization, inequality and peace building: What social work can do. In M.W. Duthie, K. Swift, & F. Turner (Eds.), *Social work and globalization, Special Issues* (123–46). Ottawa: Canadian Association of social workers.

Tsang, A.K.T., Yan, M.C. & Shera, W. (2000). Negotiating multiple agendas in international social work: The case of the China-Canada collaborative project. In M.W. Duthie, K. Swift, & F. Turner (Eds.), *Social work and globalization, Special Issues* (147–61). Ottawa: Canadian Association of social workers.

UNDP. (2007). *Human Development Report 2007/2008*. New York: UNDP.

UNDP. (2010). *Human development report*. New York: UNDP.

UNESCO. (1982). *Mexico City declaration on cultural policies*. World Conference on Cultural Policies, Mexico City, 26 July – 6 August. http://www.wwcd. org.

UNHCR. (2010). *UNHCR statistical yearbook, 2009*. Geneva: United Nations.

United Nations. (1950). *Training for social work: An international survey*. Lake Success: United Nations Department of Social Affairs.

United Nations. (1955). *Training for social work: Second international survey*. New York: United Nations Bureau of Social Affairs.

United Nations. (1958). *Training for social work: Third international survey.* New York: United Nations Department of Economic and Social Affairs.

United Nations. (1964a). *Training for social work: Fourth international survey.* New York: United Nations.

United Nations. (1964b). Patterns of social welfare organization and administration in Africa. *Social welfare services in Africa, No. 2, December.* New York: United Nations Social Development Section of the Economic Commission for Africa.

United Nations. (1964c). *Training for social work in Africa, No. 3.* New York: United Nations Social Development Section of the Economic Commission for Africa.

United Nations. (1965). *Social construction in the newly-independent countries of East Africa, No. 4.* New York: United Nations Social Development Section of the Economic Commission for Africa.

United Nations. (1966). Family, child and youth welfare services in Africa. *Social welfare services in Africa, No. 5, December.* New York: United Nations Social Development Section of the Economic Commission for Africa.

United Nations. (1967a). *Directory of regional social welfare activities.* New York: United Nations Social Development Section of the Economic Commission for Africa.

United Nations. (1967b). The status and role of women in East Africa. *Social welfare services in Africa, No. 6, June.* New York: United Nations Social Development Section of the Economic Commission for Africa.

United Nations. (1969). Youth employment and national development in Africa. *Social welfare services in Africa, No. 7, November.* New York: United Nations Social Development Section of the Economic Commission for Africa.

United Nations. (1971a). *Training for social welfare: Fifth international survey.* New York: United Nations.

United Nations. (1971b). Integrated approach to rural development in Africa. *Social welfare services in Africa, No. 8, July.* New York: United Nations Social Development Section of the Economic Commission for Africa.

United Nations. (2010). *United Nations Millennium Goals.* http://www.un.org/millenniumgoals/.

United Nations General Assembly. (2000). *General assembly resolution, MDG's.* http://www.un.org/millennium/declaration/ares552e.htm.

United Nations Millennium Development Goals (UNMDG) (2011). *United Nations Millennium Development Goals report*. New York: United Nations.

Vanbalkam, W.D., & Goddard, T. (2007). Sustainable and dynamic development. In G. Anderson & A. Wenderoth (Eds.), *Facilitating change: Reflections on six years of education development programming in challenging environments* (253–67). Montreal: Universalia Management Group.

van Hook, M.P. (1994). Educational challenges in Southern Africa: Implications for social work. *International Social Work, 37, 4*, 319–31.

van Wyk, B., & Higgs, P. (2007). The call for an African university: A critical reflection. *Higher Education Policy, 20*, 61–71.

Venkataraman, J. (1996). *Indigenization process of alcoholism treatment from the American to the Indian context*. Unpublished doctoral thesis, University of Illinois, Urbana-Champaign.

Venter, E. (2004). The notion of ubuntu and communalism in African educational discourse. *Studies in Philosophy and Education, 23*, 149–60.

Wallace, T. (2004). NGO Dilemmas: Trojan horses for global neoliberalism? *Socialist register, 40*, 201–19.

Walton, R.G., & Abo El Nasr, M.M. (1988). Indigenization and authentization in terms of social work in Egypt. *International Social Work, 31*, 135–44.

Walsh, C. (2010). Development as *Buen Vivir*: Institutional arrangements and (de)colonial entanglements. *Development, 53, 1*, 15–21.

Waters, M. (2001). *Globalization*, 2nd ed. London: Routledge.

Weenie, A. (2000). Post-colonial recovering and healing. In J. Reyhner, J. Martin, L. Lockard, & W.S. Gilbert (Eds.), *Learn in beauty: Indigenous education for a new century* (65–70). Flagstaff: Northern Arizona University.

What's Up? South! (2002). *What's Up? South! World Map*. http://www.seeingmaps.com. Amherst: ODT.

Wicker, E.R. (1958). Colonial development and welfare, 1929–1957: The evolution of a policy. *Social and Development Studies, 7, 4*, 170–92.

Willinsky, J. (1998). *Learning to divide the world: Education at Empire's end*. Minneapolis: University of Minnesota Press.

Williams, C. (1987). *The destruction of black civilization: Great issues of a race from 4500 B.C. to 2000 A.D*. Chicago: Third World Press.

Williams, L., & Sewpaul, V. (2004). Modernism, postmodernism and global standards setting. *Social Work Education, 23, 5*, October, 555–65.

Wilson, M.G. (1992). *What difference could a revolution make? Group work in the new Nicaragua.* Group work reaching out: People, places and power. Binghamton, NY: Haworth Press.

Wilson, M.G., & Whitmore, E. (2000). *Seeds of fire: Social development in an era of globalism.* Winnipeg: Fernwood.

Wintour, P., & Elliott, L. (2008). G8 sets goal of 50% cut in greenhouse gases. *Guardian Weekly,* July 11–17, 1–2.

World Bank. (2005). World development report. Washington, D.C.: World Bank.

World Bank. (2006). World development report. Washington, D.C.: World Bank.

World Bank. (2007). World development report. Washington, D.C.: World Bank.

World Bank. (2009a). *Accelerating catch-up: Tertiary education for growth in Sub-Saharan Africa.* Washington, D.C.: International Bank for Reconstruction and Development.

World Bank. (2009b). World development report. Washington, D.C.: World Bank.

World Bank. (2010). World development report. Washington, D.C.: World Bank.

World Hunger. (2011). World hunger education service. http://www.worldhunger.org/africa.htm.

Worldwatch. (2003). Rich-poor gap widening. Retrieved May 22, 2004. http://www.worldwatch.org/topics/vsow/2003/11/12.

Yimam, A. (1990). *Social development in Africa 1950–1985.* Aldershot: Avebury.

Yunus, M. (2007). *Creating a world without poverty: Social business and the future of capitalism.* New York: Public Affairs.

Zaman, M. (2002). Are we getting lost in exclusive anti-poor, adjustment lending policy cycles? http://www.esrftz.org/ppa/documents/aa_1.pdf.

Notes

Introduction: Situating the Context

1 I use 'western'/'non-western' terminology in this book. 'Western' means countries who have industrialized and who have taken on the values and beliefs of European society and are considered 'developed' in modernization terminology. This includes Europe, North America, Australia, and New Zealand. 'Non-western' countries are those who may or may not have industrialized but have kept much of their own values and beliefs and tend to be societies that are collective in nature. These countries are referred to as 'underdeveloped' in modernization terms. No terminology is perfect and I felt this was the best terminology to use.

2 The stool, in Ghanaian society, is carved from native hardwood and is used to denote the office of the chief or the king. Usually an important symbol is carved between the upper and lower sections of the stool. The symbol shows the degree of skill of the carver and the status of the owner (Sarpong, 1971).

3 Neo-liberal policies are defined as a set of economic policies that are dominating the world today. The assumption is that successful economic development can be obtained, and any country in the world can make it to the top of the economic ladder. The market is central in governing economic, social, and political life (Wilson & Whitmore, 2000). Multinational corporations influence social and economic policy and assume that they govern societies instead of societies governing them (Wilson & Whitmore, 2000).

4 The term 'umbilical cord' implies a dependent attachment to something for survival. A child is attached to the mother in the womb in order to stay alive. This metaphor challenges African social work to come out of the womb, detach itself from its mother, or western social work education and practice, and start to live and breathe on its own, growing and developing into its own unique structure.

5 When I use the term 'research group' in the body of the book, I am referring to the Ghanaian research group that was involved in my PhD research project.

I. Historical Context

1 Structural adjustment programs were implemented in many countries in Africa to reduce foreign debt. The programs include cutting government spending, increasing export, trade liberalization, devaluing currency, privatization, removing price controls and state subsidies, and balancing the budget. These programs were enforced with penalties if not adhered to by the country. Education, health, and social welfare were particularly affected by these programs.

2 The meaning of periphery in this context refers to the profession of social work as being outside the core of

society. Society has not embraced the profession and made it one of its core professions.

II. Cultural Identity

1 Chancellor Williams, an African American, wrote the book *The destruction of Black civilization*, looking at the issues around the black race from 4500 B.C. to A.D. 2000. The book is a summary of sixteen years of research in which he did field studies all over Africa. He set out to answer the following questions: 1) How did all-black Egypt become all-white Egypt?; 2) What were some of the specific details in the process that so completely blotted out the achievements of the African race from the annals of history; 3) How and under what circumstances did Africans, among the very first people to invent writing, lose this art almost completely; 4) Is there a single African race, one African people?; 5) If we are one race or one people, how do you explain the numerous languages, cultural varieties, and tribal groupings: 6) Since, as it seemed to me there is far more disunity, self-hatred, and mutual antagonisms among Blacks than any other people, is there a historical explanation for this; and 7) How, in puzzling contrast, is the undying love of blacks for their European and Asian conquerors and enslavers explained? I found the book to be quite passionate, forceful, and angry. Some of his writing seems harsh, but I felt it was important to include it as an important work concerning the history of black civilization.

III. Hegemony of Western Knowledge

1 The term 'hegemony' comes from Gramsci's understanding of cultural hegemony in which one social class or group dominates another and the dominated are oppressed.

2 Engelbrecht (2006) defines this term as "a migration or emigration of professionally trained individuals or knowledge workers … they leave for other nations, because of unfavourable conditions where they are living. It is a human capital flight, a term which refers to financial capital that is no longer invested in the country where its owner lives" (p. 129).

3 *Sarvodaya* (everybody's welfare), *Swarajya* and *Lokniti* are Indian terms that reflect Ghandian principles.

4 Ghandian principles are: 1) complete unity and integrity of body, mind, and soul in the individual human being; 2) all social action should be governed by selflessness, non-attachment, nonviolence, and active service; 3) no society, state, or any other institution has any worth or importance apart from its part in contributing to the growth of the individuals of which it is composed; 4) the means are at least as important as, and often even more important than, ends; 5) Faith in God is the foundation of all moral values.

5 *Aotearoa* is the Maori name for New Zealand and when a New Zealander is asked where they come from, often they will say Aotearoa New Zealand to give respect to the indigenous peoples of New Zealand.

IV. Neo-Liberal Policies

1   The IFIs are divided into three categories: 1) Bretton Woods institutions; 2) regional development banks; and 3) financial institutions of the European Union. In the African situation, the Bretton Woods institutions, made up of the International Monetary Fund, the World Bank Group, and the World Trade Organization (formerly GATT), are the important institutions for the African context.

2   'Structural adjustment programs' were part of the IFIs' economic plan for economic growth. When countries could not pay their debts, these programs were implemented so governments could pay back their debt. This did not work for African nations who were in debt from the time of independence. Their debts continued to rise despite the programs. What is important to social work is that some of the first programs affected by government cutbacks were in health, education, and social welfare.

3   Since 1996 two other reforms have occurred in this program. In 1999 a review of the initiative strengthened the links between debt relief, poverty reduction, and social policies. In 2005, a supplemental program, Multilateral Debt Relief Initiative (MDRI), to the HIPC initiative was introduced to allow for a hundred per cent relief on eligible debts by the IMF, World Bank, and the African Development Fund for countries who completed the HIPC process.

4   The G8 is the group of the most powerful countries in the world. These countries are France, Germany, Japan, Italy, the United Kingdom, the United States, Russia, and Canada. The European Union has a representative as well. Due to the imbalance between the westernized world and the so-called developing world, France and the United Kingdom have expressed interest in adding five more countries: Brazil, China, India, Mexico, and South Africa.

5   THEMBA means hope in the Zulu language.

VI. Creating Culturally Relevant Education and Practice

1   A term used by the Brazilian educationalist, Paulo Freire. It refers to "learning to perceive social, political and economic contradictions, and to take action against the oppressive elements of reality" (Freire, 2007, p. 35).

2   At this point I want to say that in 1999 a group of stakeholders came together to look at revising the BSW curriculum and to create a MSW curriculum. The research group took these into consideration and were pleased with what had been revised. However, the lack of lecturers has meant that some of these courses have not been taught, and this again emphasizes the relationships between the economic policies of Ghana and their effect on education.

VII. The Future of Social Work in Africa

1   I want to recognize the important work that Wangari Maathai did for Africa and her fight to preserve the environment. Her 2011 death is a major loss to Africa.

Index

A

Department of Social Work (University of
    Ghana), 145, 175
  lack of resources, 135
dependency, xxviii, 112, 114, 117, 126, 133
dependency on western social work education
    and practice, 40
dependency theory, 111–12
desegregation, 17
deterritorialization, 115
'developed,' 109
developing nations, 15
  agricultural sectors, 97
  demanding to be part of decisions made
      by IFIs and G8, 97
  imbalance between West and, 117
  lending options, 97
development, xx, 8, 16, 62, 92, 107–28. *See
    also* aid; social development
  community (*See* community development)
  donor-controlled, 118
  empowering local people to use their own
      resources, 119
  enriching further an already privileged
      minority, 122
  inclusive and equitable, 116
  meeting needs of donors, 119
  political agenda, 111
  qualitative dimension, 118
  social dimension, 122
  social policy and, 16
  social work and, 116–20
  unintended consequences, 14
  western development organizations,
      49–50
'development' (term), 110
development agencies, 114
Development and Social Issues I and II
    (courses), 164
development era, 109
development projects
  administered by overseas organizations,
      108
  beneficiaries, 117–18
  bureaucracy, 114
  failure to listen to local people, 109
  promoting dependency, 114
  western 'experts' and, 114

development theories in the context of Africa
    (course), 163
development theory, xv, 111, 164
  criticism, 111–12
development theory and practice (course), 155
development through modernization, 109–13
Directory of social welfare activities in Africa
    (UN monograph), 15–16, 23
disability, 116, 145, 161
disabled persons, 36
displaced persons, 26, 162. *See also* refugees
domestic violence, 145
Drake, S.C., 19, 70
drama, 157
dreamers and dreaming, 8, 60, 136
dynamic development, 127
Dzobo, xviii

E

East Africa case studies project, 22
Eastern and Southern African Association of
    Social Workers, 166
Economic and Social Council, 16
Economic Commission for Africa, 16
Economic Community for West African
    States (ECOWAS), 32
economic prosperity, spread of, 98
education, 17–18, 26, 36, 122, 134, 164. *See
    also* social work education
  African-centred, 3
  bank machine type educational system,
      6–7
  colonial legacy in higher education, 4 (*See
      also* western knowledge)
  deficiencies in formal education system,
      26
  Eurocentric university education, 2–3, 5
  lack of funding for higher education, 148
  race education, 54
  tool for assimilation, 74
  universal education, 4, 96
  western-educated Africans, xv, xvii,
      74–76
  western-educated teachers, 75, 83
  western education, 39–40, 101, 132

HIPC index, 93–94, 99
hire retirement rates, 10
History and philosophy of social work (course), 146
HIV/AIDS, xvi, 96, 145, 151, 164
HIV/AIDS orphans, 81, 104
homeless children, 36
Horton, Africanus, 2
hospitality, 57, 134
housing, 36, 145
Human Development Index, 89, 92
human resources, 18, 89, 115, 123, 132–33
human rights, 6, 45, 57, 67, 84, 104, 124, 134, 182, 186
human rights and African cultural rights conflicts, 161–63
hunger, 96
Hutus, 54

I

IASSW, x, 24, 28, 147
IASSW Code of Ethics, 98, 161, 166
IASSW conference in Durban (2008), 71, 131
IASSW international symposium (Toronto 2007), xxv
IASSW workshop (Durban, 2008), xxvi
identity, 47–48
    re-identifying of, 57
identity crisis, 41, 43, 59, 61
identity development and psychological defense, 149
ideology of oppression, 6
Ife, J., xxviii, 15, 62, 79, 86, 99, 149–50
IFSW, x, 174
IFSW Code of Ethics, 98, 161, 166
IFSW/IASSW Ethics in Social Work, 84
ignorance, 6–7
illiteracy, 16, 145
ILO regulations, 56
imbalance between national democracy and international economic order, 105
imbalance between traditional and western knowledge, 77, 85, 136
imbalance in international trade, 112
imperialism, 76

The important role of supervision in social welfare organizations (ASWEA document), 21
independence, 2, 104
India
    at 2008 world trade talks, 97
    lending money to African countries, 97
Indian code of ethics, 84, 161
indigenization of social development concepts, 26, 35
indigenized approaches in social work, xviii
indigenous best practices, 81
Indigenous Community Development Movement, 120
indigenous cultures, 59, 115, 188
indigenous knowledge and practice, 46, 131–32
indigenous NGOs, 182
Indigenous social work around the world (Gray), 80
indigenous teaching materials, 16
indigenous ways of knowing, 77, 79, 82
individualism, 77, 134. *See also* communal *vs.* individual oriented cultures
industrialization, 19
industrialized western model of social and economic development, 110
Institute for African Studies, 136, 155, 158
institutional structures, 144
institutions affecting social work education in Africa, 11–12, 169
Integrated approach to rural development in Africa (UN monograph), 18
interconnectedness of all things, 47
intercontinental relations, 144
interdisciplinary approaches, xxvii, 31
International Association of Schools of Social Work. *See* IASSW
international cooperation, 27
International Federation of Social Workers (IFSW), x, 174
    Code of Ethics, 98, 161, 166
International Financial Institutions (IFIs), 90, 93, 98–99
    destructive power over Africa, 91
    imposed Structural Adjustment Programs, 8

imposition of conditionality, 94
losing power over their economic empire,
97
new form of colonization, xv
New Policy Agenda, 124
reforms, 104
social work training, 149–50
International Monetary Fund (IMF), 90–91,
96, 105, 150
and the crisis in tertiary education, 9
inequities rooted in, 103
macroeconomic frameworks imposed on
poor African countries, 94
International Social and Development Centre
(ISODEC), 168
international voluntary organizations, 23
internationalization, 115
internationalization of education, 4
Internet
efficiency problems in Africa, 102
not accessible for average person, 175
intra-continental cooperation, 168–69
Inuit, 59
IT techniques, 164
Ivory Coast, 14, 17, 19
'Ivory Tower,' 3

J

Jongh, Jan de, 122
Jonhson, James, 2

K

Kabeera, B., 58, 151, 160, 163, 166
Karberg, Walter, 30
Kenya, 14, 22
Kenyan tea, 93
kings, xiv
kinship institution, xiii, 34
knowledge. *See also* western knowledge
academic, xviii
African knowledge and culture, 182
burying of unpopular knowledge, 52
as a gift, 6

indigenous knowledge and practice, xviii,
46
indigenous ways of knowing, 77, 79
subjugated knowledge, 51
knowledge from living, xviii
knowledge-intensive development, 9
knowledge-making, 75
Kreitzer, L., xiv, xv, xviii, xix, xxviii, 8, 19,
21, 36, 38, 81, 84–85, 117, 125, 158,
160, 175
Kwaku, A., xix

L

labour unrest, 145
Laird, S., 120, 150–51, 155, 163, 169
land, 123
language, 159
cultural language, 148
important to cultural identity, 87
language and course titles, 145–46
laws changing or abolishing cultural practices,
57, 68
lecture style teaching, 7, 23, 165
liberalization, 115
liberation of the African mind, 40
Liberia, 13
Liberian refugee camp in Ghana, 152
life expectancy at birth, 17
lineages, xiii
listening, 109, 127
literacy, 35
illiteracy, 16, 145
local case studies, 147–49
local markets, 113
Lombard, A., 163
Los Angeles Times, 105

M

Maathai, W., 39, 44, 46, 48, 50, 59, 72,
104–5, 188
The Challenge for Africa, 181
Madagascar, 22
Mafile'O, 61, 133
Makere University in Uganda, 10

power issues within ethnic groups, 159
preventive rather than remedial practice, 20, 36, 63
primary school, 8
primitive / civilized dichotomy, xiv, 54, 74, 133, 182
private exploitation of natural resources, 92
privatization, 97–98, 115
    of social programs, 95
professional associations, 23, 144. *See also* names of specific associations
    codes of ethics, 161
    involvement in African unity, 62
    roles of, xx
professional associations in Africa, 167–68
professional identity, 61–63
Professional imperialism (Midgley), ix, 15, 78
professional practice, 65–67
profit-maximization principle
    replaced by social-benefit principle, 103
Program of Action to Mitigate the Social Costs of Adjustment (PAMSCAD), 92
Protestant Ethic, 77
proverbs, 148
puberty rites, xiv, 67
public ownership
    revival in, 97–98
public perception of social work In Ghana, 135
Puplampu, K.P., xviii
push-pull effect, xxvi, 58

Q

qualitative research, 83, 179
quantitative research, 150–51
queen mothers, xiv, 58, 158, 174
queen mothers and social workers
    collaboration between, 158

R

race, 74, 115
race doctrine, 53
race ideology, 54
race policies, 54

racial classification, 54–55
racial equality, 2
racial identity, 50, 53
racial ideology, 54
racial pyramid, 17
racism, x, 3, 6
Radical Right, 95
radio and TV, 160, 166, 172
Ramsay, Richard, 84, 161
Ray, Donald, xiii
Realities and aspirations of social work education in Africa (Ethiopia 1976), 24
recession, 1980s, 91, 123
Reconstruction and Development Programme (RDP), 123
rectification (equalizing rich from poor), 17
rectification (rural and urban areas), 17
"Redemption Song" (Marley), 71
rediscovery and recovery, 60
rediscovery of history and culture, 59, 132–37, 140, 148
rediscovery of indigenous knowledge for teaching and practice, 131–32
redistributive justice, 105
refugee camps, 163
refugees, 151–52, 162
Relationship between social work education and national social development plan, 22
religious belief systems
    ancestors in, xiii
remedial model of social work education, 36, 63, 122
remedial social services, 22, 120
renaming university courses to reflect African culture, 87
research, 16, 24, 27, 137
    Participatory Action Research (PAR), xvii, xviii, 137, 141, 171
    power relations within, 151
    qualitative research, 83, 179
    quantitative research, 150–51
research and evaluation methods, training in, 28
research capabilities, 26
"research or development fatigue syndrome," 118, 137
rich / poor gap, xvi, 17, 90, 111, 114, 159

ritual animal slaughter, 161
The role of agriculture and rural technology in national development (seminar), 31
role-playing, 23, 136, 165
Rosenfeld, Jona, 30
Ross, E., 50, 57, 81, 161
Rostow, W.W., "The Stages of Economic Growth," 110
rural and urban issues
power issues, 159
rural community in Ghana
changes, 66
sense of helplessness concerning poverty, 107
rural development, xxvi, 18, 27–28, 121–22
rural economics, 123
community economic programs, 103
rural exodus of youth, 18
rural life and community action, 16
Russia, 56
Rwanda, 54, 74, 166
community-based counselling services, 163
reconciliation process in, 152, 160
returnees to, 58, 151
Rwandan genocide, 55, 151
Rwandan social workers
role to play concerning the Gacaca courts, 160

S

Sackey, V., xvii
Said, Edward, 76
Sammi of the Arctic, 59
Sautoy, P., 35
saving face, 57, 134
School of Social Work in Osu, 36
school social work (course), 164
scientific racism, 3, 53
"secular African-controlled university," 3
Sefa Dei, G.J., 8–9, 96
self-determination, 84
Seminar of Social Work in West Africa conference (1962), 70
Sewpaul, V., 58, 65, 151, 160, 163, 182

sexual orientation, 116
sharing of resources, 110
Shawky, Dr., 22, 62
Sierra Leone, 19, 22
skewed development, 115
skewed globalization, 117
slave trade, 52, 90
Smith, L., 60–61, 88, 98, 138, 145, 148–49, 186
social action, 2
social activism for social change, 159
social archaeologists, xix
social-benefit principle, 103
social business approach, 103, 119–20
social change, 2, 31
Social Darwinism, 77
social development, 28, 120, 163, 170, 184
indigenization, 26, 35
social development approach to social work, 24–26, 65, 71, 123
'social development' as term, 22, 30
social-development-based practicum, 153
social development education, 24, 27
Social development training in Africa (ASWEA conference, Ethiopia), 26
Social development Training Institutions, 28
'social development workers' as term, 22
social justice, 84–85, 104, 183
social planning, 26, 95
Social planning in national development (seminar), 30–31
Social reconstruction in the newly-independent countries of East Africa (UN monograph), 17
social welfare approach, 20, 65
'social welfare' as term, 22, 63
Social welfare education and practice in developing countries (seminar), 30
social welfare for children and youth, 18
social welfare institutions, 120–21, 147
colonial social welfare system, 33, 36
social welfare issues in African context, 11
social welfare personnel, 13–14
social welfare services, 16
cutbacks, 135
missionaries, 34

social work, x, xxvi, xxviii, 18
  advocating for poverty reduction policies,
      116
  an art and a science, 185
  balance in the African and western
      approaches to, 184
  brought in by colonists, 34
  need to be indigenized, 24
  needs to change with society, 138
  preventive rather than remedial practice,
      20
  promoting social and economic well-
      being, 13
  public awareness campaign, 166
  role in strengthening civil society, 116
social work and law (course), 164
social work and power issues (course), 154,
    159
social work and refugees (course), 155, 162–63
social work and social action (course), 154,
    159
social work curriculum, xvii, 27–28, 138
  African-centred curricula, 4, 8, 145, 175,
      187
  African textbooks, 98
  blend local and international content, 79
  culturally relevant (See culturally relevant
      curricula)
  curriculum development, 10, 14, 83
  curriculum development (teaching
      materials to help in), 26
  economics, 98
  on family welfare and planning for
      African schools of social work,
      23, 26
  local, 65
  for rural development, 27
  social work values and ethics, 126
  specific to needs of Africans in different
      countries, 26
  sustainability, 138
  universal guidelines, 65
  western curriculum, x, xxviii, 3, 11,
      22–23, 62, 78
  in world of NGOs, 125
social work education, xxvi, 134

blend western with traditional African
    values and practices, 130, 134
common problems, 20
continuous evaluation of, 61, 186
critical conscientization, 186
dominant values, 77
lack of adequate financial backing, 20
lack of local literature for teaching
    purposes, 20
need to critique NGO sector, 123
opens doors to work overseas, 101
professional training, 63–65
remedial model of, 36, 63, 122
social development education, 24, 27
student exchanges with other parts of
    Africa, 154
students empowered to think for
    themselves, 7
teaching skills of African teachers, 24
western knowledge and, 39–40, 77–83
social work educators, 28
  holding on to the western education, 132
Social work in Ghana (video), 172
"Social Work in West Africa" (conference
    1962), 19
social work interventions, 158
  culturally relevant education and practice,
      79, 82, 129–79
  traditional, 157–58
social work journal (established), 21
social work profession, xvi, 19, 134, 185
  Ghana, 38
  internal and external barriers, 130
  part of global solidarity movement, 125
  value to national development and social
      planning, 188
social work schools in western world
  seeking to export programs, 79
social work training. See social work education
social work values and ethics, 77, 126
social work values and ethics in African
    society (course), 154, 160
social workers
  active role in political and social arena,
      99, 159, 165
  advocating for poverty reduction policies,
      116

T

Tandon, R., xviii
Tandon, Y., xiii, xiv
Tanganyika, 14
Tanzania, 22, 97, 120
Tasfaye, Dr., 24
teacher / student relationships, 23
Techniques of teaching and method of field work evaluation (Ethiopia 1974), 23
Tema Harbour, 31
tertiary education, 9–10
Tettey, W.J., xviii
textbooks, 14, 68, 79
    African social work textbook, 165
    limited finances for publishing, 148
    western social work training texts, 14, 139
THEMBA (There Must Be an Alternative), 105
Togo, 19, 22
Tongan social work, 61, 132
traditional African culture
    balancing with modern culture, 60
    complexity, 44
    destructive to some people, 57
    respect for, 149
traditional authority or elders, 118
traditional authority structure, 158
traditional family and community supports, 66
traditional healers, 81, 157
traditional health clinics, 157
traditional knowledge
    believed to be primitive, 74
    blending together of modern and, 182
    devalued by modernization, 55
    repressed by colonialism, modernization, and globalization, 75
    undermined, xv
traditional leaders
    chiefs, 54, 58
    chieftaincy system, xiii, 58, 157
traditional local leaders, 35
traditional mechanisms for social change (course), 154–55
traditional mechanisms for social intervention, 158

traditional medicine, 161. *See also* African approach to healing
traditional practices that cause ethical dilemmas for social workers, 157, 161
traditional social systems, xiv
Training for social development (ASWEA conference, Ethiopia 1985), 27
Training for social work in Africa (UN monograph), 17
transition periods, 68
transitional change, 66–67
transparency/honesty/trust, 126
trauma counselling, 152
trickle down, 110–11
trokosi system, 67, 145
Truman, Harry, 109
truth in indigenous African society, xviii
Tutsis, 54–55

U

Ubuntu, 162
Uganda, 14, 22, 104
    moved away from IMF cash, 97
umbilical cord with western theory and practice, xix, xxviii, 86, 140, 183
unaccompanied minors, 162
'under-developed' (term), 109
UNDP Human Development Report (2010), 92
unemployment, 123, 145
unequal globalization process, 116
UNESCO, 48
UNESCO World Conference on Cultural Policies, 45
unfair trade laws, 93
Union of South Africa. *See* South Africa
United Arab Republic, 17
United Nations, 8, 23, 39, 110
    assumed western social work knowledge was universal and transferable, 15, 77
    ASWEA representatives, 27
    Millennium Development Goals (MDG), 96
    sent western consultants to non-western countries, 14–15

western curriculum. *See under* social work curriculum

western development organizations
  attitude towards Africa, 49–50

western-educated Africans, xxvii, 74, 76. *See also* African elites
  fed system of colonialism, 75
  perpetuated idea that western knowledge was best, 75
  undermined local knowledge and expertise, xv

western-educated teachers, 75
  teach and practice in western way, 83

western education. *See under* education

western experts, 77–78, 114

western knowledge, xvi, 15, 140
  Africa slow to discard, 79
  believed superior to local knowledge, 77
  challenges to the universality of, 15
  hegemony of, xv, 73–88
  post-colonial challenges to, 76
  role in development of African social knowledge, xx
  tool of European imperialism, 85
  western way of knowing, xviii

western knowledge and social work education, 77–83

western social work
  considered superior, 130
  ineffective for many communities, 79–80
  Judeo-Christian background, 78
  medical model methods, 78

western social work curricula, x, 11, 78

western social work education and practice
  dependence on, xxiii, 40
  has not worked well in Africa, 39
  transferable, 39

western theory, xvi, 15
  balancing with African indigenous knowledge and traditions, xxiii, 140

western theory and practice, xix, xxviii, 86, 140, 183

westernization, 74, 110, 115

White Paper for Developmental Social Welfare in South Africa, 123, 163

Whitmore, E., xv, 90, 110–11, 115

Williams, L., 65

Willinsky, J., xiv, xv, 44, 51–54, 74–76, 86, 146

Wilson, M., xxviii, 125

Wilson, M.G., xv, 90, 110–11, 115

'winterthorn,' 187–88

witches villages, 67

Wits University historical archives, 175

women, 36
  female genital mutilation (FGM), 67
  female participation in labour force, 26
  legal and political rights of, 18, 67
  PAMSCAD's failure to help, 92
  participation in community life, 18
  traditional culture and, 57

women and children, 123, 153

women in development, 27–28, 149

women pounding fufu, 155–56

women's movements, 157

World Bank, xvi, 8–10, 90–91, 96, 103–4
  policies contributed to the crisis in tertiary education, 9
  poverty and, 94–95

world recession, 91, 123

World Trade Organization, 103, 105

world trade talks (2008), 112
  collapse, 97

World War II, 12

Y

Yimam, 28

Youth employment and national development in Africa (UN monograph), 18

youth migration to cities, 18, 66

youth mobilization for national development, 16

Yunus, M., 93, 95, 99

Z

Zambia, 22

Zimbabwe, 2, 56, 58, 147, 170

Zulus, 162

www.ingramcontent.com/pod-product-compliance
Lightning Source LLC
Chambersburg PA
CBHW050412280326
41932CB00013BA/1836